A
SEARCH
FOR
ENEMIES

A SEARCH FOR ENEMIES

America's Alliances after the Cold War

Ted Galen Carpenter

CATO INSTITUTE
Washington, D.C.

Library of Congress Cataloging-in-Publication Data

Carpenter, Ted Galen.
  A search for enemies : America's alliances after the cold war / Ted
  Galen Carpenter.
      p.   cm.
  Includes bibliographical references and index.
  ISBN 0-932790-96-8 (cloth) : $22.95.—ISBN 0-932790-95-X (paper) :
  $12.95
  1. United States—Foreign relations—1989– 2. Alliances. I. Title.
  E881.C37   1992
  327.1'16—dc20   92-36517
                                                                        CIP

Printed in the United States of America.

CATO INSTITUTE
224 Second Street, S.E.
Washington, D.C. 20003

Contents

Preface

One of the most important issues facing Americans is the need to assess the nation's security strategy and global role now that the Cold War has come to an end. A crucial component of that assessment is determining whether it serves the best interests of the American people to maintain the various military alliances that Washington created during the long struggle against the Soviet Union. Unfortunately, neither the Bush administration nor most members of the foreign policy community seem interested in evaluating the relevance, risks, or benefits of U.S. alliances. Their premise is that all of Washington's Cold War era security commitments are still needed despite the wholesale transformation of the international system, and they are searching for new missions and new enemies to justify those commitments.

This book takes an entirely different approach. It adopts the foreign policy equivalent of zero-based budgeting, insisting that because of the dramatic changes caused by the Soviet Union's collapse, all alliances must be justified anew, regardless of any utility they may have had during the Cold War. The analysis is limited to cases in which the United States has an explicit treaty obligation to defend other nations. Those obligations include three multilateral alliances—the North Atlantic Treaty Organization (NATO); ANZUS, which links the United States, Australia, and New Zealand; and the Rio Treaty, which provides a collective defense arrangement for the Western Hemisphere. They also include four important bilateral security treaties—with Japan, South Korea, the Philippines, and Pakistan.

Washington has many other less formal military commitments, of course. There is little doubt, for example, that the United States would go to the aid of Israel or Saudi Arabia, even in the absence of a treaty obligation, if either nation faced subjugation. An assortment of base access agreements, military aid agreements, presidential doctrines, or merely informal understandings could serve as pretexts for intervening in regions that U.S. policymakers deem relevant to America's interests. Such obligations are, however, beyond the scope of this book.

I owe a debt of gratitude to many people who helped make the book possible. Ed Crane, president of the Cato Institute, has unceasingly supported my efforts to criticize the foreign policy status quo and to develop alternative strategies more consistent with the traditional American values of limited government and individual liberty. William A. Niskanen, David Boaz, Alan Tonelson, Jeffrey R. Gerlach, Eric A. Nordlinger, Doug Bandow, and Christopher Layne provided helpful comments on an earlier draft. Beth Modahl, Steven Kydd, and Kristen Krash spent many hours assisting with the research. My editor, Elizabeth W. Kaplan, deserves great credit for improving the quality of the manuscript. Any remaining errors of either fact or interpretation are, of course, entirely my own.

Most of all, I wish to thank my wife, Barbara, and our children, Lara, Amber, and Brian, for their unwavering enthusiasm for this project and the patience they exhibited when the author sometimes seemed obsessed with his topic.

Introduction

Lord Salisbury, the noted British statesman, once observed that the commonest error in politics is clinging to the carcasses of dead policies. Salisbury's observation applies with special force to current U.S. security strategy. The passing of the Cold War and the collapse of the Soviet Union may be the most important developments of the 20th century. Washington's reaction to those events, which have shaken the international system to its foundation, has been to cling tenaciously to old policies and familiar institutions. Despite President George Bush's rhetoric about a "new world order," U.S. policy is mired in the futile attempt to maintain "global stability." Bush summarized that simplistic policy orientation after the November 1991 NATO summit in Rome: "The enemy is unpredictability. The friend is stability."

Although international stability may be appealing in the abstract, the risks and costs of trying to achieve it are excessive. One of the greatest costs is that of perpetuating a host of obsolete Cold War era military alliances, including such multilateral arrangements as the North Atlantic Treaty Organization (NATO), the Australia–New Zealand–United States (ANZUS) accord, and the Rio Treaty, as well as bilateral defense pacts with Japan, the Republic of Korea, the Philippines, and Pakistan. The NATO commitment alone cost American taxpayers nearly $130 billion a year during the final stages of the Cold War. Even with the scaled-down U.S. troop presence in Europe that the Bush administration projects, the annual price tag will still be at least $90 billion. Washington's obligation to defend Japan, South Korea, and other East Asian allies costs another $40 billion a year.

The financial consequences of maintaining such alliances can be measured in another way. The United States currently spends nearly seven times as much on the military as does any other member of the Group of 7 (G-7) industrial powers—and eight times as much as either Germany or Japan. Indeed, it spends some 60 percent more than all the other G-7 countries combined. A nation that faces daunting domestic problems—a ballooning federal budget deficit, an overtaxed citizenry, and a sluggish economy—can ill afford that kind of disparity. We must ask whether in the post–Cold War world the United States really has seven times the security interests of other major industrial powers.

Washington's Cold War era alliances also have the potential to entangle the United States in a host of obscure conflicts that have little relevance to America's legitimate security concerns. The ongoing transformation of NATO from an alliance to deter Soviet aggression against Western Europe into a regional crisis management organization is a case in point. That new mission blurs the boundaries of NATO's traditional theater of operations and threatens to involve the United States in volatile and intractable ethnic conflicts in Eastern Europe and the former Soviet Union. The commitment to defend South Korea puts American forces on the front lines in one of the most dangerous areas of the planet—even though the strategic rationale for assuming such a grave risk has vanished.

The U.S. campaign to preserve a global network of alliances is based on the assumption that other major international actors will be cooperative junior partners in U.S.-led security efforts. But the belief that Japan and the West European powers will continue to follow Washington's leadership as they did throughout the Cold War is erroneous. Consistent with international relations theory and history, Cold War era solidarity has begun to dissolve now that there is no longer a credible common threat to promote cohesion among the "free world" allies. U.S. leaders cannot assume that the diplomatic, economic, and military agendas of the other G-7 powers will always coincide with our own—much less that those nations will routinely defer to Washington's policy preferences.

Although America's Cold War era allies would undoubtedly like to retain the cost-free security insurance provided by the United States, they have already begun to pursue increasingly independent political and military policies. The European Community rather unceremoniously edged Washington to the diplomatic sidelines during initial efforts to deal with the Yugoslavian crisis. France and Germany have expanded their joint military brigade to approximately 35,000 troops—an action that is the first step toward the creation of an all-European force—and have sought to strengthen the Western European Union, a potential rival to NATO. Even Japan—long diffident about playing a leadership role in security matters—has begun to be more assertive.

Instead of welcoming such signs of growing self-reliance on the part of other major democratic capitalist powers—or at least adjusting gracefully to the changing realities—U.S. officials have often reacted petulantly. National Security Adviser Brent Scowcroft chastised the members of the European Community for adopting "independent" positions on security issues and presenting those positions to the United States as faits accomplis. Similarly, Secretary of State James A. Baker III criticized the notion of security cooperation between Japan and the members of the Association of Southeast Asian Nations. The Bush administration expended considerable diplomatic capital to thwart French efforts to create a rapid reaction force under the auspices of the European Community rather than NATO and viewed with suspicion the expansion of the Franco-German military brigade.

Such responses are most revealing in light of Washington's long-standing habit of prodding U.S. allies to share security burdens. Apparently, the U.S. concept of burden sharing means only that other great powers should pay a larger percentage of the costs of policies adopted by Washington, not that they should take greater responsibility for defending their own security interests, much less adopt independent strategies for doing so.

Instead of seeking to preserve an expensive system of U.S.-dominated alliances, the United States should view the eclipse of Soviet power as an opportunity to adopt a less pretentious and more cost-effective policy. For the first time in 50 years, there is no powerful challenger, such as Nazi Germany or the Soviet Union, that could pose a grave threat to America's security, nor is there a potential threat of that magnitude visible on the horizon. The absence of a would-be global hegemonic power is a watershed development that should fundamentally alter U.S. defense policy.

The post–Cold War world may well be a disorderly place, as many regions are still confronting the legacy of the imperial age during which numerous artificial, unstable political entities were created. Moreover, a host of ancient disputes, grievances, and conflicts that were submerged in the larger Cold War struggle between East and West are now resurfacing. Without a powerful rival to exploit the turmoil, however, the United States will find that most of those parochial quarrels are irrelevant to its own security interests. Washington can afford to view them with detachment, intervening only as a balancer of last resort if a conflict cannot be contained by powers in the affected region and is expanding to the point of threatening America's security.

The vastly changed international system means that Washington's network of Cold War era alliances is an expensive anachronism. It makes little sense to maintain 150,000 U.S. troops in Europe to defend Western Europe from a Warsaw Pact that no longer exists. When NATO was established in 1949, the European democracies, still devastated and demoralized by World War II, faced an aggressively expansionist Soviet Union. Today, Western Europe is economically powerful and politically vibrant, while the Soviet Union is extinct. Given their economic and military resources, the members of the European Community should certainly be able to defend themselves against any current or future secondary threat.

A similar transformation has occurred in East Asia. When the United States first undertook the defense of South Korea in the 1950s, that country was an impoverished, war-torn hulk confronted by a communist North Korean adversary backed by the Soviet Union and China. Today, South Korea is an economic dynamo with twice the population and more than 10 times the gross national product of North Korea. Moreover, North Korea is becoming increasingly isolated as both Beijing and Moscow seek to forge closer political and economic ties with the South. Given such conditions, it is absurd to contend that South Korea cannot build whatever military forces are needed for its security and must, therefore, remain a U.S. protectorate indefinitely.

It is even more difficult to justify keeping Japan a protectorate. Japan has the world's second largest economy as well as one of the most dynamic and technologically sophisticated. Yet Tokyo spends an anemic 1 percent of its gross national product (GNP) on the military while the United States spends more than 5 percent. Given the increasingly fierce competition between American and Japanese firms in a host of international markets, we can ill afford to burden our economy with excessive military expenditures to protect Japan or, more probably, to prevent Japan from playing a larger political role in world affairs.

4

Other U.S. alliances in East Asia, most notably ANZUS and the bilateral security treaty with the Philippines, are equally obsolete. Even if it once made sense to protect those countries from the Soviet Union or other potentially expansionist communist powers, that rationale has disappeared.

Much the same is true of U.S. security commitments elsewhere in the world. The security treaty with Pakistan is a Cold War relic. It was designed to protect Pakistan from Soviet aggression or subversion—a danger that is now utterly fanciful. Yet by preserving the treaty, Washington risks entangling the United States in a possible conflict between Pakistan and its arch rival, India—a war that would have no relevance whatsoever to America's legitimate security interests. Risking such an entanglement is especially foolhardy since both South Asian nations probably have nuclear weapons.

Closer to home, Washington insists on preserving the Rio Treaty and the Organization of American States despite the lack of any credible security threat from outside the hemisphere. When the Rio Treaty was signed in 1947, memories of Nazi and fascist subversion in various parts of Latin America were fresh, and it appeared that the Soviet Union would pose an even more formidable threat. The emergence of a communist regime in Cuba in the late 1950s— especially the development of a close military alliance between Havana and Moscow—seemed to validate those fears. Today there is little risk that a powerful adversary of the United States will seek to use the other hemispheric nations as political or military pawns. There may still be a few home-grown Leninists (e.g., the Shining Path guerrillas in Peru), but they are hardly strong enough to pose a serious threat to the security of the United States. The Rio Treaty, like most Cold War era security arrangements created by the United States, is now an alliance in search of an enemy.

Instead of viewing the changes in the international system as an opportunity to shed security burdens and downsize a bloated military budget, U.S. officials seek new missions to justify the perpetuation of old alliances. For example, they insist that NATO and the U.S. troop presence in Europe are needed to prevent instability in Eastern Europe—essentially a "scarecrow" function. Even if that mission were worth $90 billion a year, the civil war in Yugoslavia demonstrates that a U.S. military presence has little ability to deter the kind of ethnic conflicts that are likely to plague Eastern Europe in the post–Cold War era.

5

It would not be in our interest to intervene in such conflicts in any case. Most Americans accepted the costs and risks associated with the NATO commitment during the Cold War, but the rationale for that commitment was the need to prevent an expansionist Soviet Union from gaining control of the population and technological assets of Western Europe and then using that additional strength to pose an increased threat to America's own security. Accepting the risks and costs of a vague mission to preserve stability in Eastern Europe is another matter entirely. Although ethnic, religious, and territorial disputes might be extremely important to the parties involved, they would rarely affect even the European, much less the global, geopolitical balance and are therefore not threats to America's security. Taking the risk of becoming entangled in the ancient and intractable conflicts of Eastern Europe is not merely unnecessary; it would be foreign policy masochism.

The same is true of the U.S. treaty obligation to defend the Republic of Korea (ROK). In a Cold War context, it was possible to argue that a North Korean attack on the ROK would pose a threat to America's security because such an attack would in reality be an expansionist probe by a Soviet or Chinese surrogate. That is no longer a plausible scenario. Pyongyang may still harbor aggressive ambitions, but even if it were to launch an attack on the South, the resulting conflict would now be a parochial one between the two rival Korean states. It need not and should not have global geostrategic ramifications. In a post–Cold War setting, South Korea is, at most, a peripheral U.S. interest, whose defense does not warrant spending billions of dollars and risking thousands of American lives.

The determination to preserve Cold War era alliances in a vastly changed world is in part a reflection of ossified thinking by the Bush administration and members of the U.S. foreign policy community. Many of them reflexively cite the supposed lessons of the 1930s, without asking whether they are applicable to the world of the 1990s. The need for early action against any aggressor, collective defense arrangements among "peace-loving" nations, and a dominant U.S. leadership role are the major components of their policy catechism.

In addition to those outmoded premises, there are less savory reasons that so many portions of the foreign policy community want to perpetuate Washington's Cold War era alliances. A network of vested interests sees those alliances as the essential justification for maintaining large military budgets and an assortment of other lucrative arrangements. The various factions in that network have no desire to see their power, prestige, and financial positions eroded, and they have been potent lobbyists for preserving a U.S. strategy of global intervention.

It is time to recognize that, with the disintegration of the Soviet Union, the mission of America's Cold War alliances has been accomplished. U.S. policymakers should now move to create a new defense strategy that is appropriate for a post–Cold War setting and that does not waste American resources or needlessly risk American lives. We cannot afford to maintain alliances for the sake of having alliances. Instead, we should seize the opportunity afforded by the end of the Cold War to adopt a new policy of strategic independence.

Strategic independence should have three guiding principles. The first would be a definition of "vital" security interests that is narrower than the vague and casual one used during the Cold War. A vital interest ought to have a direct, immediate, and substantial connection with America's physical survival, political independence, or domestic liberty. The second principle would be an emphasis on flexibility and autonomous U.S. decisionmaking. Washington should avoid alliances, especially those with imprecise, long-term obligations, since they can limit America's options when a significant U.S. interest is at stake or entangle the United States in irrelevant conflicts. They also lock the United States into commitments that may make sense under one set of global conditions but are unnecessary or undesirable under another. The final principle would be to resist pursuing ambitious international "milieu" goals—especially "stability," which lies at the heart of President Bush's new world order. America would undoubtedly be happier in a world composed entirely of peaceful democratic states, but that goal is unattainable at acceptable cost and risk to the United States. Moreover, although such a transformation of the international system might be desirable, it is not essential to America's security.

Strategic independence would not be just another sterile exercise in "burden sharing." Washington has tried to get its many Cold

7

War allies to pay more of the expense of collective defense efforts for the past four decades—without a great deal of success. (The Bush administration's ability to cajole them into paying for much of the Persian Gulf operation is an impressive, but probably unique, exception. Even those contributions were obtained only after unprecedented diplomatic browbeating.) If meaningful burden sharing was difficult to attain during the Cold War, when the U.S. defensive shield was valuable to allies facing a looming Soviet threat, it is likely to prove even more difficult in the post–Cold War world. The value of Washington's military protection to the allies has depreciated markedly in the past two years, and their willingness to pay more for that protection can be expected to decline as well. For the same reason, the notion that maintaining an extensive U.S. troop presence in Europe and East Asia will give Washington "leverage" on trade and other economic issues is an illusion. The U.S. presence is no longer important enough to induce the Europeans or the Japanese to make more than cosmetic concessions.

Instead of burden sharing, Washington's goal should be burden shedding. A burden-shedding policy would entail the gradual but complete devolution of responsibility to America's allies for the defense of their respective regions. Although the exact pace and timing of security devolution should be determined in consultation with the allies, the ultimate result should not be subject to negotiation—much less an allied veto.

Just as strategic independence is not burden sharing, it is also not isolationism. The United States can and should maintain extensive diplomatic, cultural, and economic ties with the rest of the world. Washington must also maintain sizable, capable military forces and be prepared to take decisive action if a serious threat to America's security does emerge. A judicious, albeit aggressive, pruning of security commitments is needed, not the creation of a hermit republic.

The most difficult adjustment for U.S. officials will be to accept other powers' playing larger roles in regions where America abandons its strategic hegemony. It is predictable that the major European powers, acting either collectively through the European Community or individually, will adopt more assertive positions. Similarly, Japan is likely to eventually play a political and military role commensurate with its status as an economic great power.

Such changes may be unsettling for the United States as well as for smaller powers in the affected regions. Attempting to preserve U.S. dominance, however, would involve serious risks. For example, perpetuating a large-scale U.S. military presence in the western Pacific could ultimately create dangerous frictions in U.S.-Japanese relations. A majority of Japanese favored the American security shield throughout the Cold War because it offered reliable protection from a menacing Soviet Union and spared Japan from spending scarce resources on the military. But with the demise of the Soviet threat, it will not be long before many Japanese begin to wonder why such large numbers of American forces remain. Eventually, the suspicion (not entirely unfounded, if one can judge from the comments of some outspoken U.S. military leaders) will grow that they are there to "contain" Japan. That suspicion could poison the entire range of U.S.-Japanese relations. Many Germans are likely to harbor a similar suspicion and feel alienated from the United States once the last Russian forces leave German territory, if Washington still insists on maintaining a sizable military presence there.

A policy of strategic independence would be based on a more modest and sustainable security role for the United States and on a realistic assessment of the post–Cold War international system. It would take into account the fundamental changes that have occurred in the world in recent years and seek to position the United States to benefit from the emerging multipolar political, economic, and military environment.

The new strategy would make it possible to defend America's security interests with a military force of approximately 875,000 active duty personnel—compared with the current force of some 2 million and the force of 1.64 million contemplated by the Pentagon for the mid-1990s. A policy of strategic independence would enable the United States to reduce its military budget from $291 billion in fiscal year (FY) 1992 to approximately $125 billion a year (measured in 1992 dollars) over a five-year period. The beneficial economic impact of a "peace dividend" of that magnitude, if returned to the private sector in the form of tax reductions, would be enormous.

After those reductions, the United States would still be spending at least three times as much on the military as any other G-7 nation. The reductions seem radical only in the context of the bloated Cold War era military budgets that have come to be considered normal.

But the Cold War is over, and with its passing we must change our ideas of what constitutes normal defense spending. Instead of marginal changes in military budgets that are still largely based on Cold War era assumptions, the American people should insist on the defense policy equivalent of zero-based budgeting. That approach would require the adoption of a coherent defense strategy based on the realities of the post–Cold War international system and a careful assessment of what is actually needed to protect the nation's security.

America cannot afford to pursue the mirage of a new world order, nor can it tolerate the continuing hemorrhage of its wealth to subsidize the defense of prosperous allies who are now capable of defending themselves. Instead of searching for phantom enemies to justify maintaining obsolete security commitments, the United States should welcome the chance to achieve strategic independence.

1. NATO: A Cold War Anachronism

For more than four decades, NATO has been the flagship of the alliances that Washington created to contain the power of the Soviet Union. NATO was in many ways the stereotypical Cold War military institution. It would have been difficult to imagine either its creation or its continuation outside the geopolitical context of the Cold War. In the initial euphoria that followed the sudden disintegration of Moscow's East European empire, it seemed likely that NATO would follow the Warsaw Pact into oblivion. After all, a series of stunning events had utterly transformed the political landscape of Europe and erased the original rationale for NATO—the defense of Western Europe from a powerful and aggressively expansionist Soviet Union.

Predictions of NATO's demise have proven to be premature. NATO partisans are so determined to preserve the alliance and America's military presence on the Continent that they embrace an assortment of implausible and frequently contradictory policies. Since the Soviet Union's East European empire began to unravel in the summer of 1989, Bush administration officials and numerous members of the foreign policy community have conducted a frantic search for alternative justifications for the alliance. The range of suggestions NATO's supporters have made is testimony to both their creativity and their desperation. Unfortunately, if they succeed, the American people will be saddled indefinitely with an expensive and risky military commitment that is no longer necessary. The willingness of NATO enthusiasts to thus sacrifice America's well-being is a study in ossified thinking as well as the politics of vested interests and institutional self-preservation.

Die-hard Atlanticists believe that despite the political transformation of Eastern Europe, NATO and the U.S. military presence on the Continent should be permanent geopolitical fixtures. President Bush eliminated any doubt on that score after the November 7–8, 1991, NATO summit in Rome, when he stated that the security interests of the United States and Europe were "indivisible" and, therefore, the Atlantic alliance could not be replaced "even in the long run."[1] On an earlier occasion, he had insisted that the U.S. troop presence in Europe would be needed for a century or more. Both themes—the permanent nature of the alliance and the assertion that the continuing deployment of U.S. conventional forces must be an integral part of NATO's strategy in a post–Cold War setting—were made explicit in the communiqué that emerged from the Rome summit. "In an environment of uncertainty and unpredictable challenges, our Alliance, which provides the essential transatlantic link as demonstrated by the significant presence of North American forces in Europe, retains its enduring value."[2]

NATO's more ardent supporters simply do not care that the alliance's original reason for existence has become irrelevant. NATO was created in 1949 to protect a weak, war-devastated Western Europe from a rapacious Soviet Union that had already extinguished liberty in Eastern Europe. The subsequent U.S. troop commitment that began in late 1950 has continued to the present day, although Western Europe long ago ceased to be incapable of providing for its own defense. Most of NATO's American founders would probably be astonished to learn that the alliance was preserved after Europe's complete recovery and in the absence of a Soviet threat. The expectation of such officials as George F. Kennan, the principal architect of Washington's containment strategy, and Gen. Dwight D. Eisenhower, NATO's first military commander, was that a democratic Europe would eventually assume responsibility for its own defense. Eisenhower wrote shortly after assuming his post, "If in ten years, all American troops stationed in Europe for national defense purposes have not been returned to the United States, then this whole project will have failed."[3]

The contrast between that attitude and the policies adopted by the Bush administration could not be more striking. At every turn, the administration and a large portion of the U.S. foreign policy community have strenuously resisted suggestions that America's role in NATO be radically reduced—much less eliminated. Despite the obvious liberalizing trend throughout Eastern Europe and the Soviet Union at the end of the 1980s, the administration's initial reaction was to propose reducing U.S. forces in Europe by less than 15 percent—from 320,000 to 275,000. Even after Moscow's East

European empire had collapsed entirely, Washington envisaged, in the negotiations that led to the Conventional Forces in Europe (CFE) Treaty with the USSR, a U.S. troop level of 195,000 in the European theater, including some 170,000 in Central Europe (i.e., Germany). National Security Adviser Brent Scowcroft stated in 1990 that the 195,000 figure for superpower forces would be a ceiling for the Soviet Union but a floor for the United States. Under the pressure of tightening constraints on the military budget and growing calls from members of Congress for more substantial troop reductions, the administration reluctantly agreed to further reductions by the mid-1990s. Nevertheless, the Pentagon insists that the United States must station no fewer than 150,000 troops on the Continent for the foreseeable future. That reduction would decrease the cost of the U.S. NATO commitment from the nearly $130 billion a year Washington spent during the final stages of the Cold War to a "mere" $92 billion.

Such tenacious rear-guard actions are only one indication that NATO's supporters, in a practical demonstration of the public choice economic theories that won James Buchanan the Nobel Prize in 1986, have circled the wagons in a desperate attempt to preserve their beleaguered institution. They have also been astonishingly creative in coming up with new reasons both to maintain NATO and to keep U.S. troops in Europe.

During the initial stages of the post–Cold War period, they warned that the Soviet threat might reemerge and insisted that NATO must be preserved to guard against that danger. Events steadily undermined that argument, however. As communist regimes were ousted in one East European nation after another, Moscow agreed to the reunification of Germany, and the internal political and economic weaknesses of the Soviet Union became evident to even the most hardened cynics, it was increasingly difficult to argue that the USSR posed a serious expansionist threat. The formal disbanding of the Warsaw Pact in July 1991 confirmed that the Cold War division of Europe had come to an end. U.S. military experts conceded that the warning time for any Soviet military offensive against Western Europe (in the unlikely event one could be mounted at all) would be measured in years rather than days, and the Red Army would have to fight its way through its erstwhile East European allies before it could reach Western

Europe. The rapid unraveling of the Soviet Union's political structure in the aftermath of the unsuccessful hard-line communist coup in August 1991—especially the replacement of the USSR with the amorphous Commonwealth of Independent States (CIS)—buried the remaining arguments about the need for NATO to counter a lingering Soviet threat.

Since the changes in Eastern Europe and the former Soviet Union have discredited that rationale, NATO supporters have fallen back to the final Atlanticist redoubt—finding an "alternative mission" for the alliance. Their creativity in formulating alternative missions is boundless—and sometimes unintentionally humorous. Former assistant secretary of state Robert D. Hormats, for example, stated that Western leaders must "expand the range of issues on which NATO engages the common efforts of the European and North American democracies—from student exchanges, to fighting the drug trade, to resisting terrorism, to countering threats to the environment."[4] Hormats was not alone in believing that a military alliance can be transformed into a combination student exchange placement agency and public-sector version of Greenpeace. Former U.S. ambassador to NATO David Abshire also insisted that NATO "could coordinate the transfer of environmental-control and energy-conservation technology to the East, thereby benefiting the global ecology."[5] Not to be outdone, the *Wall Street Journal*'s Karen Elliott House suggested that NATO troops could distribute food and other humanitarian aid in the former Soviet Union—as a sort of Red Cross with tanks.[6]

The proposed objectives are not necessarily without value. Student exchanges, cleaning up pollution, and providing humanitarian aid are all worthy goals. But what do they have to do with maintaining an elaborate transatlantic military alliance? The fact that NATO partisans would grasp at a host of nonmilitary reasons for preserving the alliance suggests how desperate they are and how weak the substantive security justifications for NATO have become in the post–Cold War era.

More serious proposals for a new alliance mission typically emphasize using NATO for "out-of-area" contingencies or promoting "stability" throughout Europe. The out-of-area justification has taken a variety of forms. Star Wars guru Gen. Daniel Graham, for example, proposes that NATO be used to prevent the proliferation of ballistic missiles and weapons of mass destruction among aggressive or unstable Third World states.[7] (How NATO's continued existence—much less the presence of U.S. tank and infantry divisions on the Continent—would be relevant to such a mission Graham leaves a trifle vague.) Other pro-NATO spokesmen contend that the alliance was useful to the U.S. military effort during the Persian Gulf crisis. At the very least, they insist, American troops and equipment stationed in Europe as part of the NATO commitment would be closer to the scene of future crises elsewhere in the world (i.e., the Middle East), and their deployment would save Washington valuable time. NATO's supporters also hold out the more ambitious prospect that the alliance might become a mechanism for coordinating a Western response to breaches of the peace outside the European theater.

The favorite alternative mission, however, is the preservation of stability in Europe. Even during the earliest stages of the post–Cold War period, President Bush asserted that NATO and the U.S. military presence would be needed in the future, not to deter a Soviet-led invasion (which he conceded had become highly improbable), but to guard against "uncertainty" and "unpredictability."[8] At the Rome summit, he insisted, "We demonstrated that NATO does not need a Soviet enemy to hold it together," adding that in the future the alliance must be "able to protect any ally against any threat."[9]

The shift of NATO's role from deterring or repelling Soviet aggression to undertaking regional peace-keeping and enforcement obligations has become the dominant theme of the search for a new mission. How vague that new role may be can be gathered from the comments of a senior NATO official. "We no longer face the threat of a massive attack against NATO territory, but there remains a *potential* uncertainty and unpredictability, which *might* lead to instability, tension and risk to the European security."[10] The same official noted that NATO's new strategy would focus on "crisis management" and that the planned 70,000-member "rapid reaction force" would be ideally suited for deployment in various hot spots in Central and Eastern Europe.

The most ambitious formulation of a Continent-wide peace-keeping mission has been made by NATO Secretary General Manfred Woerner. In an October 1991 interview, he stated that NATO would eventually be transformed from an alliance to deter Soviet aggression into a new arrangement to emphasize "stability and risk assurance" for the entire European continent—the "focal point of a pan-European security system." Woerner went on to say that as an expanded defense community, NATO may ultimately put peacekeeping forces in places of ethnic conflict or border disputes from the Atlantic Ocean to the Ural Mountains.[11] That change, he stressed, would soon render irrelevant the long-standing debate about NATO's theater of operations.

Woerner was only slightly ahead of his colleagues—or at least more candid—in advocating such a breathtaking expansion of NATO's mission, but the alliance is clearly moving in that direction. Indeed, the broad outlines of Woerner's program could be discerned in the strategy adopted at the November 1991 Rome summit. The geographic scope of NATO's security concerns was clearly expanding. In the days leading up to the summit, NATO officials stressed that although they were not yet prepared to extend formal membership invitations to the nations of Eastern Europe, the alliance would establish an extensive liaison operation to coordinate security policies with those governments. The final communiqué confirmed that goal, outlining various steps, including the creation of the North Atlantic Cooperation Council, to develop "a more institutional relationship of consultation and cooperation on security issues."[12] Subsequently, several East European states—as well as the Ukraine and Russia—have indicated an interest in eventual full NATO membership.

Indeed, as early as the June 1991 meeting of NATO foreign ministers, there were indications of a subtle but crucial expansion of the alliance's security sphere when the members stated that any attempt to undermine the freedom and independence of the East European nations would be a matter of "direct and material concern" to NATO.[13] Although that message was primarily directed at hard-liners in the Soviet Union who might still entertain notions of reconquering the satellite empire, it had potentially broader security implications—especially given the potential for conflicts among the East European states.

The culmination of efforts to expand NATO's geographic interests came at the June 1992 foreign ministers' conference in Oslo. The assembled officials adopted a resolution making troops available for future peace-keeping or peace-enforcement operations approved by the Conference on Security and Cooperation in Europe (CSCE). That decision raises the possibility that NATO forces may become embroiled in conflicts in Eastern Europe or the former Soviet Union, given the proliferation of disputes in those regions.[14]

The adoption of the will-o'-the-wisp of stability as NATO's raison d'être and the creeping expansion of the alliance's geographic coverage have been accompanied by shrill U.S. opposition to any manifestation of West European independence in security matters. As early as February 1991, Brent Scowcroft complained that the West European countries were increasingly acting through the European Community on security issues and then presenting a common front to the United States.[15] His aggrieved tone implied that the Europeans were being presumptuous in daring to have security interests different from those of the United States—not to mention in having the temerity to challenge Washington's preeminence in the transatlantic alliance.

A few months later, the Bush administration expended considerable diplomatic capital to cajole its European allies into agreeing to create a rapid reaction force under the auspices of NATO. France had proposed that such a force be established under the authority of the European Community, and until Washington exerted its pressure, Germany and other key members of the community had seemed inclined to go along. More recently, the Bush administration reacted with alarm to the Franco-German initiative to create a joint force of approximately 35,000 personnel. That action was viewed as setting up the nucleus of an independent European security organization that might compete with NATO.[16] Washington's apprehension about European intentions became all too evident when Bush departed from the text of his prepared remarks to the Rome summit and admonished the European members of NATO, "If, my friends, your ultimate aim is to provide independently for your own defense, the time to tell us is today."[17]

Incredibly, the United States insists on maintaining an expensive commitment to NATO despite the collapse of the threat that caused the alliance to be created. Washington flirts with new, open-ended peace-keeping missions in one of the most volatile regions of the world—missions that would have only the most remote relevance to America's own security interests—and, instead of welcoming signs of greater European initiative and self-reliance on security issues—a development that could relieve the United States of many of the military burdens that it bore throughout the Cold War—it discourages such actions. In all respects, Washington's current policy bears almost no resemblance to America's long-term goals when NATO was first created.

Washington's Original Intent

Accounts of the negotiations that led to the North Atlantic Treaty indicate that European leaders, especially British foreign secretary Ernest Bevin, sought to entangle the United States as firmly as possible in arrangements for the defense of Europe.[18] U.S. policymakers, however, contemplated a limited and restrained security commitment. The administration of Harry S Truman remained undecided about the need for formal U.S. membership in an alliance until the summer of 1948. Several policymakers, including State Department officials George Kennan and Charles E. Bohlen, argued that there was no need for comprehensive security arrangements and insisted that an informal association with the Brussels Pact— a security alliance formed in March 1948 by France, Britain, and the Benelux nations (Belgium, the Netherlands, and Luxembourg)— would be sufficient.[19]

Even though advocates of a more cautious U.S. security commitment to Europe lost out to the administration's Atlanticist faction, there was still a pervasive assumption that America's NATO commitments would be strictly limited. To reassure nervous Europeans and enable them to get on with their economic recovery programs under the Marshall Plan, the United States was prepared to contribute to the security of the West European nations and to help rebuild their defense forces. The West Europeans were expected to assume primary responsibility for their own defense, especially once their economic recovery was complete.

U.S. officials saw NATO as a predominantly European operation, to which the United States would provide assistance, if necessary. W. Averell Harriman, America's representative to Europe under the Economic Cooperation Administration, typified that attitude when he expressed confidence that by assisting the Europeans to "help themselves in defending their own countries," there would be developed "a military establishment over a period of years which will help to establish a balance of power in Europe, *backed up*, of course, by the military establishment that the United States will have."[20] Others stressed the primacy of European responsibility to an even greater extent. One pro-NATO senator stated that U.S. officials must make it clear that American adherence to the North Atlantic pact did not "put upon us the responsibility of taking care of the whole of Europe in case of trouble."[21]

U.S. leaders were also cautious about the duration of Washington's obligations. Administration officials and the treaty's Senate supporters repeatedly suggested that even the relatively limited U.S. commitments should be temporary. The Europeans wanted a long-term commitment from the United States; they sought a treaty that would be binding for at least 50 years, if not indefinitely. U.S. negotiators insisted that the pact be binding for no more than 20 years and that it be subject to revision after 10 years.[22]

Most proponents of the treaty seemed determined that the United States reap the eventual benefits of restoring a European balance of power. Secretary of Defense Louis Johnson expressed his hope that a strong European force would someday permit "a diminution of our own Military Establishment," although he cautioned that such an outcome was at least "3 or 4 years" away.

> My hope of reducing, and it must in some way be reduced, the great cost of the Defense Establishment lies in seeing these countries grow to the point that we can reduce. That is one of the most persuasive arguments with me in getting behind this program. It offers a chance to bring the cost down within the limit of our economy.[23]

When Johnson expressed the need to reduce the "great cost" of America's military, the defense budget consumed 5 percent of the nation's gross national product; more than four decades later, the figure is virtually the same.

American leaders gave European security a high priority but balked at the allies' attempt to establish a suffocating embrace. The Americans insisted on maintaining a degree of flexibility and wanted to be certain that the alliance did not constitute a free ride for the Europeans. An unspoken assumption was that America would provide aid and protection only if the West European nations made a vigorous effort to improve their military capabilities.

19

Most significant, that is the way Truman administration officials described the North Atlantic pact to the Senate and the American public. For example, supporters offered numerous assurances that no significant numbers of American troops would be stationed in Europe. One of the most graphic assurances came from Secretary of State Dean Acheson in response to a question from Sen. Bourke Hickenlooper. The Iowa Republican noted that Acheson had earlier confirmed that the West Europeans would provide the vast majority of armaments for the collective defense effort. "I presume that refers also to the manpower," Hickenlooper observed. He then pressed Acheson on that point, asking if the United States would be "expected to send substantial numbers of troops over there as a more or less permanent contribution to the development of these countries' capacity to resist?" Acheson replied without hesitation, "The answer to that question, Senator, is a clear and absolute 'No.' "[24]

Acheson's assurance was only one of many given by Truman administration officials and other prominent supporters of the treaty. Gen. Omar Bradley echoed Acheson's comments. Not only did he deny any obligation to station, or intention of stationing, additional U.S. forces on the Continent, he clearly regarded the occupation force in Germany as a temporary phenomenon. When a senator asked whether there was any intention of maintaining those forces during "the full 20 years of the pact," Bradley responded, "No, sir."[25]

Proponents of the North Atlantic pact presented a very clear image of the treaty and America's obligations under it. Senators who passed judgment on the document and citizens who followed the ratification debate were led to believe four important points about America's impending NATO membership: First, the treaty did not involve an automatic commitment to go to war if the allies were attacked; the United States would retain its ability to decide on an appropriate response. Second, there was no obligation or expectation that the United States would station troops in Europe. Third, after the initial phase in which the United States would help the European nations to rearm, Western Europe would become increasingly self-sufficient militarily. Finally, a strong Western Europe would ultimately enable the United States to reduce the scope of its own burdensome military efforts. The idea of a pact that called for modest and, for the most part, short-term U.S. obligations was potent. It contributed significantly to the ease with which the North Atlantic Treaty was ratified.

Temporary Commitments Become Permanent

Less than two years later, America's obligations expanded significantly, and the process of transforming NATO into a permanent enterprise in which the United States would bear most of the responsibilities and burdens began. Three factors acted as catalysts for the transformation in 1950–51: the slow pace of European rearmament efforts, a growing concern among administration officials that the West Europeans could not forge an adequate conventional defense force without the addition of West German manpower, and the fear that the Korean conflict might explode into a global war at a time when the Europeans were not yet capable of defending themselves.

Under intense pressure from the European members of NATO to make a more tangible demonstration of the U.S. commitment, the National Security Council (NSC) adopted NSC-82, a document that outlined an expansion of the U.S. military role in the alliance. Concern about strengthening allied confidence in the U.S. commitment to Western Europe's security was evident in Washington's agreeing to send four divisions of troops to Europe and assume the command of NATO forces.[26] Those developments represented a departure from previous American policy, but NSC-82 tempered the change in several ways. Washington's willingness to assume a more visible and vigorous military posture was contingent on the other NATO members' demonstrating a more serious commitment to the common defense effort.

> The United States should make it clear that it is now squarely up to the European signatories of the North Atlantic Treaty to provide the balance of the forces required for the initial defense. Firm programs for the development of such forces should represent a prerequisite for the fulfillment of the above commitments on the part of the United States.[27]

The conditional nature of the new American obligations was equally evident in the appointment of a supreme NATO commander. To encourage the creation of an effective multinational defense force, the United States agreed to assume initial command responsibilities. But the Truman administration attached several important provisos, including the integration of West German manpower into NATO's defenses, and there was no inclination to retain command indefinitely.

> It is our objective to assist the European nations to provide a defense capable of deterring or meeting an attack. When this objective is achieved it is hoped that the United States will be able to leave to the European nation-members the primary responsibility, with the collaboration of the United States, of maintaining and commanding such force.[28]

Truman's public announcement of his decision to dispatch additional American troops to Europe similarly emphasized the contingent nature of the new U.S. commitments.[29] In private discussions with European diplomats, Acheson stressed that closer European cooperative political action would be necessary to forge an effective integrated defense force and that the allies must be certain that problem would be resolved "at the time when our troops . . . would no longer be necessary in Europe and went home."[30] The assumption that placing a U.S. garrison in Europe and appointing an American as NATO commander were merely interim measures, which would allow the West European states time to build an effective deterrent to Soviet aggression, was not uniquely Acheson's; it pervaded American strategic thinking.[31]

In the years following the adoption of NSC-82, the temporary U.S. obligations became indelible features of NATO. Although impressive conventional force goals were adopted at the alliance's Lisbon conference in 1952, the Europeans conspicuously failed to attain those goals and thus remained unable to provide for their own defense. NATO's deterrent became increasingly Americanized and nuclearized, thereby guaranteeing extensive, ongoing U.S. involvement in the Continent's security.

The additional alliance commitments undertaken by the United States in 1950–51 have now acquired such permanence that to question their continuation is considered radical. But it was not until the middle and late 1950s that President Eisenhower and other U.S. officials finally resigned themselves to an indefinite prolongation of the American troop presence in Europe and long-term command responsibilities for NATO's military forces. Even then,

Eisenhower privately favored the withdrawal of U.S. troops within a few years.[32]

Learning to Love U.S. Preeminence

As Washington's commitments became ever more permanent, U.S officials became increasingly accustomed to dominating the affairs of the alliance. Being the acknowledged "leader of the free world" was as much an emblem of U.S. prestige as it was a burden, and nowhere did flaunting that status acquire greater importance than in NATO. Thoughts of encouraging greater European military self-sufficiency gradually but inexorably faded during the administrations of Presidents John F. Kennedy and Lyndon B. Johnson.

How jealously U.S. leaders guarded Washington's preeminence became evident when French president Charles de Gaulle began to insist on a larger decisionmaking role for his country. Soon after his ascension to power in 1958, de Gaulle challenged what he believed was "Anglo-American domination" of NATO policy. (That was not a new grievance; as commander of the French free forces during World War II, he had voiced similar complaints about a U.S.-British axis.) De Gaulle's initial objective was to gain an equal status for Paris in controlling the nuclear weapons that were playing an increasingly important role in NATO's deterrent strategy. As the only members of the alliance with nuclear weapons, Britain and the United States had the ability to involve the other signatories in dangerous brinksmanship without their consent, according to de Gaulle.

He also began to express skepticism about the reliability of the U.S. nuclear guarantee to the European allies. Such a guarantee might have been credible when the United States had a nuclear monopoly—or at least an overwhelming advantage over the Soviet Union—but by the late 1950s that advantage was fading rapidly as Moscow expanded its own strategic arsenal. De Gaulle openly wondered whether a U.S. president would risk the incineration of American cities to protect Europe.[33] Those were pertinent concerns, and they suggest that de Gaulle was motivated by more than a petty desire to enhance the prestige of France in NATO affairs (although that undoubtedly was an important factor as well). His doubts underscored the fact that U.S. and European security interests were not identical, despite the effusive rhetoric that emanated from some of the more imaginative Atlanticists. Equally important, his discontent with France's (and Europe's) dependence on the United States for its basic security needs would soon be shared by other European allies and become an increasingly common theme in the transatlantic relationship.

De Gaulle's rebellion was the first indication of NATO's impending obsolescence. Instead of viewing his complaints as an omen of serious problems, U.S. officials considered him an upstart who sought to sow dissension in an otherwise harmonious alliance. His proposal to create a three-nation directorate to govern NATO security policy—especially nuclear weapons policy—was firmly rebuffed by U.S. and British officials. He fared no better with other efforts to dilute Washington's dominant decisionmaking role.

U.S. leaders regarded de Gaulle's challenges with growing hostility. Officials in the Kennedy and Johnson administrations habitually termed his position needlessly "disruptive" of the Atlantic alliance.[34] The posture of the American leaders suggested that they equated "alliance solidarity" with an automatic West European deference to U.S. policy preferences. Apparently, they had forgotten, or were deliberately disregarding, America's original intent in joining NATO: to give Western Europe time to recover from the effects of World War II and to regain the ability to provide for its own security with, at most, residual U.S. support. Instead, keeping Western Europe a de facto U.S. protectorate was now regarded as not only normal but immutable, and any manifestation of European independence on security issues was something to be suppressed. That uncompromising stance backfired badly when de Gaulle not only began to develop an independent French nuclear arsenal in 1960 but ultimately withdrew France from NATO's integrated military command (although not from the alliance's political structure) in 1966.

The intellectual rigidity of U.S. political leaders concerning America's preeminent position in NATO was equally evident in their reaction to the Mansfield Amendment. France's decision to depart from NATO's military structure stimulated a reassessment of America's role in the alliance. That reassessment focused on the burden-sharing issue. Would-be reformers and outright critics of NATO made a serious effort to return to something resembling the original concept of NATO by reducing the number of U.S. conventional forces stationed in Europe. The legislative expression of that goal was the Mansfield Amendment, named after its sponsor, Senate majority leader Mike Mansfield (D-Mont.).

The first of Mansfield's proposals, introduced in August 1966, provided for the withdrawal of some 150,000 U.S. military personnel from Europe. The reaction of the Johnson administration was immediate and intensely hostile. In his memoirs, Johnson recalled his reluctance to make even modest cuts in U.S. forces stationed in Europe, "since I regarded any reduction as dangerous."[35] Johnson's principal foreign policy advisers were equally determined to defeat Mansfield's initiative. National Security Adviser Walt W. Rostow, for example, viewed Senate support for the Mansfield Amendment as "the makings of a powerful isolationist coalition" and concluded that a major effort had to be made to repel that challenge to the status quo.[36]

A striking aspect of Rostow's reaction was his equation of the Mansfield resolution with isolationism. The proposal was actually quite modest. It did not envisage a total withdrawal of U.S. conventional forces from Europe, merely a reduction of less than 50 percent. That action would still have left more U.S. troops on the Continent than had been there when the "temporary" dispatch of forces occurred in 1950–51. Mansfield did not favor the termination of U.S. alliance obligations. Indeed, the language of his resolution emphasized that reductions could take place "without adversely affecting either our resolve or ability to meet our commitments under the North Atlantic Treaty." Yet that mild reform of Washington's NATO role was viewed by the Johnson administration and Atlanticists in the foreign policy community as the epitome of reckless isolationism. (That was neither the first nor the last time the epithet "isolationist" was used to discredit advocates of change. Such name calling has been the knee-jerk response of the foreign policy establishment to virtually every suggestion that Washington downsize its NATO commitment.)

Rostow's justification for maintaining a large U.S. troop presence also had a familiar ring. Although he conceded that there was an ongoing "diffusion of power" in the international arena away from both Moscow and Washington (indeed, he was one of the earliest scholars to note the trend toward a multipolar system), he did not fully appreciate its implications for the transatlantic security alliance. Europe might someday be able to provide for its own security, Rostow conceded, but "now and for the foreseeable future, western Europe lacks the political and economic cohesion to generate military forces capable of substituting effectively for the American nuclear and conventional component of NATO."[37] Those words were written more than two decades after NATO's creation and after a period of unprecedented economic growth for the West European nations. Mansfield and other critics of NATO must have wondered, if the Europeans were not ready to assume responsibility for their defense in the late 1960s or early 1970s, when would they be? Apparently not in the 1990s, if the Bush administration can be believed.

The earliest versions of Mansfield's proposals were nonbinding "sense of the Senate" resolutions and, therefore, posed more of a symbolic than a substantive threat to the status quo. That changed in May 1971 when Mansfield suddenly tried to attach the measure as an amendment to the Draft Extension Act. The administration of President Richard M. Nixon reacted with alarm—National Security Adviser Henry Kissinger described the amendment as "a very serious threat to our entire foreign policy"—and went to extraordinary lengths to mobilize leading figures in the Atlanticist community to lobby the Senate. Again the reasoning of U.S. officials revealed how much they had come to assume that European dependence and a massive U.S. role in the defense of Europe were permanent features of the transatlantic relationship. Kissinger even made the astonishing observation that "our conventional forces in Europe [need] to be enhanced not reduced; the Mansfield amendment would dismantle them."[38] The administration's concerted lobbying effort paid off; the Senate rejected the Mansfield Amendment by a vote of 61 to 36—the closest it would ever come to passage.

The determination to preserve U.S. preeminence in the alliance (even at the price of continuing to bear enormously expensive military burdens) became more pronounced in the 1980s. At times the positions adopted by the administration of Ronald Reagan bordered on the bizarre. Administration officials strongly opposed an amendment, introduced in 1984 by Sen. Sam Nunn (D-Ga.), to reduce U.S. forces in Europe by 90,000 if the European allies did not significantly increase their conventional forces. The administration even opposed the much milder proposal sponsored by Reps. Patricia

Schroeder (D-Colo.) and Andy Ireland (R-Fla.) after the approval of the Intermediate Nuclear Forces Treaty in 1988. The Schroeder-Ireland measure merely proposed withdrawal of the U.S. units that had been sent to Europe to operate and protect the intermediate-range missiles that were being removed. With the Reagan administration's opposition to that action, the reflexive protection of the NATO status quo reached new, and absurd, heights.

Such a tenacious defense of Atlanticist orthodoxy, however, failed to stem a rising tide of discontent with the U.S. role in NATO. Some critics focused on the relatively narrow issue of burden sharing, contending that the allies enjoyed a lucrative "free ride" on the U.S. security guarantee.[39] Other critics, especially conservatives and neoconservatives, not only argued that NATO was an excessive financial burden on the United States, but that weak and vacillating European allies unnecessarily inhibited Washington's foreign policy options in the ongoing rivalry with the Soviet Union.[40] More sophisticated analysts noted the divergence of U.S. and West European security agendas, the changing dynamics of the international system, and the growing desire of the Europeans to achieve greater autonomy in the security realm. Such trends, those analysts concluded, indicated that NATO was becoming increasingly obsolete and counterproductive from the standpoint of advancing America's true long-term interests.[41] Those diverse assaults indicated that discontent with Washington's NATO policy did not suddenly flare up after the opening of the Berlin Wall; it had been building for many years.

In the decades since the signing of the North Atlantic Treaty, U.S. officials have gradually lost sight of the original objective. America did not become a member of NATO to shoulder onerous and expensive military obligations forever or to maintain the trappings of "alliance leadership" no matter what the costs, risks, or lack of relevance to America's own security. It undertook such obligations for a specific purpose: to prevent the USSR from dominating a populous region, whose economic potential and technological sophistication would have been a rich prize for Moscow, until the Europeans recovered to the point that they could protect themselves. That mission clearly has been accomplished. Present efforts to preserve NATO spring from a different source: the desire to protect a waning U.S. dominance in the transatlantic relationship.

Weaknesses of the Out-of-Area Mission Justification

As the traditional rationale for NATO has faded, supporters of the alliance have advocated two prominent alternative missions. One is to use the alliance to address out-of-area problems.[42] Former president Nixon is an outspoken advocate of that role.

> [NATO's] creators did not envision that by specifying that the NATO commitment applied to Europe and North America, the alliance would operate only within a strict boundary. . . . Today, as demonstrated in the Persian Gulf, challenges to Western interests can arise half a world away. If NATO adheres mindlessly to artificial geographical restrictions, we will simply be shooting ourselves in the foot, compromising our interests to legalism. . . . While European defense must remain NATO's core mission, so-called "out of area" security cooperation must become its cutting edge.[43]

There are several problems with the out-of-area justification for NATO. Most important, NATO members have always had difficulty agreeing on policy responses to non-European security issues. The generally pro-Arab tilt of France, Italy, and some other European states, for example, has stood in sharp contrast to the strongly pro-Israeli orientation of Washington and London since the early 1970s. Similarly, the Reagan administration tried without success to convince its NATO partners that Marxist insurgencies in Central America posed a security threat to the entire democratic West. Not only did many of the West European governments reject that notion, they even provided financial aid to Nicaragua's Sandinista dictatorship.

Allies who were unable to reach a policy consensus on out-of-area issues during the Cold War are not likely to do so in a post–Cold War setting. Previously, Washington could at least raise the specter of the Soviet threat and argue that policy disagreements risked weakening the alliance. It is testimony to the diverging perspectives and security interests of the United States and the West European nations that such arguments usually proved ineffective. Without a Soviet threat, the prospects for common policy objectives in regions outside Europe will probably diminish, not improve.

Atlanticists who are tempted to cite the response to the Persian Gulf crisis as a model for NATO collaboration in out-of-area operations should examine that episode more carefully. Washington was able to secure cooperation from the European allies only with the greatest diplomatic exertion. Even then, support for the U.S.-led war effort was (with the exception of Britain) grudging and half-hearted. Except for Britain and France, none of the NATO signatories provided more than token military forces. Although Germany gave financial aid, it steadfastly refused to contribute troops, citing alleged constitutional constraints on military operations outside the NATO theater.

It was also significant that the allies gave military and financial help individually, not as part of an official NATO operation. Secretary of State Baker's efforts early in the gulf crisis to solicit a coordinated NATO response (using the argument that Iraq posed a threat to alliance member Turkey) were politely but firmly rebuffed by the alliance partners.

The refusal of the NATO members to use the alliance for an out-of-area operation against Saddam Hussein dims hopes that they would be willing to do so on other occasions. Several atypical factors converged in the gulf crisis to maximize the chances of NATO unity. First and foremost was oil. Several economists and oil experts have debunked the notion that Iraq's takeover of Kuwait—or even a subsequent takeover of Saudi Arabia—would have given Baghdad a stranglehold on the economies of the West (see Chapter 8). Nevertheless, most Westerners and their governments apparently believed the alarmist scenarios. The West Europeans, therefore, had an unusually strong incentive to authorize a NATO response, since they assumed that an important economic interest was threatened.

The egregious nature of Iraq's aggression should also have generated widespread support for an out-of-area NATO mission. Saddam repeatedly managed to play the role of the quintessential international villain. His effort to expunge Kuwait from the map, his seizure of Western hostages, and his blustering threats to use chemical weapons all reinforced Bush's contention that Saddam was a new Hitler who had to be stopped.

Despite those advantages, Washington was unable to gain allied consent to use NATO against Iraq. Moreover, although the European allies all endorsed Washington's leadership once the fighting began, several NATO members (including France and Italy) had expressed vehement disagreement with U.S. policy right up to the eve of Operation Desert Storm. They favored giving economic sanctions a longer time to succeed, hinted that some Kuwaiti territorial concessions might be appropriate, and repeatedly urged the United States to avoid military action except as a last resort.[44] If the United States could not convince NATO as an organization to undertake out-of-area operations in the gulf crisis, there should be little expectation that it can do so in future episodes, since U.S. and West European perspectives are likely to be further apart.

NATO's inability to deal with problems outside Europe also means that the alleged advantage of stationing U.S. troops on the Continent for possible redeployment elsewhere during a crisis is mostly illusory. A European host government might object strenuously if U.S. forces stationed in its country, ostensibly for NATO security missions, were dispatched to implement a policy that the host government opposed. It is indicative of the sensitive nature of this issue that U.S. and other NATO leaders rarely invoke the out-of-area justification for a continuing U.S. troop presence when they address European audiences. They realize that there is scant public support anywhere in Western Europe for using the Continent as a staging area for U.S. forces whose mission would be unrelated to the defense of Europe.

NATO's "Stability" Mission: Dangers for the United States

The inadequacies of the out-of-area justification have caused most supporters of the alliance to emphasize another alternative mission: preserving stability in Europe. Even NATO's most ardent admirers generally concede that there is little danger that Moscow will attempt to regain the East European empire, much less mount an invasion of Western Europe.[45] The possibility exists, of course, that Russia's fragile experiment in democracy may fail. Even if a new authoritarian regime came to power, however, it would face daunting internal economic limitations and a radically changed European geopolitical environment. The political structure of the Soviet Union has been shattered, and the various republics and the former East European satellites can be expected to defend their newly acquired independence tenaciously. Russia has only two-thirds the population of the old USSR and a comparable proportion of the economic output. Moreover, it is evident that previous U.S. estimates of the size of the Soviet economy were wildly inflated. In short, Russia's economy is about the size of Italy's, hardly an adequate foundation for achieving expansionist territorial ambitions. Moscow's economic woes have also had an adverse impact on the capabilities of its military forces. The once powerful Soviet military has fragmented along national lines, and its readiness has rapidly declined. Although a future authoritarian regime might want to restore the imperial "glory" of the USSR, it would face enormous obstacles. A new Russian threat to Western Europe would be merely a weak echo of the menace once posed by the Soviet Union.

Most Atlanticists recognize that Russian expansionism is not a credible rationale for maintaining NATO, so they portray the alliance as an indispensable force for general European stability. In its narrowest form, the stability rationale stresses the political chaos that may follow the breakup of the Soviet Union. Atlanticists are apprehensive about the possibility of fighting among the various republics as they assert their independence and grapple with a variety of problems, including border disputes—a Yugoslavian scenario writ large. An even greater worry is what will happen to the nearly 30,000 strategic and tactical nuclear weapons in Moscow's arsenal—now deployed in Russia, the Ukraine, Belarus, and Kazakhstan—if the central command established by the new CIS breaks down.[46]

Those are not trivial concerns, but the maintenance of NATO has little relevance to the resolution of such problems. The outcome of the political ferment in the former USSR will be largely determined by developments within the CIS. The United States and the West European nations will have an influence only at the margins.

Uncertainty about the command and control of CIS nuclear weapons underscores NATO's irrelevance and obsolescence in another way. The credibility of extended deterrence (the U.S. nuclear shield used to protect the European allies) was questionable enough in the relatively stable geostrategic environment of the Cold War when only Moscow needed to be deterred. Any implied promise to risk the destruction of American cities to deter several, possibly unstable, nuclear-armed republics is considerably less credible. Again, the issue is not whether there are security problems in Europe but whether NATO has much relevance to the management of those problems.

The stability rationale for a U.S.-led transatlantic alliance is much wider, however, than the need to deal with the proliferation of nuclear weapons and political turbulence in the CIS. Marian Leighton, senior analyst at National Security Research, Inc., concisely states the underlying rationale for a broader mission.

> The 40-plus years of peace that Europe has enjoyed since NATO's creation contrast markedly with the instability that generally plagued the continent from the time of Bismarck until the end of World War II. The NATO alliance, with U.S. military power as its foundation, is the chief instrument of European stability and should not be jettisoned simply because war in Europe now seems a remote possibility.[47]

A number of other experts have also stressed the more general stability mission. John Lewis Gaddis, one of America's most distinguished foreign policy scholars, even suggested that the Warsaw Pact could maintain stability in Eastern Europe while NATO did so in Western Europe.[48] (Amazingly, he made that suggestion just months before Warsaw Pact leaders voted to dissolve the organization.) Several other writers have proposed that the Eastern European nations be granted NATO membership, and some enthusiastic advocates of stability have even suggested that Russia be admitted.[49] Gradually, the preservation of stability throughout Europe has become NATO's new raison d'être.[50]

The insidious transformation of NATO from an alliance to deter Soviet aggression into a comprehensive regional peace-keeping body does not serve the best interests of the American people. Most Americans accepted (albeit reluctantly) the costs and risks associated with the U.S. commitment to NATO throughout the Cold War when the rationale was the need to prevent an expansionist great power (the Soviet Union) from gaining control of the population and industrial capacity of Western Europe. Were the USSR to do so, it was generally conceded, the already serious Soviet threat to America's own security could become lethal. The burden-sharing critics made telling points about the dubious wisdom of allowing the Europeans to free ride on the U.S. security guarantee, and Washington's insistence on making a U.S.-dominated NATO the sole vehicle for dealing with European security issues was a terribly short-sighted policy. Nevertheless, the argument that it was worth risking war and spending tens of billions of dollars each year to defend the security of Western Europe and thereby thwart a dangerous rival was at least plausible.

Embracing the risks and costs of a quixotic crusade to preserve stability in Eastern Europe and the CIS is another matter entirely.[51] It is difficult to imagine how becoming entangled in ancient and intractable ethnic quarrels, religious conflicts, and territorial disputes in regions that have never been deemed relevant—much less essential—to the security of the United States constitutes a worthwhile mission for the American republic. Assuming such burdens would be an exercise in masochism as well as futility.

Indeed, the prospect of instability throughout Eastern Europe is an argument for eliminating the U.S. military presence on the Continent. If we undertake the stability mission, there will be almost unlimited possibilities for dangerous entanglements. The ongoing turmoil in Yugoslavia is an indication of what to expect. The current fighting between Serbs and Croats (and Serbs and Slavic Moslems) is only one of the possible conflicts in and around that unhappy country. Another Yugoslavian republic, Macedonia, could cause problems for neighboring Bulgaria, Greece, and Turkey—all of which possess sizable territories claimed by Macedonian nationalists.[52] Although only dimly remembered in the United States, disputes over the status of Macedonia led to two major Balkan wars in the years immediately preceding World War I.

The situation elsewhere in Eastern Europe is scarcely any better. Poland has already complained about the alleged mistreatment of the Polish minority by the newly independent Lithuanian government. Hungary harbors longstanding grievances against Romania for that country's discrimination against its Hungarian minority. Brutal ethnic warfare has already convulsed Moldova and the Republic of Georgia, and Moscow has barely been able to dampen major fighting between Armenia and Azerbaijan. Disagreements between Moscow and Kiev over the political status of Crimea are potentially dangerous. Eastern Europe was a turbulent, contentious, and frequently violent region before communist regimes suppressed those conflicts and imposed a semblance of order. Suppression, though, is not the same as resolution, and ancient disputes have rapidly resurfaced in the postcommunist period.

Eastern Europe may well become a cauldron of political and military chaos in the coming years.[53] That is unfortunate, but there is little the United States, or NATO as a collective entity, will be able to do about it. It is hubris to assume that NATO can keep the lid on a volatile region that has just escaped the domination of a hegemonic power. The Soviet Union barely succeeded in maintaining temporary order despite its military occupation of most of the region and imposition of the most draconian forms of totalitarian control. Washington can scarcely hope to do so with far more restrained and limited means.

Moreover, there is no compelling reason for the United States to intervene in disputes between small European states or among competing factions within those states. The delineation of power and territory between Croats and Serbs, the unity or breakup of Czecho-Slovakia, or whether Moldova remains independent or merges with Romania may be extremely important issues to the parties involved. And we can all grieve if (as the Croats and Serbs have done) they are determined to settle their differences with violence. But such internecine or bilateral conflicts do not affect the global—or in most cases, even the European—geopolitical balance and, therefore, do not impinge on vital American security interests. Indeed, it would be better to insulate the United States from a conflict—between, say, Hungary and Romania over the status of Transylvania—than to preserve security arrangements that might entangle American troops in it. That principle would apply not only to NATO but just as readily to gratuitous U.S. involvement in regional or civil conflicts through such organizations as the CSCE.[54]

The West European powers have at least some tangible interests at stake in East European disorders (e.g., the prospect of being inundated by refugees), and they may want to pursue a common policy through the CSCE, the Western European Union (WEU), or the European Community. (Even the West Europeans would be wise to be cautious about becoming entangled in the conflicts of their eastern neighbors, however.) The greater relevance of such conflicts to the West Europeans is strong argument for a European-directed rather than a U.S.-directed security arrangement. It is precisely because developments in Eastern Europe affect the United States less immediately than the they do the West European nations that a U.S.-dominated NATO is a singularly inappropriate organization for dealing with problems in that region.

NATO's Hidden Agenda: Containing Germany

For some Americans and many Europeans, the stability argument is a diplomatic euphemism for keeping Germany subordinate.

NATO must be preserved and the United States must maintain troops in Europe, it is argued, to contain German power. Some have gone beyond that point and seem to regard Germany as a candidate to replace the USSR as the principal long-term threat to world peace. In the earliest days of the post–Cold War era, Edward C. Meyer, former chief of staff of the U.S. Army, stated bluntly that a reunified Germany (along with a more assertive Japan) would pose the major future threat to U.S. security.[55] Others have been only slightly more circumspect, and the necessity of preserving NATO to protect Europe (and the world) from Germany has become an article of faith among many NATO supporters. Columbia University political scientist James Chace was one of the earliest proponents of that view. According to Chace, German reunification automatically required "a revamped NATO, whose purpose is no longer simply to deter the Soviet Union from aggressive moves against Western Europe. In fact, what will be needed is a cooperative arrangement with the Soviet Union that will allay Soviet and European fears of both German revanchism and German military and economic power."[56]

The passage of time has not noticeably mollified Germanophobes on either side of the Atlantic. William E. Odom, former director of the National Security Agency, argues that only the linkage of Germany to a U.S.-led NATO can ensure peace in Europe. Whenever Germany has acted on its own, he contends, it has pursued an expansionist policy and threatened the well-being of its neighbors.[57] Leslie H. Gelb speaks cryptically but ominously of "a power vacuum that can only be filled by Germany" in the event of NATO's "premature" demise, and he sees the Franco-German corps as a possible threat to the alliance's preeminence in security matters. "NATO remains the only group on the horizon," he concludes, "that can keep the door closed to renewed militarism and saber-rattling."[58] Others are far less subtle than Gelb. Columnist Richard Cohen, citing everything from German chancellor Helmut Kohl's tardiness in officially guaranteeing the sanctity of the Polish-German border to incidents of violence against foreigners by small neo-Nazi factions, asserts bluntly, "Germany, whether it likes it or not, remains on parole."[59] Gen. Robert Oakes, commander of U.S. air forces in Europe, suggests that Germany needs American troops to keep it from misbehaving.[60] Kenneth Adelman, former director of the Arms Control and Disarmament Agency, opines that "age-old concerns remain about a unified Germany of the future acting like the unified Germany of the past."[61]

The editors of *The Economist* find even Bonn's enthusiasm for a federal Europe a cause for suspicion, despite the dilution of national sovereignty that would accompany the creation of such an entity. "A federal Europe, with Germany at its heart, offers Germans the chance to extend their power and influence in all directions." *The Economist* derisively dismisses counterarguments as made "from a safe distance across a stretch of water from continental Europe."[62]

The idea that NATO is essential for constraining German power is hardly new; from the beginning, the alliance has had an implicit "double containment" mission (keeping Germany as well as the Soviet Union in line). Lord Ismay, NATO's first secretary general, reportedly remarked that the alliance existed to "keep the Russians out, the Americans in, and the Germans down."[63] There was even a noticeable lack of initial enthusiasm among the Federal Republic's allies for the prospect of reunification after a beleaguered East Germany opened the Berlin Wall in November 1989. It was only when it became evident that there was overwhelming sentiment in both German states for reunification and that Kohl's government was adamant about ending the nation's artificial division that the United States and the other NATO members grudgingly accepted the inevitable.[64] They realized that further resistance would provoke an acrimonious breach with Bonn and possibly jeopardize NATO's continued existence.

Concern about a "German threat" is not entirely irrational. The competitive nature of the international system makes it likely that a strong, capable power such as Germany will gradually become more assertive in promoting its own political and economic interests.[65] Bonn's determination to recognize the independence of Croatia and Slovenia despite opposition from other members of the European Community—and the United States—is an indication of that trend.[66] It is a measure of Germany's influence that it was ultimately able to persuade the rest of the European Community to follow its policy. Since Germany is already the strongest and most dynamic economic power in Europe—and its relative military strength is also increasing as the CIS republics dismantle the military establishment they inherited from the Soviet Union—the other European powers may have reason for some uneasiness.

Nevertheless, it is easy to overstate both the probability and the scope of a "German threat." The size of Germany's military forces and the levels of military spending are actually declining. Moreover, there is a strong pacifist streak in German public opinion. Kohl's efforts to change the country's Basic Law (constitution) to authorize German forces to participate in UN or CSCE peace-keeping operations has encountered strong opposition. It is indicative of the continuing legal and political constraints on military activities that Bonn, despite its hard-line stance on the conflict in Yugoslavia, has made it clear that there will be no contribution of German forces if the international community decides to intervene. At least for the foreseeable future, Germany's assertiveness is likely to be confined to the diplomatic and economic arenas, hardly the hallmark of a dangerous expansionist power.

Much of the concern about Germany is a mixture of obsolete historical analogies, ethnic prejudice, and self-serving rationales to justify the preservation of NATO. Atlanticists have really entered the conceptual Twilight Zone when they think it reasonable that NATO's primary mission in the 1990s ought to be the containment of the alliance's most vibrant European member. Such a mission would require German cooperation, or at least acquiescence, to avoid the very proliferation of tensions and confrontation that NATO supposedly wants to prevent. Although there may be some guilt-ridden Germans who are willing to collaborate in the hobbling of their own country, most Germans are much more likely to react to allied distrust with anger and resentment. American troops may have been welcome guests during the Cold War when Germany was divided and the Federal Republic confronted a powerful Soviet adversary. (Although even then, a significant minority of Germans viewed those troops more as an army of occupation than as partners in a genuine collective defense effort.) That welcome is likely to wear very thin once the last CIS soldiers leave German soil. A May 1992 *Frankfurter Allgemeine Zeitung* survey found that 57 percent of Germans want the U.S. troops out of their country by 1995.[67] The perception that American forces intend to remain as "parole officers" to monitor Germany's behavior has enormous potential for embittering U.S.-German relations.

Above all, the United States and other nations must not view Germans as congenital aggressors.[68] The nightmare of Nazi Germany resulted from the convergence of conditions that were unique to the interwar period (the artificial subjugation to Britain and France, resentment of the draconian Treaty of Versailles, and an unprecedented global economic depression). Unfortunately, Germanophobes on both sides of the Atlantic frequently act as though Germans are born with a double dose of original sin. A more realistic appraisal is needed. Germany is no more likely to pursue an expansionist agenda than any other great power. Indeed, given the bruising experiences of two disastrous military defeats in this century, and the more recent experience that cultivating a dynamic economy and astute diplomacy can be a safer and more reliable source of influence, Germany may be among the countries least likely to embark upon the risky path of aggression.

Although history can never be forgotten, it also cannot justify obsolete alliances. The doctrine of collective guilt—and the imputation of guilt to later generations that had nothing to do with the sins of the Nazis—is inherently unjust. There ought to be a statute of limitations. Otherwise, we would need a mechanism to constrain a potential Napoleonic revival in France. The German containment thesis seems more the product of reflexive historical suspicions and the search for a "necessary enemy" to justify NATO's continued existence than of any reasonable geopolitical analysis.

Washington's Hidden Agenda: Keeping Europe Dependent

If containing Germany is NATO's hidden agenda, maintaining U.S. preeminence in the alliance and thwarting European efforts to create an independent security policy is Washington's hidden agenda. Ever since NATO was established, U.S. political leaders have urged the Europeans to assume more responsibility for their own defense and to pay a larger portion of the cost. Washington has also expressed its support for greater European unity on both economic and security matters. Such official enthusiasm for a strong "European pillar" to support NATO, however, has concealed—at least since the mid-1950s—a profound ambivalence about the Europeans' taking greater initiative. What U.S. leaders apparently want is the best of both worlds: a democratic Europe strong enough to relieve the United States of some of its security burdens but not strong enough to challenge U.S. primacy.[69]

That is an unrealistic expectation. During the Cold War the European nations had little choice but to accept U.S. leadership on major security issues, however much that dependence may have rankled at times. The magnitude of the Soviet threat inhibited any inclination to risk disrupting alliance solidarity. As historian Ronald Steel observes:

> From the beginning NATO has always been a kind of Lincoln's Cabinet: every member would solemnly express its opinion, but the American president had the only vote that mattered. This was perfectly reasonable. The United States provided the nuclear deterrent and the central core of NATO's land forces against the Soviets. In return, the Europeans let the United States make all of the big decisions.[70]

However, U.S. control has never been quite as complete as many U.S. officials have assumed or desired. The Europeans have frequently chafed at Washington's domination of NATO policy as the region's prosperity has grown, and they have become adept at achieving a surprising degree of autonomy in their foreign policies. The ostentatiously independent strategy adopted by Charles de Gaulle and his successors was the most obvious example, but there were others. Bonn's Ostpolitik—the policy of outreach to East Germany and the rest of the Soviet bloc in an effort to create a more normal relationship—in the 1970s and 1980s was pursued despite Washington's uneasiness and barely disguised opposition. Many of the European allies openly resisted U.S. policy preferences on such issues as building the Soviet gas pipeline, the Arab-Israeli dispute, relations with left-wing regimes in Latin America, and East-West trade.

Without the common Soviet threat to sustain alliance cohesion, the divergence of U.S. and West European security interests will accelerate. The actions of the major European powers in the past two years confirm that trend. The effort by Paris and Bonn to expand their 4,200-man joint military brigade to a force of approximately 35,000 troops and their insistence that the WEU "become an integral part of the process of European union" are indicative of the movement toward greater security independence. France and Germany may profess to believe that the joint brigade will not undercut NATO, but the reality is otherwise—as most confirmed Atlanticists recognize.[71] Former secretary of defense Caspar Weinberger may have been more emotional than most when he asserted that the "extraordinarily undesirable independent army proposals" of Kohl and President François Mitterrand of France "rightly cause consternation in the United Kingdom and among American and other strong supporters of NATO," but he expressed the consensus view of NATO partisans.[72]

As Weinberger's comments suggest, Britain and some of the smaller West European states are less enthusiastic than Bonn or Paris about diluting the U.S. security role in Europe. But even those countries are beginning to recognize that the era during which a U.S.-dominated NATO had a monopoly on European security issues is over. Several of the positions adopted at the Rome NATO summit confirmed that trend. Even as the alliance signatories were pledging eternal fidelity to NATO, the European members insisted on language that recognized the development of a distinct "European security identity and defense role" and acknowledged the growing importance of the WEU and the CSCE—both of which will inevitably be European-directed organizations.[73] The policies adopted by the members of the European Community at their historic meeting in Maastricht in December 1991 also pointed toward the creation of a separate European security identity. Although the final document reflected compromises between the countries that wanted a strongly "Europeanist" foreign policy and those (primarily Britain and Denmark) that sought to preserve as much as possible of the transatlantic connection, the substantive result was a commitment to greatly strengthen the WEU. Britain and the rest of the Atlanticist faction received little more than the familiar rhetorical sop that increasing the power of the WEU was consistent with creating a strong European pillar within NATO.[74]

The pertinent question is whether U.S. leaders and members of the American foreign policy establishment can adjust to growing European self-reliance with at least a semblance of grace. Unfortunately, they seem determined to criticize and if possible sabotage every meaningful measure the West European nations propose for taking greater responsibility for the security of their region. U.S. officials are reluctant to acknowledge that a strong, prosperous Western Europe will ultimately adopt security strategies tailored to its own distinct interests. Those strategies will be increasingly independent of the United States and may sometimes even run directly counter to U.S. wishes. Indeed, that is one of the most significant implications of the end of the Cold War. The post–Cold

War international system does not lend itself to a true transatlantic security partnership. Although U.S. and European interests overlap, they are by no means congruent; even the modest convergence of interests that existed during the Cold War has begun to dissipate. It is unrealistic to expect the European nations to remain deferential junior partners in a security system run by Washington.

Instead of coming to grips with that sea change in the U.S.-European relationship, members of the American foreign policy establishment search for cosmetic reforms that will preserve the substance of U.S. dominance. Thus, there are frequent calls for a greater sharing of decisionmaking authority and for the appointment of a European as the commander of NATO forces. Such reforms might have a degree of symbolic importance, and at one time they might even have been useful transitional measures, but the time for such tepid changes is long past. Limited reforms cannot disguise the fundamental divergence of U.S. and West European security interests or objectives in a post–Cold War environment. At best, such reforms are exercises in the politics of delay.

Attempts to preserve a waning U.S. primacy are not cost free. The most obvious cost is financial. Ninety billion dollars or more a year is a lot to pay for the prestige of "alliance leadership." There are also hidden costs. Efforts to reassert U.S. dominance could provoke acrimonious disputes that would dwarf the burden-sharing controversies of the 1970s and 1980s. Moreover, there could easily be a spill-over effect from security to other arenas; a wide array of trade relations and diplomatic and cultural ties could be damaged. Such a development would be unfortunate for all concerned.

Washington's approach, which foreign policy analyst Alan Tonelson has aptly described as a "smothering strategy,"[75] also has unfortunately retarded the development of European collective defense arrangements that will be increasingly needed in the coming years. That problem has become all too evident in the European Community's attempt to deal with the Yugoslavian crisis. The EC members aggressively took the lead in efforts to end the internecine fighting in Yugoslavia. Their initiative was an implicit recognition that NATO was an inappropriate vehicle for dealing with the crisis— that it was legitimately a European rather than a transatlantic concern. There was also more than a little irritation in Bonn and some other European capitals at Washington's initial ham-handed efforts to dominate the diplomatic process, epitomized by Secretary Baker's remarks in Belgrade on June 21, 1991, in which he clearly tilted in favor of the central Yugoslavian government—even as that government began to topple.

It soon became apparent, however, that the European Community lacked both a sufficient policy consensus and the institutional mechanisms needed to handle the crisis. Efforts to arrange a cease-fire among the warring factions foundered throughout the summer and fall of 1991. The community fared little better in deciding on a menu of sanctions to be invoked if diplomatic measures continued to prove unsuccessful, although it ultimately endorsed a UN-imposed arms embargo in late 1991 and an array of UN economic sanctions in May 1992.

Atlanticists cite the European Community's difficulties in dealing with the Yugoslavian turmoil as evidence that U.S. leadership is indispensable and that NATO must be maintained. The caustic observation of an unnamed administration official that the EC governments "could not organize a three-car motorcade if their lives depended on it" typified the contemptuous attitude among members of the U.S. foreign policy elite.[76] But the community's limitations are largely the result of the domination the United States has exercised in security matters since the 1940s. Ronald Steel exaggerates only slightly when he notes, "For all practical purposes Europe's defense and diplomacy were run from Washington."[77] Instead of encouraging its allies to strengthen independent European security institutions such as the WEU, the United States has viewed them as threats to NATO's (and hence Washington's) preeminence.

We can never know whether the West Europeans would have been better able to adopt unified and effective policies for dealing with the Yugoslavian conflict if Washington had not clung so tenaciously to its smothering strategy. Trying to formulate common policies and create institutional arrangements from scratch in the midst of a major foreign policy crisis, however, is hardly the optimal situation. Unfortunately, that is what the members of the European Community have had to do. The longer Washington insists that NATO eclipse the WEU, the CSCE, and any other competing organization, the longer it will take the European states to become competent security actors. Given the number of troubles that can be anticipated throughout Eastern Europe, continued U.S. domination is a dangerous policy that creates an institutional vacuum. It is neither in America's nor Europe's best interest to perpetuate Western Europe's artificial security dependence on the United States.

The Bush administration also appears to be operating under the illusion that preserving the NATO commitment will give the United States "leverage" on economic and political issues. Secretary of Defense Richard B. Cheney has hinted at that motive, contending that the United States must have "a sizable military presence in Europe to maintain American political ties with Western Europe."[78] Similarly, Gen. John Galvin, NATO's military commander, admitted that the U.S. strategy was to maintain a troop commitment to NATO "in order to get a seat at the table and a certain amount of influence."[79]

The most blatant attempts to apply that thesis came in rapid succession in early February 1992 from a congressional delegation and Vice President Dan Quayle. Sen. Richard Lugar (R-Ind.), one of 11 senators and representatives attending a conference in Munich, stated that the Europeans did not seem to appreciate the consequences of intransigence on trade issues. "If they don't back down, it could undermine NATO and American participation in the alliance. We're heading for a precipice that Europeans don't understand." In a similar vein, Quayle led a drive to convince the allies that no issue was more important to NATO than preventing a breakdown of the General Agreement on Tariffs and Trade (GATT). The current round of negotiations had long been stymied by a U.S.-EC stalemate on European agricultural subsidies. Quayle cautioned the Europeans against clinging to their demands, noting ominously, "Trade is a security issue."[80]

But Washington's ability to translate its dominance in the transatlantic security relationship into comparable influence on such issues as trade, monetary policy, and out-of-area diplomatic initiatives has long been overrated.[81] Except during the initial decade of the Cold War, when U.S. dominance was overwhelming, the European states have typically made just enough concessions on those matters to prevent a breach in the alliance.

If the United States encountered difficulties in exercising meaningful leverage during the Cold War when the value of its military guarantee to the Europeans was quite substantial, it is likely to encounter far more severe problems in the post–Cold War era. The value of the U.S. conventional military presence, and even the protection afforded by the U.S. nuclear shield, has depreciated markedly with the demise of the Soviet threat. Washington cannot threaten that if it is not given a prominent seat at the European table when economic and political policies are determined, the United States will pick up its troops and go home. At the height of the Cold War that might have been an alarming prospect to most Europeans—if they believed we would actually withdraw. Now such a threat would provoke little more than mild concern—and might even be greeted with yawns in some circles.

It is already evident that Washington's clout with the major European actors on issues as diverse as aid to the republics of the former Soviet Union and monetary policy is extremely limited.[82] A small but telling incident in December 1991 underlines the nature of the new relationship. As reported by syndicated columnists Rowland Evans and Robert Novak, President Bush telephoned German chancellor Kohl to dissuade him from extending diplomatic recognition to the breakaway Yugoslavian republics. But Kohl "was too busy with the annual convention of his Christian Democratic Union Party to pick up the phone." U.S. officials, long accustomed to deference from America's German ally, were enraged at such a snub to the president of the United States. "It's a [expletive deleted] outrage," fumed one high-level administration official.[83] Actually, it is merely another indication that the major European nations are no longer going to be at the beck and call of the United States.

The European reaction to the clumsy attempts of Vice President Quayle and the congressional delegation to use the threat of U.S. withdrawal from NATO to obtain concessions on GATT was an even clearer sign. Dutch foreign minister Hans van den Broek scorned the U.S. tactic. "It does not work to say we better agree on GATT or else America will leave NATO," he stated bluntly.[84] The Europeans might wish to retain some security tie with the United States as a long-term insurance policy and as a modestly valuable defense subsidy, but U.S. protection is no longer viewed as a vital need. If U.S. officials believe they can parlay the NATO security commitment into influence on economic and political matters, they are in for a rude awakening.

Former American ambassador to the United Nations Jeane Kirkpatrick laments, "The most important conversations about the future organization of the Western world are taking place without any U.S. participation."[85] That is to be expected. Although the United States may sometimes be a guest at the policy deliberations of the European Community, its NATO leadership role will not give Washington an equal voice, much less a veto. The days when the United States could act as paterfamilias to the European nations are over.

Beyond NATO

The United States faces both an urgent need and an unprecedented opportunity to make a bold change in its European policy. NATO was created to bolster nervous Europeans whose nations still suffered from the devastation of World War II. But Western Europe achieved full economic recovery long ago and is now a prosperous and politically stable region capable of forging military forces adequate to meet any likely danger. The members of the European Community have a collective population of more than 342 million and a collective gross domestic product of nearly $6 *trillion*.[86] It is ludicrous to suggest that a community with those characteristics cannot manage problems that arise from disorder in Eastern Europe or defend itself from threats that might emanate from sources outside the European region.

NATO's principal purpose was to deter an attack by an aggressively expansionist Soviet Union, a threat that seemed at least plausible under Stalin and his successors. Today the Soviet Union has disintegrated, and its successor, the Commonwealth of Independent States, which will be preoccupied by internal economic and political problems for years to come, will undoubtedly be much less aggressive. There is simply no longer a credible superpower threat to the security of Western Europe. Under such vastly changed conditions, a U.S.-dominated NATO protectorate is an anachronism, and the time has come to devolve full responsibility for the security of Europe to the Europeans.

There is certainly no justification for perpetuating the expanded NATO commitments undertaken temporarily in the early 1950s. At the very least, U.S. officials should insist on a return to the original concept of NATO: conditional U.S. support for a predominantly

European defense effort and no permanent U.S. garrison on the Continent. If that level of American involvement was deemed sufficient in 1948–49, during the most virulent phase of the Cold War and at a time when the West Europeans could afford to make only meager military efforts, it should certainly be sufficient in the post–Cold War environment.

Indeed, it is difficult to make a credible case for maintaining even the original level of commitment envisaged by NATO's American architects. If the mission of protecting Western Europe from the USSR has been fulfilled, then the alliance—in contrast to American political, economic, and cultural engagement in Europe—is no longer needed. There should be every incentive to celebrate NATO's success, give the alliance a long-overdue retirement party, and enjoy the financial benefits of reduced military obligations. Washington should welcome, not resent, such signs of European initiative and independence as the Franco-German military brigade and efforts to strengthen the WEU. Devolution to the Europeans of responsibility for the security of their own region was the original long-term objective of the U.S. officials who helped create NATO, and that objective was consistent with American interests. It is certainly not in the best interests of the American people to transform NATO into a peace-keeping organization to intervene in a host of obscure East European ethnic conflicts that do not have even the most tenuous connection with America's security requirements.

Some moderates who support the alliance concede that it will not play a major long-term role in Europe's security affairs, but they insist that it has an important "transitional" role to play in the immediate post–Cold War period.[87] That is a debatable proposition, but it is not nearly as indefensible as the position taken by President Bush and other die-hard NATO partisans. Their campaign to preserve NATO suggests that obsolete institutions are even more durable than old soldiers, who, according to Gen. Douglas MacArthur, "never die, they just fade away." NATO is not fading away; it is trying to achieve organizational immortality.

2. Japan: Smothering an Ally

Washington's determination to maintain a dominant military position in Europe despite the cost involved is echoed in U.S. policy toward Japan. Remnants of the American occupying force that presided over the rebuilding of Japan after World War II are still in place. All told, more than 45,000 Americans are currently stationed on bases in Japan, including 15,000 Air Force personnel, 1,800 Army, 6,300 Navy, and 22,000 Marines; Japan is home port to another 10,000 personnel from the U.S. Seventh Fleet as well.[1]

The financial price tag of the defense commitment to Japan is substantial. The total cost of Washington's security obligations in East Asia is nearly $40 billion a year, and approximately one-half of that sum is attributable to the defense of Japan.[2] That figure is actually a conservative estimate, for it includes only the cost of U.S. conventional air, naval, and ground forces stationed in the western Pacific for the defense of the Japanese archipelago and units designated as reinforcements in the event of hostilities. It does not, for example, include the cost of the U.S. forces that help protect Japan's oil lifeline to the volatile Persian Gulf.

The ostensible reason for the U.S. military presence throughout the Cold War was to protect Japan, as well as other U.S. allies in East Asia, from the neighboring communist giants—the Soviet Union and China. That motive gradually emerged as the dominant one, but it was never the exclusive one. Initially, the primary U.S. objective was to disarm Japan and demilitarize Japanese society, and that objective remained important, though secondary, even during the Cold War. Just as NATO had a double containment mission, so did the U.S. military presence in Japan. Washington sought to protect Japan, but it also intended to forestall a resurgent Japan from posing a security threat in East Asia.[3]

America's Cold Warriors clung to the argument that a U.S. military presence was needed in the western Pacific to counter a lingering Soviet threat even more stubbornly than they clung to similar arguments for preserving the NATO commitment. Months after the collapse of Moscow's East European satellite regimes, some policy experts still insisted that Cold War tensions had not abated in East Asia. A May 1991 study by the conservative Heritage Foundation, for example, concluded that it was not yet appropriate to negotiate arms control agreements with the Soviets comparable to the Conventional Forces in Europe Treaty.[4] University of California political scientist A. James Gregor was equally pessimistic. "In the euphoria engendered by the conviction that 'history' was at an end, Americans have failed to adequately assess the threat environment that prevails in East Asia." Nothing that Moscow had done had significantly reduced the Soviet armed forces' offensive capabilities in that region, he insisted. Those forces remained "formidable."[5]

Milder notes of caution were expressed by more prominent members of the U.S. foreign policy establishment. Former chairman of the Joint Chiefs of Staff Adm. William Crowe, writing in the spring of 1991, argued: "The major strategic issue is still the USSR. It is not clear how the United States should cope with the remaining, and in some respects growing, Soviet military capability in the Asian-Pacific area."[6] Former U.S. ambassador to China Winston Lord conceded that Soviet military withdrawals from various portions of East Asia were taking place, but he cautioned that those promising developments were "not as pronounced, nor as advanced in Asia, as they are in Europe." Moreover, "while force levels are declining, modernization is continuing, and the capability of these forces is therefore improving." According to Lord, it would be "most premature" to make any large-scale reductions in the U.S. military commitment to the noncommunist states of the region.[7]

Such views were reflected in the attitude of the Bush administration. Under Secretary of Defense Paul D. Wolfowitz told the Senate Armed Services Committee in the spring of 1990 that there had been "relatively little or almost no change in the Soviet threat in the Far East" and that "the welcome trends we have seen in Europe have not transformed the security situation in Asia as dramatically as they have transformed the European landscape."[8] Although Wolfowitz was willing to endorse a 10 percent reduction of U.S. forces in the region over a three-year period (including some reductions in units stationed in Japan), he warned against any deeper cuts. That limited reduction was made possible, he emphasized, by the increasing capabilities of America's allies, not by any significant changes in the threat environment.

The increasingly evident economic and political collapse of the Soviet Union, however, inexorably undermined the "Soviet threat" justification for retaining Washington's security commitments to East Asia, just as it did similar arguments for preserving NATO. A year after Wolfowitz's testimony, Richard H. Solomon, assistant secretary of state for East Asian and Pacific Affairs, emphasized a markedly different rationale for maintaining a large U.S. military presence. "Were the Soviet presence to disappear tomorrow," he stated, "in the emerging security environment, our role as regional balancer and honest broker, would, if anything, be more important than ever."[9] Solomon's statement seemed more than a little surprising given that for more than four decades Washington had invariably cited the Soviet expansionist threat as the reason for the network of bilateral military obligations in East Asia.

As in the case of the European commitments, advocates of the status quo are engaged in a vigorous effort at threat procurement. Some have fastened on China as the new military menace in the region.[10] Several of Beijing's recent actions—most notably its irresponsible role in furthering the proliferation of ballistic missiles in the Middle East and elsewhere in the developing world—are legitimate cause for concern. Nevertheless, there may be more than a little cynicism on the part of those who use the "China threat" justification for continuing a large-scale U.S. military presence in East Asia. After all, it was not long ago that China was held up by a succession of U.S. administrations and many in the American foreign policy community as an essential counterweight to Soviet power, a force for stability in East Asia, and a de facto U.S. ally.

More important, it is difficult to portray China as a serious military factor for at least the next decade. Alarmists note that Beijing's military budget has increased by nearly one-third in the past three years. What they fail to mention is that the increase was from $5.88 billion in 1988 to $7.56 billion in 1991.[11] Even the latter amount is scarcely sufficient to build or sustain an East Asian military juggernaut. The People's Liberation Army is antiquated, and both the air force and the navy are relatively small and oriented more toward territorial defense than power projection.[12] Beijing's modest nuclear arsenal gives it some advantage over its nonnuclear neighbors, but it is not large enough to be a reliable vehicle for international blackmail, much less for intimidating Russia or other nuclear-armed states. Despite recent nuclear tests, there is no reliable evidence that China has plans to greatly expand its arsenal. To the contrary, Chinese officials have declared their intention to sign the Nuclear Nonproliferation Treaty and have expressed an interest in multilateral negotiations that would reduce the arsenals of all powers that now have nuclear weapons.

Finally, China lacks the economic and political foundation to pursue serious expansionist ambitions. Despite the benefits that have flowed from the economic reforms adopted under Deng Xiao Peng, China's gross national product is still a mere $422 billion—just slightly larger than Spain's. Politically, the country has even more daunting limitations. Given its serious unresolved domestic divisions and tensions, exemplified by the Tiananmen Square episode in 1989, China is more likely to follow the Soviet Union down the path of chaos than it is to become an effective expansionist power.

With the end of the Cold War, the threat environment in East Asia does not justify Washington's large military deployments. In particular, it is inappropriate for Washington to continue bearing expensive military burdens for Japan—a nation that has emerged as a veritable economic great power over the past two decades and has a gross domestic product that now stands at $2.97 trillion, second only to that of the United States.[13] Yet despite periodic burden-sharing complaints, most U.S. officials are even more apprehensive about the prospect of Japan's playing a larger and more independent military role than they are about the members of the European Community doing so.

Smothering Japan

The desire to have Japan militarily dependent on the United States has been a consistent feature of U.S. policy for more than 4½ decades. Ever since the U.S. victory in World War II, Washington has repeatedly discouraged Japan from taking significant military initiatives. The post–World War II occupation government, led by Gen. Douglas MacArthur, engaged in a comprehensive effort to root out all vestiges of Japanese militarism. One of MacArthur's first actions was to supervise the complete disarmament and demobilization of Japan's armed forces in accordance with the explicit wishes of the Allied leaders at the Potsdam meeting. President Harry S Truman's directive to MacArthur implementing the Potsdam declaration stated, "Japan is not to have an Army, Navy, Air Force, Secret Police organization, or civil aviation."[14]

The MacArthur regency went far beyond those initial steps. Most of the provisions of Japan's so-called Peace Constitution were drafted by members of MacArthur's staff. The most important provision, suggested by pacifist elements in Japan (including the interim prime minister, Baron Shidehara) and strongly supported by MacArthur and his superiors in Washington, was article 9.

> Aspiring sincerely to an international peace based on justice and order, the Japanese people forever renounce war as a sovereign right of the nation and the threat or use of force as means of settling international disputes.
>
> In order to accomplish the aim of the preceding paragraph, land, sea, and air forces, as well as other war potential, will never be maintained. The right of belligerency of the State will not be recognized.[15]

Washington's goal of keeping Japan demilitarized carried over into the Cold War period, despite concern about securing allies to help contain Soviet power. The 1951 U.S.-Japan Security Treaty was never viewed as "mutual" in any meaningful sense. To a much greater extent than the North Atlantic Treaty, the U.S.-Japan treaty was blatantly one-sided; the United States would protect a pacifist and largely disarmed Japan from aggression by the Soviet Union or China. Article 1 of the treaty was especially revealing, for it not only gave the United States the right to station troops in and about Japan, but unlike the North Atlantic Treaty, the mutual defense treaty with South Korea, and similar agreements, it authorized the use of those forces "to contribute to the maintenance of international peace and security in the Far East" as well as to protect Japan. Moreover, U.S. forces could be used not only to defend Japan from external attack but also to assist the Japanese government in suppressing "large-scale internal riots and disturbances in Japan, caused through instigation or intervention by an outside Power or Powers."[16] That provision was in direct contrast to the treaty with South Korea, ratified by the U.S. Senate in 1954, that explicitly restricted U.S. obligations to helping repel *external* attacks. In short, the entire tone of the Japanese treaty suggested that Japan was a barely trusted and closely guarded U.S. protectorate—a smothered ally.

In essence, Washington assumed primary responsibility for Japan's conventional defense and exclusive responsibility for nuclear deterrence. Japan was to provide some help in repelling any conventional aggression against its territory but had no responsibilities for assisting in the defense of the United States. The 1960 security treaty that replaced the 1951 document did not alter that relationship in any meaningful way. A powerful Japanese military partner was neither sought nor welcome.

Japan's Ambivalent Response

Japan's reaction to the policy of U.S. military paternalism has been one of profound ambivalence. Although essentially imposed by an occupying power, the Peace Constitution became—and largely remains—popular with the Japanese people. Part of that popularity is explained by widespread public revulsion at the militarism of the 1930s and 1940s, which brought catastrophe to Japan. The disastrous experience of World War II left most Japanese war weary and determined never to tolerate a repetition. The aversion to war, assiduously cultivated by U.S. political and military leaders during the late 1940s and early 1950s, is still shared by a significant percentage of the Japanese public. Relying on the United States for its defense enabled Japan to replace the imperialist and militarist values that had dominated Japanese society in the years before World War II with values that emphasized pacifism, democracy, and economic success. U.S. statesmen sought to create a new Japan that was dedicated to peaceful commercial pursuits, and they succeeded beyond their expectations.

Eschewing a large military role has also served more tangible Japanese interests. Willingness to be a protectorate of the United States throughout the Cold War was an economic bonanza for Tokyo. Japan was able to concentrate on its recovery from World War II and, later, to build one of the most modern and dynamic economies in the world instead of spending its resources on armed forces. The U.S. defense subsidy since the conclusion of the security treaty in 1951 has saved Japanese taxpayers more than $800 billion (measured in 1992 dollars). That figure may, in fact, be conservative. There were some economies of scale in having the United States, which had a large military infrastructure for missions around the world, provide protection for Japan. If Tokyo had had to build the conventional and nuclear forces necessary to fully replace that protection, it would probably have cost considerably more than the $20 billion annual price tag of the U.S. shield. From the standpoint of minimizing military expenditures, being a U.S. dependent has been very good indeed for Japan.

There were also more subtle advantages. Research and development (R&D) spending has been higher in the United States than in Japan since the 1940s (although that gap has virtually disappeared in recent years), but the distribution shows striking differences. A much larger percentage of American R&D funds has gone into military projects. During the 1980s, approximately 30 percent of such expenditures in the United States went for military purposes. The figure for Japan was less than 1 percent.[17] Because Japan has relied on the United States for its defense, its own R&D spending has been devoted overwhelmingly to the development of civilian products. The same is true of R&D talent. In Japan the best scientists and engineers gravitate to the civilian economy; in the United States they frequently end up working for defense contracting firms on a variety of weapon systems. (Indeed, defense firms can typically outbid consumer products companies for the best talent and simply pass the additional costs on to the Pentagon—and hence, the taxpayers—in the form of higher price tags for the weapons produced.) The impact of such differential military burdens on the economies of Japan and the United States is noticeable. While U.S. firms have succeeded in building a military technology second to none, Japanese companies—spared the diversion of talent and resources to military pursuits—have been able to concentrate to a much greater degree on building the highest quality consumer products. Japanese political and economic leaders would have had to have been uncharacteristically obtuse not to grasp the importance of that advantage.

Despite the aversion to militarism and the significant fiscal and economic benefits of being a U.S. protectorate, Japanese political elites have grown increasingly uncomfortable with such dependence. Even during the early years of the post–World War II era, Japan's new democratic government sought to apply article 9 with some flexibility. A literal interpretation of that provision would seem to prohibit the existence of armed forces for any purpose whatsoever. But even General MacArthur did not see it in that light.

> Nothing in article 9, . . . prevents any and all necessary steps for the preservation of the safety of the nation. Japan cannot be expected to resist the overweening law of self-preservation. If attacked, she will defend herself. Article 9 was aimed entirely at eliminating Japanese aggression.[18]

On another occasion, he elaborated on that point and seemed to favor a modest but reasonably active Japanese military role, even going so far as to endorse the creation of a defense force consisting of 10 divisions and corresponding air and sea elements.

> Should the course of world events require that all mankind stand to arms in the defense of human liberty and Japan comes into the orbit of immediately threatened attack, then the Japanese, too, should mount the maximum defensive power which their resources will permit. Article 9 is based upon the highest of moral ideals, but by no sophistry of reasoning can it be interpreted as complete negation of the inalienable right of self-defense against unprovoked attack.[19]

MacArthur's comments were revealing on two counts. The most obvious was his rather "loose constructionist" interpretation of article 9. The other was his care to couch his support for limited Japanese rearmament in terms of a multilateral effort to resist aggression. That was an early expression of Washington's narrow view of what would be an acceptable military role for Japan. Some Japanese military capabilities were acceptable—as long as they remained limited in scope and were part of a U.S.-directed strategy to contain aggression (i.e., Soviet expansionism).[20]

Japan did, in fact, cautiously begin to develop a military capability consistent with the principles that MacArthur outlined. When U.S. troops stationed in Japan left to fight in the Korean War, MacArthur helped to set up a small armed force—the Police Reserve Corps. That organization gradually expanded and became a full-blown military apparatus in 1954. To avoid the sticky problem of the restrictive language of article 9, however, the Japanese government did not establish an army, air force, or navy. Instead, in an example of doublespeak worthy of George Orwell, Tokyo designated those military units Self-Defense Forces (SDF).

The constitutionality of Japan's embryonic military establishment was challenged in the courts. But judges, perhaps compelled by political realities, consistently ruled that the rearmament effort did not violate article 9. According to journalist James Fallows, "Japan has worked its way toward its current sizable military force through a series of judicial and political 'reinterpretations' of the Constitution. The crucial legal concept has been the idea that no nation can renounce the right to defend itself against attack, much as no individual is allowed to sell himself into slavery."[21]

Despite the creation of the SDF, Japan's military effort was barely visible throughout much of the Cold War era. Government policy limited defense spending to 1 percent of the nation's GNP, and until the 1970s Japan's economy was relatively small— although growing at a healthy rate. One percent of such a modest GNP did not buy a large military establishment. That began to change, however, in the mid-1970s. Japan's rapid economic growth rate had produced a sizable economy—and hence a considerable pool of funds to support the military. Also in the mid-1970s, the Japanese political elite began to adopt a new attitude: Japan should have forces capable of making more than a token contribution to the defense of the home islands.[22] In 1981 Japan committed itself to defend the sea lanes out to 1,000 nautical miles from the archipelago and began to build the forces needed to accomplish that mission. An additional impetus to Japan's defense output came in 1987 when the government, responding to mounting U.S. pressures for more burden sharing, decided to lift the 1 percent barrier within three years.

Today, the SDF have more than trivial capabilities. There are more than 246,000 active duty personnel, along with a modern 200-ship navy and an equally modern air force that includes some 422 combat aircraft.[23] Nevertheless, Japan remains the most lightly armed of any of the great powers in the international system. Noticeably absent are bombers, short- or intermediate-range missiles, aircraft carriers, and other weapon systems that would be capable of projecting force outside the immediate vicinity of the Japanese archipelago. Equally important, Japan still spends a meager 1.1 percent of its GNP on defense. That figure is substantially less than even the small percentage of GNP devoted to the military by the European members of NATO. Germany, for example, spends 2.6 percent, France 3.2 percent, and Britain 4.4 percent.[24]

Japan now seems to be searching for its own political and military identity. There is a growing inclination to play an active role in world affairs, in spite of the supposed constitutional restrictions on the use of military force. One manifestation of that desire has been Japan's aggressive foreign aid budget. In 1989 Japan contributed over $6.77 billion in bilateral foreign aid and another $1.7 billion through multilateral aid programs—more than any other nation in the world.[25] To many Japanese, giving foreign aid has been an acceptable way of asserting Japan's influence in the world without having to address the thorny issue of a more extensive military role.

In recent months there have even been intriguing hints of efforts to lay the foundation for a more independent security strategy. For example, Tokyo has quietly moved to expand its own intelligence operations in an attempt to wean itself from dependence on U.S. analyses of threats to Japanese interests. Former deputy minister of defense Seiki Hishhiro, one of the architects of the new intelligence plan, noted that "in the cold war era the world moved in teams, and as a member of the American-led team, our judgment was not so important. Now Japan needs its own ability."[26] The new intelligence operation is quite extensive. Not only will the foreign ministry create an International Information Bureau with as many as 200 analysts, but the Self-Defense Agency is establishing a separate unit patterned after the Pentagon's Defense Intelligence Agency. A high-level Japanese official has indicated that the new unit will focus particularly on North Korea, China, the members of the CIS, and, perhaps most significant, the Persian Gulf.

There are other indications of cautious advances. During briefings with Malaysian and Indonesian officials, Japan's vice–foreign minister, Koji Kakizawa, suggested the creation of a Southeast Asian peace-keeping force under UN auspices, noting that such an arrangement would enable the SDF to operate in the area and conduct joint training exercises with regional forces.[27] That "private suggestion" followed a July 1991 proposal by then prime minister Toshiki Kaifu to establish a security dialogue with the members of the Association of Southeast Asian Nations (ASEAN), indicating that Kakizawa's suggestion was more than just a casual comment.

Japan's recently announced plans to acquire and store more than 30 tons of plutonium over the next nine years have also attracted notice and raised questions about Tokyo's underlying motives. Japanese officials insist that the plutonium is needed for the nation's ambitious nuclear power program, which will include the building of several breeder reactors. Although it would be premature to dismiss that explanation and conclude that Japan intends to use the plutonium to create weapons, Japanese officials were disturbingly vague about how such a large quantity of plutonium would be used for civilian purposes. Japanese leaders were also unresponsive to suggestions that the material be placed under international control.[28]

Taken individually or collectively, those developments do not prove that Japan has embarked on a concerted effort to develop an assertive political and military posture. They do, however, suggest that Japan seems to be hedging its bets. An independent intelligence apparatus, for example, is a crucial prerequisite for an independent security strategy. Similarly, a stockpile of plutonium gives Japan the option of developing a nuclear weapons arsenal if the political leadership subsequently decides that the U.S. nuclear shield is no longer reliable or that the U.S.-Japanese alliance is no longer in the country's best interest. The underlying reason for Tokyo's recent actions appears to be a quest for more options in the security realm.

At the same time, it is important not to overstate the significance of such moves. Anti-military, if not outright pacifist, sentiment remains strong throughout Japan. In the midst of the Persian Gulf crisis, more than two-thirds of Japanese voters opposed sending troops to participate in the operations of the international coalition. Opposition in the Diet was strong enough to prevent Prime Minister Kaifu from sending even a small contingent of noncombat personnel to the gulf.[29] Similarly, in December 1991, the Diet forced the withdrawal of a plan by the new prime minister, Kiichi Miyazawa, to permit members of the SDF to participate in peace-keeping missions authorized by the United Nations—even though he had made the adoption of that measure one of the highest priorities of his government.[30]

Miyazawa had better luck the following June, but only after a bruising battle with opposition lawmakers committed to the Peace Constitution. The Diet finally approved a bill permitting the dispatch of military personnel abroad to play a role in international peace-keeping operations. Restrictions imposed by the bill, how-ever, were quite severe. Only one 2,000-member unit was desig-nated for such operations, and it was to be deployed for strictly limited, noncombatant tasks.[31]

Despite still potent anti-militarist sentiment, there are signs that parliamentary and public attitudes have begun to change. The out-come of the Gulf War demonstrated to many Japanese that military power was still an important factor in a nation's ability to exercise influence in the international arena. Washington's success in orchestrating a decisive military victory undercut the arguments of people in Japan and elsewhere who had contended that economic strength was an adequate substitute for military power. While Washington acted, Tokyo found that—for all Japan's economic capabilities—it could not significantly affect the outcome of events in a region that provided the bulk of Japan's oil supply.[32] Yoichi Funabashi, diplomatic correspondent of the Tokyo daily *Asahi Shim-bun,* described the chagrined reaction of many Japanese.

> A crisis almost always reveals the reality, and the Persian Gulf crisis revealed the real Japan. In the moment of truth, an economic superpower found itself to be merely an auto-matic teller machine—one that needed a kick before dis-pensing the cash.[33]

Perhaps in response to that sobering experience, public opinion polls taken in the summer of 1991 revealed that by more than a two-to-one plurality—46 percent to 21 percent—respondents supported the SDF's playing a role beyond the protection of the Japanese archipelago.[34] It was also significant that a more active military posture was not conditioned on operating within the United Nations or some other multilateral framework. Moreover, senti-ment favoring a more extensive role seemed to be most pronounced among younger Japanese.

Japan's ambivalence about its military policy is likely to continue for some time. The most important factors determining the outcome of that national debate will be domestic. Decisions will require political judgments about various issues, including the extent of Japan's security needs, the impact of additional defense spending on the nation's economic growth rate, and the probable effect of a more assertive Japanese strategy on Tokyo's relations with East

Asian neighbors who still recall the horrors inflicted by imperial Japan.

Of course, Washington's policies will also influence that debate. Japan's long-standing reluctance to build up its military and play a more active security role must be viewed in context. The U.S. policy of providing for the bulk of Japan's security needs—combined with the policy of discouraging independent Japanese initiatives—has greatly skewed the incentives. As the gulf crisis revealed, Washington's willingness to assume the costs and risks of defending Tokyo's interests spared the Japanese people and government difficult decisions about how to protect those interests.[35] It is highly unlikely that Japan would have continued to spend such a small percentage of its GNP on the military throughout the Cold War era or have remained so diffident on matters that affected its own well-being, had it not been for the smothering strategy of the United States. Tokyo's response is aptly described by Kenneth Hunt, vice president of the International Institute for Strategic Studies. "Defence spending has tended to be set simply at levels which kept both Washington and domestic opinion not too restive."[36]

Keeping Japan a U.S. military dependent has become increasingly unhealthy for both countries. It perpetuates an expensive set of security obligations for the United States while it encourages the Japanese to act as though they can evade political and military issues forever. Yet, despite some gestures to the contrary, Washington appears determined to maintain a policy of paternalism in the post–Cold War period.

The Bush Administration's Bogus Changes

Secretary of State James A. Baker III surprised observers on both shores of the Pacific during a November 1991 speech in Tokyo when he urged Japan to play a more active role in the world—one appropriate for its status as an economic great power. "You are beginning to fully appreciate your national capabilities—and your responsibilities around the globe," Baker stated. Referring to Tokyo's policy of "checkbook diplomacy"—dispensing liberal doses of foreign aid and otherwise exploiting Japan's financial clout as a substitute for direct political or military influence—he argued that such a strategy "like our 'dollar diplomacy' of an earlier era, is clearly too narrow."[37]

Less than two weeks later, Secretary of Defense Richard B. Cheney seemed to view Japan's playing a larger role even more favorably. He not only suggested that Japan use its wealth to help the nations of Eastern Europe and the unraveling Soviet Union to make the transition to democracy and free markets, but he specifically called for increased cooperation between Japan and the United States on military matters, including sharing new military technologies and engaging in joint military exercises.[38]

At first glance it might appear that the Bush administration had boldly reversed more than four decades of U.S. policy toward Japan. That is largely an illusion. Despite the rhetoric of Baker and Cheney during their November trips to Tokyo, the administration shows few signs of departing from the traditional U.S. policy of keeping Japan militarily dependent on the United States. Clear evidence of Washington's intentions emerged in the summer of 1991 when Japanese prime minister Kaifu made a surprise proposal for a "security dialogue"—formal regional meetings on defense matters—between Japan and the members of ASEAN. Instead of endorsing that manifestation of greater initiative on the part of Tokyo, the United States reacted with thinly disguised hostility. In a speech to the annual meeting of ASEAN foreign ministers, Baker warned them against adopting new arrangements that would replace "tried and true frameworks" involving the United States. "We have a remarkable degree of stability in this region," Baker said. "We ought to be careful about changing those arrangements and discarding them for something else."[39] Privately, U.S. officials expressed opposition to the Japanese proposal because it might weaken the bilateral agreements between the United States and various nations in East Asia and the Pacific. In other words, Tokyo's modest security dialogue initiative was seen as a challenge to Washington's military primacy in the region.

Some of Baker's and Cheney's subsequent remarks also indicated that the United States had no intention of encouraging Japan to play a larger military role, except under conditions set down by Washington. Even as he urged Tokyo to become more active, Cheney stressed that the United States would maintain a substantial "forward presence" in East Asia. His rationale, outlined in an interview shortly before his November trip, was most revealing. "Our presence . . . in the western Pacific is reassuring to an awful lot of people in that part of the world. If we were to withdraw, there would be pressures on other governments to try to fill that vacuum."[40] In reality, only Japan has the ability to fill a vacuum created by U.S. disengagement. Cheney's comments were little more than diplomatic code for Washington's desire to keep Tokyo from upsetting the East Asian status quo.

Baker was a bit more subtle, but it was clear that he, too, envisioned Japan's continuing in a subordinate position. The areas of "broader global responsibilities" for Tokyo that he outlined included leadership in "building democracy, respect for human rights, stopping the proliferation of weapons of mass destruction, and in facing transnational challenges in areas such as the environment, narcotics and refugees." Conspicuously missing from that list was any suggestion that Japan might play a role in defending its own security interests that would be greater than the narrow and limited one it already plays in providing some conventional defense of the Japanese home islands. If there was any doubt that Washington did not envisage a change in the military status quo, Baker also offered the opinion that Japan had built "an appropriate self-defense capability" that "complements" U.S. forces in East Asia.[41]

Viewed in context, Baker's and Cheney's calls for Japan to become more active in security matters were rather disingenuous. Baker and Cheney, like most U.S. leaders past and present, would like to have Japan shoulder a somewhat larger share of the burden of collective defense without in any way gaining the ability to challenge Washington's dominant position in setting policy. To use the analogy of a law firm, Washington now appears willing to consider elevating Japan from a mere associate to the status of junior partner—as long as Tokyo never forgets that the United States remains the senior partner. As in the case of the effort to preserve NATO, the underlying objective is to maintain U.S. military preeminence.

America's Burden-Sharing Complaints

Even as a succession of U.S. administrations has consistently discouraged a more independent Japanese military role, there has been a growing demand in both the executive branch and Congress for more burden sharing. Richard Holbrooke, assistant secretary of state for East Asian and Pacific affairs during the Carter administration, notes the inherent contradiction in U.S. burden-sharing policy throughout the 1970s and 1980s. "Little thought was given to the long-term consequences," especially the possibility "that Japanese military capability might, over time, lead to an aggressive foreign policy from Tokyo that might even eventually be at odds with America's."[42] Holbrooke's point is valid, even if his policy conclusion—that the United States should not have encouraged Japan to increase its rearmament effort—is not.

In recent years, calls for more burden sharing have become increasingly strident. The Burdensharing Panel of the U.S. House Armed Services Committee concluded bluntly in its 1988 report that "Japan's defense contributions and capabilities are inadequate given its tremendous economic strength."[43] Defense analyst Edward A. Olsen summarized the attitude of proponents of burden sharing in the late 1980s when he charged:

> Japan's defense contributions remain decidedly minimalist, parsimonious, and inordinantly cautious. Japan is, indeed, getting a cheap ride. It benefits from an international system predicated on collective security, but refuses to pay its fair share of the costs or bear a fair share of the risks.[44]

Other critics have been less polite. Economist Melvyn Krauss, for example, branded Japan the "king of the free riders."[45]

Allegations of Japanese free riding reached a crescendo during the 1990–91 Persian Gulf crisis when Tokyo urged the United States to take vigorous military action against Iraq but refused to contribute forces to the U.S.-led coalition and initially even resisted contributing financially to the international effort. A bitter Rep. Patricia Schroeder (D-Colo.) fumed that the Japanese were "laughing all the way to the bank."[46] Japanese leaders contended that article 9 of the Peace Constitution prohibited Japan from making any military effort, but critics pointed out that Tokyo had frequently adopted a flexible interpretation of article 9 in the interest of pursuing specific policy objectives. Article 9 had not prevented Japan from creating military forces in the 1950s, expanding them significantly in the 1970s, and ultimately deploying them as far as 1,000 nautical miles away to defend the air and sea approaches to the archipelago. If Tokyo could send its forces out that far, it was not clear why they could not go farther. The limits to Japanese military operations appeared to be purely the result of political decisions, not constitutional requirements.

Schroeder and other congressional leaders charged that Japan was hiding behind article 9 to avoid subjecting its citizens to the risks of combat. That suspicion was reinforced when opposition in the Diet compelled Prime Minister Kaifu to abandon plans to send a small noncombat contingent to the gulf. Although Japan eventually contributed more than $13 billion in response to intense U.S. diplomatic pressure, that belated payment did little to quell resentment in the United States.

Anger with Japan's position on the Persian Gulf crisis quickly translated into congressional retaliation on the broader burden-sharing issue. The House of Representatives voted overwhelmingly in September 1990 to withdraw U.S. troops from Japan unless Tokyo greatly increased its financial support for the maintenance of those forces.[47] Three months later the Japanese announced a change of policy. Presumably in response to U.S. objections, they agreed to increase their contribution to the cost of maintaining U.S. forces in Japan from 40 to 50 percent.[48] The Bush administration seemed content with that gesture; Baker noted with approval that by 1995 Tokyo's support "will reach 73 percent of the nonsalary costs of maintaining our forward-deployed forces in Japan."[49] Congressional critics were considerably less willing to concede that a 10-percentage-point increase in overall support payments was "significant." Such burden-sharing controversies show no signs of abating. On the contrary, they are likely to become even more acrimonious during the 1990s unless there are substantive changes in both U.S. and Japanese military policies.

Rising Japanese Annoyance

Keeping Japan militarily subordinate while insisting on greater burden sharing is a very dangerous game. Some Japanese have always regarded their nation's military dependence on the United States as humiliating. In the past their views could be safely ignored because they represented only a small minority of public opinion. But as Japan's economic power has soared, the belief that Tokyo should play a political and military role in global affairs commensurate with its new status as an economic great power has also grown. Although pursuing an independent security agenda is still the desire of a minority, that desire is no longer confined to the reaction-ary political fringe. It is gaining currency especially among younger Japanese who have no memory of a weak and defeated Japan.[50]

Accompanying the desire for greater independence in security matters is burgeoning resentment of the United States. That resent-ment is most pronounced among right-wing politicians and their supporters. The best known anti-American spokesman has been Shintaro Ishihara, an ultranationalist member of the Diet. His 1989 book, *The Japan That Can Say No*—written with Sony Corporation cofounder and chairman Akio Morita—sold more than 1.2 million copies in Japan and created a sensation on both sides of the Pacific.[51] In that book the themes that have now become standard features of "America-bashing" pieces are all present: the United States as a decadent, crime-ridden, declining world power; allegations that Washington bullies or cynically manipulates Japan; assertions that the United States has a nefarious strategy to prevent Japan from achieving greatness; and the thesis that Japan is now strong enough, given its economic productivity and technological sophisti-cation, to cast off its humiliating dependence on the United States.[52]

Ishihara has continued his barrage. Shortly after the end of the Persian Gulf War, he published another book (written with rightist intellectual Jun Eto), *The Japan That Can Really Say No*, emphasizing Japan's great underlying strength and America's growing weak-ness. Not only did he reiterate his criticisms of the United States, but he contended that U.S. forces could not have won their military victory without the computer technology that Japan had supplied. It was "ludicrous" for the United States to regard itself as the sole remaining superpower, Ishihara wrote. After all, Washington "had to ask other countries to contribute money so that it could fight, and it depended on foreign technology to carry out its war strategy."[53]

It might be tempting to dismiss Ishihara's invective as the atypical sentiments of a fringe politician, but the popularity of his books should cause Americans to avoid such a sanguine reaction. More-over, there are signs that Ishihara's views are shared, at least to some extent, by a growing number of Japanese. Indeed, a word specifically coined to describe an attitude of extreme hostility toward the United States, *kenbei*, began appearing in the Japanese press in 1991.[54] The principal impetus for Japanese antipathy has been the ugly disputes between Tokyo and Washington about trade policy. The exchange of national insults reached a new low following President Bush's ill-fated trip to East Asia in January 1992 when the speaker of the Japanese Diet remarked that many American workers were lazy and illiterate, and Sen. Ernest Hollings (D-S.C.) responded by suggesting to a group of employees at a roller bearing factory in South Carolina that they "draw a mushroom cloud and put beneath it, 'Made in America by lazy and illiterate Americans and tested in Japan.' "[55]

There are also other reasons for Japanese animosity toward the United States, including the suspicion that the United States is seeking to keep Japan a second-rate political and military power. Journalist Kan Ito observed more than two years ago, "Constant Japan bashing in the United States has created a dangerous reaction in Japan: bitter, resentful, nationalistic America bashing. Japanese bookstores are currently offering more than 10 books that claim to prove America's 'evil design' to destroy and eliminate the Japanese challenge."[56] U.S. demands on and criticism of Japan during the gulf crisis, in particular, helped fuel Japanese resentment. "We cannot simply be checkwriting machines," a senior Japanese official fumed. "We hear America saying, 'You do the paying, and we will do the thinking.' "[57]

The attitude of arrogant triumph in which the U.S. policy community seemed to indulge during and immediately following the Gulf War produced both fear and anger in Japan. Yasuki Murakami, a professor at Tokyo University, concluded that many Japanese were fearful that Washington would try to impose a Pax Americana in which the United States "calls the shots" and other countries are forced to follow. Another Japanese opinion leader, Yoshiki Hidaka, Washington bureau chief of NHK, Japan's public television network, compared the United States to a successful gunfighter looking for his next fight—and speculated that U.S. coercive power might take the form of a full-scale trade war against Japan.[58] Australian political scientist Aurelia George accurately summarized the undercurrent of discontent.

> The popularity of the Ishihara style of strident nationalism is testimony to the sea change in Japanese public attitudes toward the United States. What is holding the relationship together is the traditional "Yoshida line" of pro-U.S. conservative politics that is still entrenched in the Foreign Ministry

and retains the majority support of the governing Liberal Democratic Party. Levels of resentment are growing, however, both inside and outside government circles.[59]

Indiscreet comments made by some U.S. political and military leaders have exacerbated Japanese distrust of Washington's motives. Maj. Gen. Henry C. Stackpole, commander of Marine Corps forces in Japan, for example, stated bluntly that "no one wants a rearmed, resurgent Japan." The United States is "the cap in the bottle," preventing Japan from embarking on that course, according to Stackpole. "If we were to pull out of the U.S.-Japan Security Treaty," he warned, "it would definitely be a destabilizing factor in Asia."[60]

A 1991 study commissioned by the Central Intelligence Agency expressed similar views, portraying Japan as a dangerous expansionist power bent on global economic domination. The authors also exhibited antipathy toward any suggestion that Tokyo play a more active military role.[61] Suspicions of Japan (albeit in more subtle form) were evident in the initial draft of the Pentagon's defense policy guidance planning document for 1994–99. The authors warned that a larger Japanese role in East Asia would be destabilizing and argued that a major purpose of U.S. strategy should be to prevent the emergence of such a political or military competitor.[62] That attitude inflamed even those Japanese who favor retaining the mutual defense treaty. Takashi Inoguchi, a professor of political science at the University of Tokyo, charged that the Pentagon document showed that "there is a great deal of interest in some segments of the U.S. policy establishment in maintaining a preeminent global military position." The United States, in his view, was creating "a covert barrier to Japan's assumption of a greater role in world affairs," although Washington "has for many years publicly argued that Japan should assume more of the collective defence burden."[63]

Manifestations of distrust by U.S. officials, based on an assumption that the Japanese are inherent aggressors and that Japan intends to become a geopolitical adversary of the United States, intensify Japanese resentment. The pieces are in place for a nasty rupture in U.S.-Japanese relations, a rupture that could go far beyond security or trade issues.[64]

Fears of East Asian Instability

U.S. officials and foreign policy experts who insist on keeping Japan militarily dependent rarely admit that the United States simply does not trust Japan. Instead, they contend that any significant Japanese rearmament would alarm Japan's East Asian neighbors, thereby producing a regional arms race and dangerous instability. President Reagan's first national security adviser, Richard V. Allen, summarized that attitude when he noted that the nations of East Asia "have painful, vivid memories of Japanese military prowess in the 1930s and 1940s." Allen concluded: "If the United States disengages, or is seen to be disengaging, albeit slowly, from Asia, and if Japan continues its dynamic regional expansion, the effect may be either that of a vacuum to be filled or a simple lateral replacement of one influence by another. I cannot see how this will benefit U.S. interests, or that of our non-Japanese allies and friends in the region."[65]

Former president Richard Nixon offered a slightly more general version of the stability thesis.

> A continued U.S. presence in Europe is important, but a continued U.S. role in the Pacific is indispensable. Without the United States, the Pacific triangle will be like a three-legged stool: unstable and potentially dangerous. The competition among Japan, China, and the Soviet Union would be unbridled, with each driven to seek preeminence in the region. The United States must serve as a stabilizer—the fourth leg of the stool—in order to advance the interests of all East Asian nations.[66]

It is true, of course, that the other East Asian nations fear a militarily resurgent Japan. Former Singapore prime minister Lee Kuan Yew was only a little more candid than other regional leaders when he urged the United States to maintain a large military presence in the region to contain Japanese power. Observing that the Japanese were once even greater warriors than they are now merchants, Lee concluded, "I do not think they have lost those qualities." The United States and other nations, he said, should pressure Japan to abide by its Peace Constitution. "It's already breached by the self-defense force, but let's not breach it further."[67]

A similar attitude is evident in South Korea. A Ministry of Defense white paper issued in October 1991 warned of a military build-up in Japan, which it said was shifting from a "defense only" orientation. Cha Young Koo, director of policy planning for the ROK government's Institute of Defense Analysis, even expressed the view that Japan was ultimately a more dangerous threat than China, even though China invaded South Korea during the Korean War.[68]

Although it would be unwise to discount the fear with which Japan is still regarded throughout East Asia, the specter of a larger Japanese military role may be less traumatic for the nations of East Asia than it might at first appear. Japanese leaders are mindful of the continuing suspicions harbored by their neighbors. It is no accident that a large portion of Tokyo's foreign aid budget has been given to the countries occupied by Japanese forces during World War II, and the Japanese are taking other steps to alleviate concerns and mend relations with neighboring states. Former prime minister Kaifu, current prime minister Miyazawa, and other officials have apologized for Japan's aggression during the 1930s and 1940s and expressed remorse for the wartime atrocities committed by imperial Japanese forces.[69] Although one might wish that such statements of regret had been made earlier, they do represent a concerted effort to at last begin to heal the emotional wounds of World War II.

Moreover, with the collapse of the Soviet Union and its replacement by the far more decentralized commonwealth, Japan can probably protect its security interests without a massive rearmament effort.[70] A modest increase in military spending, say to the level of 1.5 percent of GNP, might well be sufficient. Such an increase would produce an active duty force of 350,000 to 400,000 personnel—hardly enough for a new wave of imperialism. Only the most paranoid would be alarmed by a build-up of that magnitude.

The most worrisome development would be a decision by Tokyo to acquire nuclear weapons. That possibility cannot be ruled out in the long term—especially if North Korea or other aggressive or unstable regimes develop nuclear arsenals—but it is not inevitable. The Japanese public has a pronounced dislike of nuclear weapons, and the memories of Hiroshima and Nagasaki are not likely to fade soon. In addition, given the technological sophistication that Japan can bring to bear in the development of its military forces, Tokyo might conclude that an arsenal of precision-guided weapons, together with appropriate aircraft and missile delivery systems (and comprehensive air and missile defenses), would be sufficient to counter the nuclear arsenals of its neighbors. As the gulf war demonstrated, precision-guided conventional weapons can be extremely effective.

Finally, Japan's neighbors should realize that Japanese public opinion will help restrain any aggressive ambitions that might be harbored by a future political leader. A public that for more than four decades has resisted not only militarism but even the most modest expansion of Japan's military role is not likely to countenance a huge military build-up and an expansionist binge. Indeed, the opposite problem may surface; public opposition may inhibit Japan from doing enough to protect its own security interests.

The regional apprehension about Japan's "aggressive tendencies" parallels the attitudes in some European circles about Germany. But the Japanese are not congenital aggressors, any more than the Germans are. Imperial Japan's expansionism in the 1930s and 1940s, as horrible as it was, arose from a specific set of conditions that bears little resemblance to the current or any reasonably foreseeable situation. Both East Asian and U.S. officials must move beyond the simplistic assumption that Japan's military role must inevitably be one of extremes—either the rampant imperialism of a half century ago or the self-effacing pacifism of the post–World War II era. It is not only possible but probable that, left to its own devices, modern Japan would play a reasonably prudent role somewhere between those two extremes.

Nevertheless, there is little doubt that the smaller nations of East Asia would prefer the status quo, with the United States as regional protector. But the pertinent question from the standpoint of U.S. foreign policy should not be whether the status quo is more comfortable for the regional states but whether it is in the best interests of the American people. It is difficult to justify preserving expensive military commitments indefinitely merely to spare Japan and its neighbors the difficulties of confronting old animosities. Washington cannot permit the ghosts of World War II to dictate U.S. policy toward Japan.

Avoiding a U.S.-Japanese Conflict

U.S. leaders must recognize that attempting to preserve stability in East Asia by keeping Japan militarily subordinate runs the risk of irreparably damaging U.S.-Japanese relations. Most Japanese were grateful for the U.S. security shield during the Cold War, both because it afforded reliable protection from a menacing Soviet Union and because it spared Japan from spending scarce resources on the military. But with the dissipation of the Soviet threat, it will not be long before more and more Japanese begin to wonder why U.S. forces remain in their region. An increasing number of Japanese are already discontented with Washington's smothering strategy, and although that view is not yet held by a majority, the trend is ominous. Fanned by Ishihara and other ultranationalists, the suspicion will grow that U.S. troops are there to contain Japanese power. A *Yomiuri Shimbun* columnist observed in March 1990 that some American officials were contending that U.S. forces needed to remain in Japan to contain Japanese rearmament at the same time Congress and the Bush administration were insisting that Japan pay more for those forces. The Japanese people "cannot feel good about paying for a watchdog that watches them," the columnist concluded.[71] "Regional stability" diplomatic camouflage will not be able to neutralize such suspicions and the inevitable resentment they will provoke.

The "cork in the bottle" mission advanced by Gen. Stackpole and others is no longer a viable option for the United States. Even some of the staunchest advocates of the security status quo seem to dimly recognize the danger of a rupture in U.S.-Japanese relations. Richard Allen concedes that in a worst-case scenario Tokyo might ask the United States to withdraw its forces from Japanese territory. "For those who subscribe to the 'cork in the bottle' theory, as I do, the prospect of U.S. forces being ejected from Japan is almost too unpleasant to consider."[72] But what Allen and many other members of the U.S. foreign policy community fail to understand is that trying to preserve a large-scale U.S. military presence in East Asia may turn their greatest fears into a self-fulfilling prophecy.

Appreciation of the special concerns voiced by Japan's neighbors should not deter the United States from executing a gradual military withdrawal and accepting a Japanese build-up. Such a policy change would, of necessity, go far beyond current proposals to have Tokyo pay more of the costs of maintaining U.S. forces stationed in Japan. More important than the multibillion-dollar cost of the U.S. security role in East Asia—a modest increase in Japanese support payments would not greatly reduce that cost in any case—is the possibility that a continuing U.S. military presence may jeopardize the entire range of U.S.-Japanese relations. A strategy of disengagement would seek to avoid the quarrels and invective that already accompany burden-sharing controversies and will inevitably do so in the future.

Unfortunately, there are few indications that U.S. policymakers understand the problem. The Bush administration appears determined to cling to the sterile strategy of fostering Japanese military dependence, while expressing platitudes about the need for a new, strengthened relationship.[73] The administration's "reform" seems to consist of such cosmetic changes as withdrawing 10 percent of the troops now stationed in Japan as part of a general drawdown of U.S. forces in East Asia and badgering Tokyo to increase its support payments for the remaining units.

The present U.S.-Japanese security relationship is unhealthy for both countries. As Aurelia George observed:

> The whole pattern of U.S. pressure and Japanese response is locked in a dominant-subordinate framework that takes no account of changing power relativities in the relationship. The U.S. administration continues to view Japan as a client state and Japan feels obliged to respond accordingly. . . . If Japan's ascent and the U.S. decline continue, this pattern of relations will be increasingly anomalous and untenable."[74]

The United States needs to recognize that Japan is a great power that will, sooner or later, become the preeminent actor in East Asia and the western Pacific. U.S. leaders can adjust to that reality and maximize the chances of maintaining good relations with Japan, especially the economic ties that are so valuable to both countries, or they can insist on perpetuating the policy of smothering paternalism until the Japanese openly rebel against it. If the latter approach is adopted, both nations may be headed for tragedy.

3. Korea: The Perpetual Protectorate

Although Japan is the largest and most expensive U.S. security obligation in East Asia, the commitment to defend South Korea is a close second. The foundation for that obligation is a mutual defense treaty signed in October 1953 and ratified the following year. Article 3 of the treaty affirms that each signatory considers an armed attack on either country as a threat to its own security and will act to meet the common danger. Article 4 explicitly gives the United States the right to station military forces in South Korea.[1]

Washington's military commitment to South Korea is a direct product of the Cold War rivalry with the Soviet Union.[2] Indeed, Korea, its territory brutally sundered, (along with Germany) became one of the most prominent victims of the U.S.-Soviet struggle. After Japan's defeat in World War II, Moscow and Washington agreed to divide the Korean Peninsula at the 38th parallel for administrative convenience; Soviet units were to disarm Japanese troops north of that line, while U.S. units were to do so in the southern portion. That temporary division soon solidified, however, as Cold War tensions deepened, ultimately leading to the creation of two Korean states. The Republic of Korea (ROK) was established in the south, and its leader, conservative nationalist Syngman Rhee, enjoyed the backing of the United States. In the north, Moscow set up the Democratic People's Republic of Korea (DPRK), run by a staunch communist, Kim Il Sung, who had led guerrilla forces against the Japanese.

Although both superpowers assisted their respective clients, the degree of support differed markedly. The Soviet Union armed the DPRK to the hilt, supplying some of the most modern tanks, heavy artillery, and MiG aircraft in Moscow's arsenal. Washington was considerably more circumspect. U.S. leaders were concerned about Rhee's repeated threats to recover the northern "lost territories" by force and, therefore, declined to provide his government with weapons that could be used for offensive operations.

Rhee, however, was not the only Korean leader who was willing to use military coercion to unify the peninsula. On June 25, 1950, North Korean forces launched a series of coordinated attacks across the 38th parallel, sending the lightly armed South Korean defenders into a headlong retreat. The administration of President Harry S Truman promptly abandoned its policy of apparent indifference to the fate of South Korea and dispatched air and ground forces to help repel the attack. Within a few months, U.S.-led forces had not only pushed North Korean troops back across the 38th parallel; they had advanced all the way to the North Korean–Chinese border and seemed poised for a decisive victory. That hope ended abruptly in November when China intervened on a massive scale. Nearly three years of bloody, inconclusive warfare followed. Although the United States, China, and the DPRK—but not the ROK—finally signed an armistice in July 1953, no final peace treaty was ever concluded. The armistice left the Korean Peninsula in a twilight zone between peace and war, an armed camp on the front lines of the Cold War.

After the armistice, Washington negotiated a mutual defense treaty with Seoul and continued to station in South Korea ground forces backed by ample air and naval power and tactical nuclear weapons. U.S. force levels were finally reduced during the administration of Richard M. Nixon, but President Jimmy Carter's subsequent effort to withdraw all U.S. forces from the peninsula ended in failure. Not only is the Mutual Security Treaty still in effect, but more than 40,000 U.S. troops remain in Korea, despite the end of the Cold War. Although the Bush administration has expressed a willingness to draw down those forces to 36,000 by the mid-1990s, it resists any suggestion for deeper withdrawals—much less any notion of abrogating the treaty.

Continuing an expensive and potentially dangerous U.S. security commitment to South Korea makes even less sense than preserving NATO or the alliance with Japan. Conditions have changed radically since the United States came to the rescue of a weak and beleaguered South Korea in 1950. The Cold War rationale for undertaking that responsibility has vanished, South Korea's geostrategic significance has declined markedly, and the ROK is now fully capable of providing for its own defense. Yet U.S. leaders seem determined to maintain Washington's military protectorate over South Korea in perpetuity.

74

Flawed Justifications

Defenders of Washington's military commitment to South Korea insist that the defense of that country is a vital U.S. security interest. It is often unclear, however, what criteria they employ to reach that conclusion. A detached observer might well be puzzled by the contention that defending one half of a small peninsula on the opposite shore of the Pacific Ocean is essential to the well-being of a superpower.

The fundamental problem is that U.S. policymakers employ the concept of "vital interests" too casually. Indeed, as explained in Chapter 8, that was the central defect of U.S. foreign policy throughout the Cold War era. The continuing commitment to South Korea is a classic example of confusing a peripheral U.S. security interest with a vital one.

The belief that the ROK is vital to America's security is more a product of obsolete Cold War assumptions combined with an emotional attachment resulting from the sacrifice of American blood and treasure during the Korean War than it is a rational assessment of current U.S. security interests or requirements. Neither South Korea's economic nor strategic importance to the United States is sufficient to justify the costs and risks entailed by Washington's security commitment, especially the continued presence of U.S. forces on the peninsula.

True, the ROK is a significant trading partner, America's seventh largest; U.S.–South Korean trade came to nearly $32.9 billion in 1990.[3] Disruption of that commerce would be costly and unpleasant, but even a worst-case scenario involving the total loss of trade with South Korea would hardly devastate America's $5.5 trillion a year economy.

The concept of South Korea as an important strategic asset is even less compelling. Indeed, the very notion of the ROK as strategically vital to the United States is almost entirely dependent on the hoary but increasingly irrelevant Cold War doctrine of forward defense.

During the 1950s the United States established an elaborate network of alliances and bilateral security agreements with nations on the perimeter of the Soviet Union. The tacit bargain between the United States and its newly acquired allies, clients, and protectorates was that Washington would shield (with conventional and, if necessary, nuclear weapons) those countries from Soviet aggression. America's dependents, in turn, would provide bases for U.S. forces and augment U.S. military strength with their own forces if deterrence failed. Although the bargain was never stated in such crass terms, that was always its substance.

One can readily appreciate why America's clients found that arrangement at least satisfactory if not entirely appealing. Confronted with an aggressive Soviet Union—and its network of clients—those nations understandably felt menaced. Accepting U.S. protection spared them an unpleasant choice between risking eventual subjugation or risking economic ruin by building their own large military establishments—an effort that might still prove insufficient.

The benefits to the United States, even during the initial stages of the Cold War, were less obvious. In theory, of course, the acquisition of allies and clients increased America's ability to deter Soviet aggression or, failing that, to repel it. But many of those nations (including South Korea) were too small to alter the superpower force equation in any significant way. Indeed, in a showdown between the nuclear giants, the help provided by a small, nonnuclear power was likely to be decidedly marginal with one major exception—the utility of those nations as bases or forward staging areas for the projection of U.S. military might, especially air and nuclear power, against the USSR. Washington's network of clients also enabled the United States to test, and if possible contain, Soviet expansionist probes (or more often probes by Moscow's surrogates) without the perils of a direct superpower confrontation at the strategic nuclear level. That is what U.S. political leaders really meant when they urged Americans to support the vast array of global commitments because "it is better to fight the communists in country x than to fight them on our own shores."

But the military value of clients was eroding even as Washington built its globe-girdling alliance network. The development of long-range bombers, intercontinental ballistic missiles, and submarine-launched ballistic missiles greatly reduced the importance of a forward defense strategy. By the late 1950s the United States no longer needed bases on the perimeter of the Soviet Union from which to launch devastating strikes. Similarly, the use of clients as arenas in which to wage limited wars and keep the superpower rivalry from leading to global catastrophe became less effective. Indeed, instead of reducing the danger of an all-out war, alliances were much more likely to be, in defense analyst Earl C. Ravenal's particularly apt phrase, lethal "transmission belts for war"—converting local or regional wars into superpower confrontations. Both superpowers frequently found themselves in the midst of quarrels between clients, usually involving issues that were at most of marginal relevance to the patrons. The tense confrontation between the two Koreas is a case in point.

The value of South Korea and Washington's other small and medium-sized protectorates has been declining steadily for more than three decades. With the passing of Cold War tensions, the question of whether such clients are worth either the cost or the risk is more pertinent than ever before. And nowhere does that question need to be addressed more urgently than in Korea.

Despite repeated assertions about South Korea's importance to the United States and the need for Washington's commitment to protect that country, the actions of U.S. leaders have frequently suggested that the ROK is something less than a vital interest. Even at the dawn of the U.S.–South Korean military relationship, American ambivalence was apparent. NSC 48/2, approved by the National Security Council in December 1949, defined U.S. security objectives in the Far East and listed the ROK as one of the nations to receive military and economic aid, but it placed only "Japan, the Ryukyus, and the Philippines" inside the U.S. defense perimeter.[4] Both Secretary of State Dean Acheson and Senate Foreign Relations Committee chairman Tom Connally pointedly declined to include the ROK in that defense perimeter in their public statements during the months leading up to the Korean War.[5]

Although the Truman administration reversed course after the North Korean attack in June 1950, the way in which the United States waged the ensuing struggle suggested that the stakes were not vital. If truly vital security interests had been in jeopardy, the United States would have carried the fight to the Chinese homeland once Beijing intervened. Nor is it likely that Washington would have been content with an uneasy twilight peace that left the Korean Peninsula divided and the ROK vulnerable to another invasion by the North. Great powers do not accept such results when vital interests are involved unless compelled to do so, and the United

States, as the world's preeminent military power, clearly had other options.

The unwillingness of Presidents Truman and Dwight D. Eisenhower to treat Korea as a vital U.S. interest by waging an all-out war was understandable. Indeed, Truman should be faulted for involving the United States in the conflict at all. Even if one viewed the North Korean invasion as simply one move in a Soviet expansionist grand design (a highly simplistic interpretation), the decision that led to the expenditure of some $40 billion and the sacrifice of more than 50,000 American lives was of dubious wisdom. South Korea was never central enough to U.S. security to justify losses of that magnitude.

There are few indications that South Korea's importance to the United States has increased in the intervening years. The ROK's economic relevance has grown, but that has been more than offset by the decline in its military significance. Part of that decline is due to the decreased importance of forward defense; other factors are specific to the Korean situation. At one time North Korea could at least plausibly be viewed as a Soviet or Chinese surrogate. The protection of South Korea, therefore, was a symbol of Washington's resolve to resist the expansion of either communist giant through the use of proxies. Seoul's willingness to host U.S. forces also gave the United States a toehold on the Asian mainland and strengthened the overall U.S. military presence in East Asia.

But the role of the two Koreas began to shift in the 1970s. Rapprochement between the United States and China made it doubtful that Beijing would support, much less incite, an attempt by Pyongyang to forcibly unify the peninsula. As relations between the People's Republic of China and South Korea gradually warmed during the 1980s, the probability of a Chinese role in a North Korean offensive further receded. By 1989 more than 4,000 South Korean business leaders were visiting the PRC each year, and trade between the two nations exceeded $3 billion—some six times the amount of trade between China and North Korea.[6] Today the prospect of Beijing's encouraging a North Korean offensive is highly improbable.

Concerns about Soviet incitement were slower to fade, but during the tenure of President Mikhail Gorbachev even that danger became exceedingly remote. True, the postcommunist regime in Moscow still provides North Korea with some military hardware, and a defense treaty remains in place, but the Kremlin has steadily distanced itself from Pyongyang and moved closer to Seoul in other ways. The vast expansion of Soviet-ROK trade from virtually nothing to more than $1 billion in 1991 is only the most visible indication of change. The summit meeting between Gorbachev and ROK president Roh Tae Woo in June 1990 symbolized the growing ties—and Moscow's realization that there were few benefits to continuing to support North Korea. Moscow's subsequent decision to establish formal diplomatic relations with the ROK and to openly support Seoul's bid for UN membership cemented the rapprochement. The collapse of the old Soviet structure and the emergence of the new Commonwealth of Independent States will only accelerate those trends.

The marked improvement in Sino-American and Russo-American relations since the depths of the Cold War has also reduced South Korea's military importance. As late as the beginning of the 1980s, a North Korean attack on the ROK could at least arguably have been viewed as a Chinese or Soviet expansionist probe. Even if the debatable assumption that such a move would have impinged on significant U.S. security interests had been valid then, it no longer is.

With its massive internal economic and political problems, Russia is unlikely to embark on an expansionist course in East Asia. Although Moscow will undoubtedly keep some military forces in the region, those forces are being rapidly downsized and their readiness is eroding.[7] Russia's military expenditures are likely to be less than one-third the amounts spent by the old Soviet Union, and the entire Russian armed forces may have as few as 1.2 million active duty personnel.[8] Given Moscow's mounting financial woes, the trend toward lower military spending and smaller forces is likely to accelerate. More important, without some plausible motive for an expansionist drive, the remaining forces do not pose a serious threat to U.S. interests.

China's objectives are less clear, but there is little evidence that Beijing is about to adopt an aggressive policy. China is increasing its air and naval capabilities and may be embarking on a more serious effort to modernize the antiquated People's Liberation Army, but, as noted in Chapter 2, Chinese military capabilities are

79

quite modest. It would take a concerted and prohibitively expensive rearmament program, especially the establishment of a sizable blue-water navy, before Beijing could pose a serious threat to U.S. security interests in the Pacific.[9]

The diminished Russian and Chinese threats mean that developments on the Korean Peninsula are less relevant to the United States than at any point since the onset of the Cold War. Only if it could be established that the fall of South Korea would lead inexorably to the subjugation of Japan and America's other trading partners in East Asia (i.e., the emergence of a hostile hegemonic power in the region) would the ROK itself be more than a minor stake. But the notion that a North Korean conquest of the South would lead to the collapse of capitalist East Asia is little more than an recycled version of the simplistic and discredited domino theory. To pose a larger regional threat, North Korea would have to be acting as the agent of either China or Russia, a scenario that, in light of the domestic constraints in both countries and the policies adopted by Beijing and Moscow, is utterly farfetched.

Today, even assuming that Pyongyang would undertake a military offensive against its southern neighbor—a most risky enterprise given North Korea's estrangement from its one-time patrons—it would be a local conflict between rival Korean states. Such a conflict need not and should not have cosmic strategic ramifications.

Faced with mounting evidence that South Korea itself is not a vital U.S. interest and that neither China nor Russia poses a credible expansionist threat in the foreseeable future, defenders of the status quo have increasingly stressed an alternative justification for continuing the U.S. military presence. The commitment to South Korea is now supposedly merely one component of a larger mission to ensure stability in East Asia, which is assumed to be a vital U.S. interest.[10] Secretary of Defense Richard B. Cheney expressed that rationale succinctly during a trip to the area in early 1990: "If we were to withdraw our forward-deployed forces from the Asia-Pacific region, a vacuum would quickly develop. There almost surely would be a series of destabilizing regional arms races, an increase in regional tensions, and possibly conflict."[11]

As noted in Chapter 2, Washington's obsession with East Asian stability is frequently little more than a pretext for preserving U.S.

hegemony and preventing other nations, especially Japan, from playing more active political and military roles. But Cheney's claim that the U.S. military presence in Korea and elsewhere in the region is indispensable to stability is dubious even on its own merits. It reflects the same arrogance as the assumption that the mere continued deployment of U.S. forces in Europe will dampen the numerous conflicts and quarrels of that region. As analyst Marcus Corbin of the Center for Defense Information observed, Washington's ability to translate its military power into a force for political stability is overrated.

> If regional disputes heated up to the point of conflict, it is not at all clear that the mere presence of U.S. forces would be enough to stop them. U.S. public support for the actual use of U.S. forces in somebody else's Asian war would be highly unlikely. . . . The brief period when the U.S. could be the world's policeman is over. The paternalistic view that the U.S. should interfere in every regional problem and can solve them better than the people who live there is popular neither overseas nor at home.[12]

Assessing Costs and Risks

The factors just discussed combine to make South Korea no more than a peripheral American security interest, and since a vital interest is not at stake, it is essential to assess the costs and risks of fulfilling our commitment to the ROK. Only a very limited level of cost or risk is appropriate to the defense of a peripheral interest, and the evidence suggests that Washington's South Korean commitment substantially exceeds the permissible level in both categories. The financial cost of the U.S. military presence in South Korea is sizable. More than 40,000 U.S. military personnel, including the Second Infantry Division of the Eighth Army and 1½ air-wing equivalents of the Seventh Air Force, are stationed in the ROK. Taking into account all support and overhead expenses as well as direct costs, each active duty Army division costs more than $4 billion per year to deploy and sustain; each air wing costs approximately $1.9 billion. Consequently, the total cost of U.S. forces stationed in Korea is nearly $7 billion per year, of which the South Korean government supposedly offsets about $1.8 billion.[13]

Even that considerable sum does not fully measure the cost of Washington's security commitment to the ROK. There are other air, naval, and ground forces that exist primarily, or at least in part, to reinforce U.S. forces stationed in Korea in the event of conflict. Adding the cost of those forces brings the total cost of the commitment to South Korea to approximately $13 billion per year.

More worrisome than the expense of the South Korean commitment are the risks entailed. The Korean Peninsula is one of the most heavily armed portions of the planet. American forces are not only stationed in the ROK, most of them are deployed directly astride the route of any invasion by the North. Although the U.S. military commitment is based on the assumption that the presence of American forces (and the certainty of substantial American involvement in the event of conflict) will deter North Korea from launching an attack, Washington's policy puts the lives of those Americans at the mercy of a ruthless and unpredictable regime.

The possibility that deterrence could fail raises serious doubts about the wisdom of the U.S. military presence. Such doubts are especially pertinent now that North Korea may be attempting to manufacture nuclear weapons. It was one thing to take the risks of protecting the ROK when a North Korean attack might have been the first stage of a communist bid for global domination, however improbable that scenario seems in retrospect; it is quite another to accept the risk of becoming entangled in a local conflict with little relevance to U.S. security.

South Korean Capabilities

Incurring great expenses and risks to subsidize the defense of another country is especially unjustifiable when that country has the economic strength to create whatever military forces are needed for its security and enjoys a decisive advantage in terms of population and technological sophistication over its only conceivable enemy. Yet that is precisely the situation with regard to the U.S. security guarantee to South Korea.

When the Mutual Security Treaty was approved in 1954, the ROK was a poverty-stricken country that had been devastated by more than three years of war. The population was demoralized, and the military (although somewhat stronger than it had been when the North Koreans invaded in June 1950) was still decidedly inferior in training, equipment, and morale to its communist adversary. Moreover, Seoul had to confront not only the hostility of North Korea but the knowledge that Chinese or Soviet forces might support Pyongyang's units in the event of war. The security treaty with the United States was a tangible guarantee that the ROK would not have to deal with such powerful enemies by itself. Given the geostrategic realities in the mid-1950s and for many years thereafter, South Korea could not have provided for its own security.

That is no longer true. The ROK has become one of the world's great economic success stories. For nearly two decades its economy has enjoyed annual double-digit (or very high single-digit) growth rates, achieving a per capita GNP of more than $5,100 in 1991.

The ROK's dynamism and rapid growth contrast sharply with North Korea's stagnation and have given the South an overwhelming economic advantage over its communist nemesis. South Korea's GNP in 1990 stood at nearly $224 billion compared to the North's meager $21.5 billion.[14] In other words, the ROK has an economy more than 10 times larger than that of its enemy. It also has a decisive edge in population—some 43.4 million versus 21.3 million. In addition to such quantitative advantages, the ROK enjoys important qualitative advantages.[15] Technologically, South Korea's economy is light years ahead of the North's. South Korean firms compete successfully in global markets in a variety of products, including automobiles, computers, heavy machinery, and electronics.

Such economic strength is not a matter of merely academic interest. The large size, dynamic quality, and technological sophistication of the ROK's economy has important actual or potential military implications. For example, the sheer size of its economy means that Seoul can easily equal or surpass North Korea's military spending. If the South spends a mere 5 percent of its GNP on the military, the North must spend an astounding 50 percent just to match that effort. No country can sustain such a drain over a long period of time without risking economic collapse. Indeed, one factor in the economic troubles of the Soviet Union that contributed to its eventual disintegration was the constant burden of military spending, which apparently hovered around 20 to 25 percent of GNP throughout the 1970s and the 1980s.

Communist regimes habitually devote a disproportionate amount of economic resources to the military, and North Korea is no exception. Pyongyang's military budget in 1990 was an estimated $4.1 billion, or approximately 24 percent of GNP. Seoul's 1990 military budget of $10.62 billion was a mere 4.7 percent of GNP.[16] North Korea is caught in a military spending race that it cannot win; indeed, the South's already daunting advantage grows larger each year.

Advocates of preserving the U.S. security guarantee and troop presence, however, contend that the ROK's undeniable economic edge is not the issue. Instead, they point to the North's numerically larger military forces and cite continuing disparities in various categories of weapon systems. The reasoning of William J. Taylor, Jr., vice president of the Center for Strategic and International Studies, is typical.

> Although South Korea's military is far stronger than it was four decades ago, North Korean forces remain superior to those of the South in virtually every category. On the ground, North Korea boasts a 380,000-man advantage in personnel strength, and a better than two-to-one edge in medium and light tanks. It brandishes nearly twice as many artillery pieces as its southern counterpart and enjoys a massive advantage in multiple rocket launchers, antiaircraft missiles and surface-to-air missiles.[17]

Taylor notes further that the DPRK holds a similar numerical advantage in air and naval forces.

That argument contains several flaws. One is an excessive preoccupation with "bean counting"—a belief that raw numbers alone determine military capabilities. Although numerical factors can be important, the quality of forces is typically much more crucial. The size of Iraq's military at the onset of the Persian Gulf crisis was impressive, but most units were ill-trained, ill-equipped, and afflicted by poor morale—as some perceptive observers pointed out months before the outbreak of the war in January 1991.[18] Baghdad's large forces simply crumbled under the onslaught of a better trained, better led, and more technologically sophisticated adversary.

The qualitative disparity between ROK and DPRK forces does not appear to be as great as that between those of the U.S.-led international coalition and Iraq. Nevertheless, the assumption that North Korea is more powerful militarily merely because it is ahead in the bean count ought to be viewed with skepticism. Defense analyst Stephen D. Goose notes:

> While the North does enjoy numerical superiority in most manpower and weapons categories, that advantage is offset by other factors, most notably the superior quality and greater sophistication of South Korean weapons. Most analysts would credit ROK personnel with superior training, experience, and leadership, and most believe that South Korea would benefit from superior fighting doctrine and tactics.[19]

Other crucial factors are also often ignored by those who want to perpetuate the security ties between Washington and Seoul. For example, as the defender, the ROK would have a significant advantage in any conflict. North Korean forces would have to advance over difficult terrain against prepared fortifications and a powerful, well-armed foe determined to protect hearth and home. Most military experts have maintained that an attacking force needs at least a two-to-one advantage in personnel and firepower to prevail against a capable defending force. Even by the most crude numerical indices, the DPRK would lack that margin in several categories. A North Korean invasion would be, at best, a high-risk gamble.

Even if those who contend that Pyongyang presently enjoys military superiority over the South are correct, that does not validate the argument that Washington should maintain its security protectorate. Supporters of that policy act as though the ROK's numerical military inferiority were an immutable fact of nature. Given the large, rapidly expanding South Korean economy, however, Seoul clearly has the ability to close that gap—if it chooses to make the effort. Increasing military spending to 7 or 8 percent of GNP from the current level of 4.7 percent would create a situation that Pyongyang simply could not match. (Since Seoul has pledged to give more than $3 billion in economic aid to the republics of the former Soviet Union, it can scarcely plead "lack of funds" for a needed military build-up.) Even at the current levels of spending, the gap is likely to close, albeit more slowly. According to most estimates, ROK military spending has been outpacing that of the DPRK since the mid-1980s.

South Korean officials have no desire to make an accelerated effort, and as long as the United States is willing to subsidize the

ROK's defense by preserving the security treaty and maintaining forces to come to Seoul's rescue, they have no incentive to do so. Their attitude is exemplified by the comment of a prominent member of the ruling party at a conference on U.S.–South Korean security issues in late 1989. Responding to proposals that the ROK boost its military spending, he stated that such a diversion of resources would be undesirable because "we have needs in health and education that must be met."[20] Overburdened American taxpayers who face serious problems of their own in education, health care, and other areas may not be entirely sympathetic to that line of reasoning. The truth of the matter is that the South Korean government does not want to spend the money needed to create adequate defenses, not that it cannot afford to do so.

Incentives are vital. Apologists for the status quo profess to fear that the departure of U.S. troops would cause Seoul to despair and that South Korea would soon fall prey to North Korean aggression or intimidation. In addition to the obvious logical flaw of arguments that the ROK, although able to do so, would be so suicidal as to refuse to expand its military forces to the level needed to deter a DPRK attack, Seoul's reaction to the Nixon administration's partial troop withdrawal belies such pessimism. ROK leaders did not respond to that action with panic or defeatism. To the contrary, they launched a sustained military build-up. Military spending increased from a mere $1.1 billion in 1975 to more than $10.6 billion in 1990. There is no reason to believe that the South Koreans would display a perverse lack of prudence by not compensating for the withdrawal of the remaining U.S. units.

In their more candid moments, ROK officials concede that Seoul could become self-sufficient militarily within a few years if it increased its military spending. Defense Minister Lee Sang Hoon estimated in 1989 that by raising the military's share of GNP from 5 to 8 percent, South Korea could offset a complete U.S. troop withdrawal.[21] Although Lee did not want the ROK to undertake that effort, and such additional expenditures would slow South Korea's explosive economic growth rate, the tax burden would not be unmanageable. More important, from the standpoint of justice, the financial costs of the ROK's defense should be borne by South Korean, not American, taxpayers.

Washington's Cosmetic Changes

Faced with growing budgetary constraints, mounting congressional calls for scaling back America's expensive overseas military commitments, and South Korea's insistence on a greater say in decisionmaking, Washington has begun to alter its security role in Korea. According to Assistant Secretary of State for East Asian and Pacific Affairs Richard H. Solomon, the objective is to see that "U.S. forces make the transition from a leading role to a supporting posture in the defense of Korea by the year 2000."[22] But proposed changes in Korea are even more cosmetic than those in NATO.

Thus far, the Bush administration has agreed only to the most minimal troop withdrawals—some 2,000 Air Force support personnel and 5,000 Army personnel—as part of an overall program to scale down the U.S. military presence in East Asia by 10 to 12 percent. That reduction would still leave approximately 36,000 U.S. troops in South Korea. Apparently, there were plans for a second-stage reduction of an additional 5,000 to 6,000 troops by 1996, but that step was postponed indefinitely in November 1991 in reaction to Pyongyang's ongoing nuclear weapons program.[23] Even if the second-stage reduction is eventually implemented, there is no indication that the Bush administration is willing to carry out the Carter administration's proposal to withdraw all forces while retaining the security treaty. Indeed, some officials apparently want to keep U.S. forces on the peninsula even if the two Korean states agree to reunification.[24]

Other recent changes in Washington's policy have been more symbolic than substantive. For example, in the summer of 1991 the United States agreed to appoint an ROK general to head the southern delegation to the largely moribund Armistice Commission. There were also indications that Washington might agree to a South Korean general's becoming the head of the Combined Forces Command, which includes all South Korean units plus U.S. forces stationed on the peninsula.[25] (Having a U.S. officer technically in command of South Korea's forces has long been an affront to national pride and a source of irritation even to generally pro-American Koreans.)

The most substantive change was the apparent decision in the autumn of 1991 to withdraw U.S. tactical nuclear weapons deployed in South Korea.[26] (President Bush's arms control proposal applied to all land- or sea-based tactical nukes worldwide, but his action would have the greatest impact in Central Europe and South Korea.) The U.S. initiative raised the possibility that North Korea could be persuaded to abandon its nuclear weapons program, which appeared to be motivated in part by the perceived need to counter the U.S. tactical nuclear arsenal in South Korea.[27] There were indications that both Moscow and Beijing were prodding Pyongyang to take that step. It must be noted, however, that air-delivered nuclear weapons were not included in Washington's withdrawal program. Such weapons, reportedly carried by U.S. aircraft based throughout the western Pacific region, are likely to be a matter of continuing concern to the North Korean regime.

In their obsession with maintaining the U.S. military commitment to South Korea, Bush administration officials not only confuse a peripheral security interest with a vital one, they sometimes act as though Americans should be grateful to Seoul for letting U.S. forces defend the ROK. President Bush's statement at a news conference during his East Asian trip in February 1989 was typical: "At the request of the Republic of Korea, our forces are in Korea to deter aggression from the North. They will remain as long as the Government and people of South Korea want us to remain and as long as we believe it is in the interest of peace to keep them there."[28] A State Department position paper issued later that year was even more accommodating. "U.S. forces will remain in South Korea as long as there is a threat from North Korea and the South Korean Government and people wish them to remain."[29]

The end of the Cold War era has not materially altered Washington's attitude toward the Korean alliance. In a January 1991 address before the Korea Society in New York City, Solomon stressed that the administration had "no higher priority" than protecting the security of South Korea. "The United States intends to maintain appropriate forces in Korea so long as our two governments agree that a U.S. presence is necessary to deter a renewed outbreak of hostilities."[30]

The administration's rationale makes U.S. forces virtual hostages to politics on the Korean Peninsula. America will not be released from its mission to defend the ROK until Seoul decides that it no longer needs the insurance provided by U.S. protection or, even more improbable, decides to assume the financial burden of providing for its own defense. Moreover, the withdrawal of U.S. forces apparently cannot take place until North Korea ceases to be a threat to its neighbor. Given the breathtaking changes that have swept through the communist world in the past two years, the transformation or collapse of North Korea might occur overnight. Then again, the retrograde Stalinist regime might survive for decades. In any case, it is unwise to make the end of a U.S. security burden contingent on Kim Il Sung's experiencing a conversion to capitalist democracy or the emergence of a successor with that orientation.

Toward a Meaningful Policy Change

It should not be for Seoul to decide when U.S. troops may go home. Nor should the U.S. military presence be dependent on Korean reunification or even the advent of harmonious relations between the two Koreas—as desirable as either development would be.[31] The decision by the Bush administration in November 1991 to postpone indefinitely the second-stage troop reductions that reportedly were to take the number of U.S. troops down to 30,000 or 31,000 by 1996 is a particularly disturbing development. The ostensible reason for the postponement was North Korea's refusal to guarantee that it would not seek to develop nuclear weapons. But that is precisely the sort of linkage that may keep U.S. forces in Korea indefinitely. Unless the Pyongyang regime collapses or becomes a peace-loving capitalist democracy, there will always be some incident or source of tension that Seoul and its political allies in Washington can cite as a reason the United States cannot reduce, much less eliminate, its military commitment.

Apparently, not even reunification would be enough to release the United States from its military burdens. Many South Korean leaders would like to retain the U.S. military presence as a long-term insurance policy against an expansionist China or a resurgent Japan. Military and strategic planners in Seoul reportedly envision keeping approximately 20,000 American troops on the peninsula in a postreunification setting. "The different [policy] communities in South Korea believe that even if [the two Koreas] reunify we would still ask the U.S. to remain," stated Kim Kook Chin, the dean of research at the Foreign Ministry's Institute for Foreign Affairs and National Security.[32] Cha Young Koo, director of the Policy Planning Office of the government's Institute of Defense Analysis, is candid about the reason. "U.S. troops would be a guarantee against the militaristic policies of Japan."[33]

Such attitudes imply, quite literally, a permanent U.S. military presence in Korea. Only when the South Koreans came to trust the North Koreans, the Chinese, the Russians, and the Japanese could the United States withdraw its troops—that is to say, never.

The United States needs to move beyond the cosmetic changes the Bush administration is contemplating in the Korean commitment. Washington should establish a definite timetable (which should not exceed five years) for the complete withdrawal of all U.S. forces and the termination of the "mutual" security treaty. The specific pace of that disengagement and such issues as which units should depart first, the possible transfer of certain weapons systems to the ROK, and U.S. assistance in helping South Korean forces make the transition to self-sufficiency are proper subjects for negotiation. But the final result must not be hostage to any delay or obstructionism by Seoul, much less contingent on ROK approval. The pertinent issue from the standpoint of U.S. policy is not whether disengagement might be desired by the ROK, but whether it is in the best interest of the American people.

A five-year transition period would give South Korea adequate time to build up its forces—especially air and naval power for which it has deliberately chosen to rely on the United States—to offset the North's current numerical advantage. By that time, a North Korean invasion (which even now would be a high-risk venture) would be a suicidal enterprise. If U.S. officials are worried about the remote possibility that either China or Russia would assist an attack by Pyongyang, Washington should propose to Moscow and Beijing a U.S.-Russo-Chinese nonintervention pact. Such an agreement would confirm that none of the three powers would intervene in any conflict that might erupt on the Korean Peninsula—a posture that is in the best interest of all three countries. That measure would ensure that Seoul would only have to worry about defending itself against North Korea, a task that, given the ROK's enormous population and economic advantages, it should be able to manage without undue strain.

The Nuclear Weapons Issue

The most serious objection to severing the alliance with South Korea is that, by removing the U.S. nuclear shield, Washington would leave the ROK in a highly vulnerable position if the DPRK continues to pursue its nuclear weapons program. There is little question that North Korea has maintained such a program despite having signed the Nuclear Nonproliferation Treaty (NPT) in 1986. It has developed an extensive complex at Yongbyon, approximately 50 miles north of Pyongyang, including a building that U.S. intelligence experts believe is a plutonium reprocessing facility. Indeed, some U.S. officials concluded in early 1992 that the DPRK might be only months away from building its first bomb and that the Yongbyon reactors might be large enough to produce the material for as many as seven or eight Hiroshima-sized bombs per year by the mid-1990s.[34]

If North Korea did develop even a small nuclear arsenal and the United States severed its security commitment to the ROK, Seoul would face the unpleasant choice of risking nuclear blackmail from the North or acquiring its own strategic deterrent. From the standpoint of South Korea's security interests, the latter might be the more prudent course, and given its technological capabilities, the ROK could probably develop a deterrent fairly quickly. Indeed, Seoul apparently had an active program under way in the 1970s, which it abandoned under intense pressure from the United States. A decision to reactivate that program would have the unsettling effect of undermining Washington's long-standing global policy of preventing the proliferation of nuclear weapons. Moreover, Tokyo might also reconsider its renunciation of nuclear weapons if both Koreas as well as China and Russia had such arsenals. Being the only major nonnuclear power in an unstable neighborhood would undoubtedly make the Japanese nervous. Japan's acquisition of a nuclear capability, however, would send geopolitical shock waves throughout the region.

Although the prospect of nuclear weapons proliferation in northeast Asia is certainly not pleasant to contemplate, its likelihood should not be exaggerated. There is a reasonable chance that Seoul may be able to avoid the Hobson's choice of risking nuclear blackmail from the DPRK or contributing to proliferation. President Roh's November 1991 proposal to make the Korean Peninsula a nuclear-free zone was a serious effort to find a more satisfactory option. (Admittedly, the ROK's disavowal of any intention to acquire nuclear weapons also may have had the more insidious purpose of putting additional pressure on the United States to maintain its security commitment.) Seoul's diplomatic initiative appears to have borne fruit, as the ROK and DPRK reached an agreement in late December 1991 to renounce nuclear weapons.[35]

That agreement was the culmination of several developments during 1991 that provided some hope for peaceful coexistence of the two Korean regimes. The ability of Seoul and Pyongyang to agree to UN membership for both states and the conclusion of a nonaggression pact demonstrate that at least limited cooperation between the long-time antagonists is possible.[36]

There were other positive signs that North Korea may be abandoning its efforts to join the ranks of nuclear-armed states. North Korean leaders seem increasingly aware that the renunciation of such ambitions is a prerequisite for establishing economic relations with the outside world—a step that is vital to preventing the complete collapse of North Korea's sagging economy. The DPRK unexpectedly signed an inspection agreement with the International Atomic Energy Agency (IAEA)—the enforcement body for the NPT—in January 1992, after stalling since the mid-1980s. It also released a significant amount of data on its "peaceful nuclear research program," including a surprise revelation that it had already produced small quantities of plutonium.[37] IAEA director Hans Blix then visited Yongbyon in May to make arrangements for a full-scale inspection and reported continuing cooperation from North Korean authorities.

Those developments are encouraging. Nevertheless, Pyongyang's new conciliatory posture must be viewed with some caution and skepticism. We simply cannot be certain what North Korea's long-term intentions are with respect to nuclear weapons. It is possible that more pragmatic elements in the regime's leadership have concluded that a nuclear weapons program is too expensive, would fail to achieve meaningful political objectives, and would perpetuate the DPRK's disastrous political and diplomatic isolation.[38] At the same time, the possibility that Pyongyang is merely stalling for time until it can present the world with the fait accompli of a small arsenal cannot be ruled out. Even with IAEA access to the North Korean installations that have been identified, there is always the possibility that the DPRK has underground facilities that are not known to the international community. Iraq's ability to conceal its nuclear weapons program despite periodic IAEA inspections does not offer much comfort.

Even if the goal of a nuclear-free zone on the Korean Peninsula ultimately proves elusive, the United States should proceed with the orderly termination of its security protectorate. Nuclear proliferation—the most probable outcome if the ROK-DPRK agreement unravels—would be an unpleasant development, but it might also impose a regional version of the "balance of terror" that prevented a shooting war between the United States and the Soviet Union. Moreover, the crucial issue is not whether Seoul acquires nuclear weapons but whether Pyongyang does so. And the United States has little leverage to influence the outcome of North Korea's deliberations.

A continuing U.S. military presence in South Korea is more likely to cause the DPRK to embrace than reject the nuclear option. The most helpful steps the United States could take would be to remove its military presence so as to deprive the DPRK of that pretext and to prevail upon Tokyo, Beijing, and Moscow to exert diplomatic pressure on Pyongyang to abandon its nuclear ambitions and honor the agreement it reached with the ROK. That would certainly be a more productive course of action than the one that has been recklessly proposed in some quarters—preemptive strikes by U.S. (or U.S. and ROK) aircraft against North Korea's nuclear installations.[39] Such a step would risk igniting the very war Washington has sought to deter for nearly four decades.

Contrary to the beliefs of those who contend that the DPRK's nuclear weapons program reinforces the need for Washington's military commitment to the ROK, the possibility of a nuclear-armed North Korea should increase the incentives for U.S. disengagement. The only thing worse than risking a conventional war over peripheral interests would be to risk a nuclear conflict. That level of risk should *never* be assumed except to defend America's most vital security interests.

U.S. officials must stop operating from the premise that America's interests and those of its Korean client are congruent. Security strategy is not—or at least should not be—a philanthropic enterprise. The ROK is capable of building the military forces necessary for its own defense, and American taxpayers should not continue to shoulder that burden merely to spare South Korean taxpayers. Even more important, the Korean Peninsula is not and never has been a vital security interest of the United States. The defense of South Korea does not warrant either the expense or the risk that the U.S. military commitment entails. That was true even during the Cold War, and it is doubly true in the post–Cold War era.

4. Other Obsolete East Asian Commitments: ANZUS and the Philippines

The commitments to NATO, Japan, and South Korea were the most important alliances that Washington created during the Cold War era, and they continue to account for nearly half of all U.S. military spending. Nevertheless, there are other security commitments that were established from the late 1940s to the mid-1950s. As is the case with the "big three" alliances, U.S. officials and members of the foreign policy community still seek to perpetuate those secondary obligations, even though their relevance, which was always modest, has virtually disappeared with the end of the Cold War. Washington maintains two such commitments in East Asia: the ANZUS alliance with Australia and New Zealand and the mutual defense treaty with the Philippines.

ANZUS

ANZUS was a manifestation of the "pactomania" of the 1950s, when U.S. leaders seemed to treat alliances as an end in themselves rather than a means to some meaningful policy goal. During that period Washington also initiated such regional security agreements as the Southeast Asian Treaty Organization and the Baghdad Pact or Middle East Treaty Organization,[1] both now mercifully defunct. ANZUS, negotiated in 1951, was the first of the "little NATOs."

There was one important difference, however. Unlike NATO and most of the other defense guarantees forged by the United States after World War II, ANZUS was not primarily intended to contain the Soviet Union, which had no significant military presence in the South Pacific in the early 1950s. Indeed, the creation of that alliance is proof that policymakers as well as generals typically prepare to fight the last war. ANZUS was designed to prevent a repetition of Japan's military threat to the region, which had culminated in World War II. ANZUS was an excellent institutional arrangement for thwarting aggression by the imperial Japanese fleet. That fleet, however, had been resting at the bottom of the Pacific for several years. ANZUS has the distinction of having been obsolete the day it was formed.

In retrospect, it is apparent that Australia and New Zealand desired ANZUS less for its meager military significance than its political symbolism. Canberra and Wellington wanted to direct Washington's attention to the South Pacific. Otherwise, those nations feared, the United States, with so many defense obligations elsewhere in the world, would ignore their region. According to onetime New Zealand National party leader J. K. McLay, "The Australian and New Zealand leaders of that time wanted the United States to have a treaty commitment in our part of the world as well."[2] That attitude has also been evident in more recent years. David Lange, New Zealand's prime minister in the middle and late 1980s, for instance, insisted that ANZUS was more an affirmation of common interests than a serious military alliance. "A South Pacific NATO was not, and is not, needed."[3] Similarly, a 1986 Australian defense study (the so-called Dibb report) conceded that the possibility of Canberra's needing assistance under ANZUS was "remote."[4]

Such views are especially significant because they were expressed even before the disintegration of the Soviet Union and the end of the Cold War. If it was difficult for the principal beneficiaries to imagine a serious military purpose for ANZUS in a Cold War setting, it has become virtually impossible to do so in the post–Cold War environment.

The alliance has been virtually moribund since the mid-1980s. ANZUS began to unravel in 1984 when the Labor party came to power in New Zealand, having promised to bar any nuclear-powered or nuclear-armed vessels from visiting that country. Prime Minister Lange reaffirmed New Zealand's support for ANZUS but warned that U.S. warships would be barred unless Washington guaranteed that they were nonnuclear. When U.S. officials were unable to resolve the problem through negotiations, they decided to use the USS *Buchanan*, a conventionally powered destroyer, to test the ban in February 1985. The Lange government requested a U.S. assurance that the vessel did not have nuclear weapons, but the Reagan administration, citing a long-standing policy of refusing to confirm or deny whether U.S. vessels carry nuclear weapons, refused. New Zealand then barred the ship from its ports.

ANZUS became a casualty in the ensuing diplomatic squabble.[5] The United States canceled joint military exercises, restricted the flow of intelligence information, and in June 1986 formally suspended its pledge to defend New Zealand.[6] Although New Zealand refused to withdraw from ANZUS, leaving the alliance technically alive, the country was expelled as a member in everything but name by the other two members even before the parliament formally enacted the Lange government's nuclear ban into law in June 1987. Washington and Canberra turned ANZUS into a de facto bilateral treaty, although they left the door open for New Zealand's return to grace.

Paul Wolfowitz, assistant secretary of state for East Asian and Pacific affairs, insisted in June 1984 that ANZUS was "one of the critical factors" supporting the stability of the Pacific and warned that the health of the alliance was "vital to the global Western alliance,"[7] but there is little evidence that the Reagan administration actually believed that tiny New Zealand's rejection of nuclear weapons would seriously threaten U.S. security. U.S. officials were primarily concerned that Wellington's stance would encourage other, more important U.S. allies to adopt similar restrictions. The administration's uncompromising response to the Lange government's policy was designed to quarantine the New Zealand anti-nuclear "disease."[8]

Since the conservative National party's election victory over Labor in October 1990, there have been movements in both Wellington and Washington to resuscitate ANZUS. New Zealand's new prime minister, Jim Bolger, expressed a desire to mend the breach with the United States and even indicated that visits by U.S. naval vessels would now be welcome without an explicit "no nukes" pledge.[9] Bolger's foreign minister, Don McKinnon, is a staunch advocate of acceding to U.S. demands, and he ridicules the previous Labor government for converting New Zealand into a "modern-day Albania hiding in the South Pacific."[10] President Bush's August 27, 1991, nuclear arms control initiative, which ordered the removal of all nuclear weapons from U.S. surface ships, had the collateral effect of defusing the issue that had led to the rupture of security ties between the United States and New Zealand. The National government was sufficiently emboldened in the autumn of 1991 to announce plans to review the anti-nuclear legislation.[11] Nevertheless, Bolger and McKinnon have proceeded cautiously, since the legislation is still extremely popular with New Zealand voters, and the National party had pledged before the 1990 elections that it would not change the law.

For its part, the Bush administration is receptive to proposals for raising ANZUS from the dead, as are the usual nongovernmental enthusiasts for a global interventionist foreign policy.[12] At this point, however, revitalizing ANZUS does not appear to be a high-priority administration objective. U.S. officials would like to see the alliance revived, but only if it can be done entirely on U.S. terms. There is no inclination whatever to make concessions to bring New Zealand back into the fold.

Given the general military irrelevance of ANZUS, one might wonder why the United States would bother with revitalization initiatives at all. The old justifications for the pact—meager as they were—clearly have no validity. Supporters of ANZUS made much of the Soviet Union's naval build-up in the Pacific during the 1980s, particularly its use of Vietnam's Cam Ranh Bay. Moscow had also made a few diplomatic inroads in the region, signing a fishing treaty with Kiribati, for instance, and establishing diplomatic relations with Vanuatu, both sparsely populated Pacific island states. Despite a considerable amount of alarm in U.S. policy circles at the time, the Soviet advances were never terribly significant. With only a limited ability to project military power and scant diplomatic influence in the region, Moscow posed an unlikely, purely theoretical threat even before the dramatic changes that ultimately destroyed the USSR.

Given the turmoil in the former Soviet Union and the economic constraints on both the Commonwealth of Independent States and the Russian republic, there is little chance of military adventurism in the South Pacific. Not only have the naval units been withdrawn from Cam Ranh Bay, but Moscow's Pacific fleet seems to be in an increasing state of disarray. Indeed, that fleet, along with most other surface vessels in the once proud Soviet navy, was recalled to its home ports in January 1992 because of fuel shortages and uncertainty about the command structure. A high-level Pentagon official conceded that the Pacific fleet was docked in its home ports of Vladivostok and Petropavlovsk without fuel.[13] Even with the passing of that short-term crisis, what remains of Moscow's sea power in that part of the world will be concentrated in the northwest Pacific, far away from Australia and New Zealand, making any threat to those nations remote.

There are few other credible threats to the security of either country. New Zealand's neighbors are Australia to the northwest, Antarctica to the south, and wide expanses of ocean and scattered islands in other directions. Australia is less isolated geographically, but it too appears to face few military dangers. Defense analysts Amitav Acharya and Daniel Mulhall note that "Australia is protected from invasion by formidable air and sea barriers," which make it an unlikely candidate for invasion.[14] Canberra's relations with Indonesia have been tense at times, and Australian leaders are rightly concerned about the political instability that may accompany the end of General Suharto's long rule. Nevertheless, Indonesia is no military powerhouse, despite its sizable population. It has barely 278,000 active duty military personnel, and neither the navy nor the air force has serious power projection capabilities. Jakarta's defense budget is a mere $1.57 billion—barely 20 percent of Canberra's expenditures.[15] Aggression from Indonesia would be highly unlikely.

Security threats from other powers are even more improbable. Vietnam has a large army but lacks the naval and air forces necessary to invade a distant continent, and Hanoi is preoccupied with massive internal economic woes. Furthermore, a regional power that was unable to preserve its sway in neighboring Cambodia does not pose a credible threat to distant states in the South Pacific. China and Japan are modestly strengthening their militaries, but neither country has either the power projection forces needed to attack Australia or any incentive to launch an attack.

In such a strategic environment Australia and New Zealand should be capable of protecting their own interests. Australia has more than 68,000 active duty personnel and another 29,000 in reserve. It added six new submarines to its fleet in the middle and late 1980s; modernized its guided missile destroyers; introduced anti-mine ships; and built a western port in Perth, which makes possible a two-ocean Australian navy. It is also upgrading the weapons systems of its air force and army. True, Canberra spends only a modest \$7.57 billion (U.S.), or some 2.5 percent of GDP,[16] on defense, but that may not be an unreasonably low amount, given Australia's relatively benign threat environment. Moreover, Canberra's defense expenditures are predicated on the assumption that the United States would provide substantial military assistance if a crisis arose. Australian officials concede privately that their country could afford to spend more on defense if it became necessary and that they would do so if the United States began to disengage from the region.[17]

New Zealand's military, while substantially smaller, is also a capable force. Wellington currently spends \$810.7 million (U.S.), some 1.9 percent of GDP, on defense.[18] Although it might be advisable for New Zealand to increase that spending somewhat, and especially to enhance the capabilities of its navy, the defense budget is not entirely out of line given the country's geographic advantages. Nations such as Indonesia and Malaysia, which might pose some security concerns to Australia, are considerably less of a factor in Wellington's defense calculations.

Nevertheless, there is little doubt that the National party government would like to resume its status as a U.S. protectorate under ANZUS—in part to avoid having to increase military spending. Even the Heritage Foundation's Richard Fisher—a staunch advocate of reviving ANZUS—concedes that the "Bolger government's desire to rebuild defense ties with the U.S. stands in contrast to its questionable ability to maintain a credible NZDF [New Zealand Defense Force]. To reduce the large government budget deficit, National is contemplating cutting this year about \$65 million from the NZDF's defense budget."[19] What Fisher and other U.S. fans of ANZUS fail to explain is why American taxpayers should provide a defense subsidy to New Zealand. After all, the United States has a large government budget deficit of its own that could be trimmed by reductions in the military budget.

In addition to such considerations as the lack of a credible threat to the security of Australia and New Zealand and the ability of both countries to defend their security without U.S. assistance—if they are willing to bear the expense of doing so—there is another reason Washington can afford to dispense with ANZUS. U.S. interests in the South Pacific are far more diffuse and limited than those of Australia or New Zealand. The security of those nations—as well as that of their neighbors throughout the region—is not even arguably vital to the survival of the United States. If South Korea is only a peripheral U.S. security interest, the South Pacific scarcely reaches even that level. America undoubtedly has economic and cultural interests in the South Pacific, including extensive trade with Australia and New Zealand, and ANZUS promotes some useful political ties, but such interests were never compelling enough to go to war even in the unlikely event of a Soviet expansionist move. They certainly do not merit the expense and bother of a security alliance in the absence of a serious global threat.

The most important military value of Australia and New Zealand to the United States is their extension of the range of U.S. interventionist capabilities. Australian bases, in particular, provide an important link in the international command, control, and communications network of the U.S. military, especially for operations in the Indian Ocean.[20] Both countries also help to create a regional climate that is hospitable to Western democratic capitalist values, though one can anticipate that they would continue doing so without a formal military alliance with the United States. From the standpoint of important U.S. security interests, there is even less military justification for ANZUS now than there was when the alliance was first created.

Washington needs to stop prodding New Zealand to return to the ANZUS fold. At the same time, the United States should encourage Australia and New Zealand to increase their bilateral security cooperation and to continue playing moderating and stabilizing roles throughout the South Pacific. Given the compatibility of their security interests, it is not surprising that Australia and New Zealand had a record of bilateral cooperation even before the advent of ANZUS. Their first agreement to share military information was adopted in 1933, and they have remained close partners ever since. New Zealand predictably responded to the cutoff of U.S. military ties in the mid-1980s by expanding its bilateral links to Australia, and the latter country accommodated the wishes of its neighbor by creating a separate intelligence bureau to pass along information generated in Canberra.[21]

Both nations also have good relations with other countries throughout the region and have provided economic and technical assistance to many of them. New Zealand once administered the

Cook Islands, Nuie, and Western Samoa and has educated a large percentage of the South Pacific island leaders. Australia and New Zealand have forged important military links with their Pacific and East Asian neighbors as well. Australia helped train Papua New Guinea's armed forces, bases a number of aircraft and a small army contingent in Malaysia, and conducts occasional exercises with Thailand's armed forces. New Zealand maintains a small troop unit in Singapore.[22]

ANZUS, even more than Washington's other post–World War II military commitments, is a relic, geared to preventing domination by an imperialist Japan that long ago ceased to exist and to countering a Soviet threat to the South Pacific that never materialized. Australia and New Zealand face no challenges to their security that they cannot manage with their own military resources, and those nations, though they provide bases that are useful to a U.S. global interventionist strategy, are not vital to U.S. security. Canberra and Wellington (now that the National party is back in power) would probably like to keep the alliance with the United States as an insurance policy against the emergence of an expansionist threat in their region, however improbable that danger might be. Australia's former prime minister, Robert Hawke, expressed his desire to cling to the U.S. security blanket.

> U.S. engagement is, and will remain, important to Australia's strategic and security interests, and important to the security interest of the region as a whole. To understand that, consider for a moment its opposite—the United States walking away, or even worse being forced away—[from] a profound involvement in the region. We would feel, and we would be, much less secure.[23]

Although it is highly questionable whether Australians would in fact be less secure if the United States adopted a lower military profile in the region, there is little doubt that they would feel less secure. But it is not in the best interests of the United States to provide cost-free insurance merely to spare Australian and New Zealand taxpayers feelings of insecurity and the necessity of making additional military expenditures. The U.S. desire to preserve ANZUS is a classic example of wanting to have an alliance for the sake of having an alliance. Instead of pressuring New Zealand to rejoin ANZUS, the United States should move to formally dissolve that moribund military pact.

The Philippines

The U.S.-Philippine military relationship dates from Washington's acquisition of the archipelago at the end of the Spanish-American War. After suppressing the insurgency led by independence leader Emilio Aguinaldo, the United States established a variety of military installations in its new colony. During the following decades, the Philippines became the principal outpost of the American presence in East Asia. Although Japanese forces temporarily expelled the United States during World War II, U.S. units fought their way back in 1944 and remained after the war ended. In March 1947, a mere eight months after the Philippines received its independence from the United States, the two countries entered into an agreement covering Clark Air Base, Subic Bay Naval Base, and several minor facilities. The U.S.-Philippine military relationship was further consolidated in August 1951 with the conclusion of a bilateral mutual security treaty.

During the initial years of the Cold War, the military comaraderie that had been established during World War II in the common effort to dislodge the Japanese continued, but frictions developed as time passed. Increasing numbers of Filipinos complained that U.S. financial compensation for the Clark and Subic Bay installations was inadequate. Others suspected that Washington's support for the corrupt dictatorship of Ferdinand Marcos in the 1970s and early 1980s was motivated by a cynical desire to keep those bases regardless of the cost to the political and economic well-being of the Filipino people. After the "people power" revolution led by Corazon Aquino overthrew Marcos in 1986, complaints mounted, and it became increasingly unclear whether the base agreement would be renewed when it expired in 1991. Negotiations on a new agreement were marked by sharp, sometimes acrimonious exchanges between U.S. and Philippine officials.

The Bush administration's handling of the bases issue in 1991 and early 1992 illustrated how U.S. leaders cling to the trappings of America's Cold War era global military presence. As late as the spring of 1991, U.S. officials insisted that Clark Air Base and Subic Bay Naval Base were both essential installations. Not until the eruption of Mount Pinatubo buried Clark in ash and mud—creating in the words of one observer, "a landscape of mind-boggling ruin" that would have cost an estimated $520 million to repair—did the administration finally abandon its goal of retaining that base.[24] Administration leaders were even more determined to keep Subic, whose deep-water port and extensive ship repair facilities were deemed "irreplaceable." At the same time that they agreed to withdraw from Clark, they negotiated a new agreement with the government of president Aquino to extend the lease on Subic for 10 years.

A spirited and often bitter debate erupted in the Philippine Senate as soon as the agreement was submitted for ratification, and it was obvious from the outset that the treaty was in trouble. Several anti-base senators charged that the Aquino government had failed to extract enough compensation for extending the U.S. presence and hinted that they might be persuaded to vote for ratification if Washington's offer were sweetened. Other opponents made it clear that the fundamental issue was one of national pride and sovereignty. To them the U.S. base symbolized a continuing colonial paternalism that was unhealthy for the Philippines' development as a independent and self-reliant country. Sen. Agapito Aquino, the president's brother-in-law, captured that sentiment when he urged the United States to understand that "the absence of authentic sovereignty on our part translates into a very real incapacity to stand on our own feet, a palpable inability to grow up, a political adolescence perpetually tied to the purse strings of America, a crippling dependence, an anachronistic colonial and Cold War mentality." In a similar but harsher vein, Sen. Juan Ponce Enrile castigated the treaty as "an insult to our race." He added, "I cannot live with a treaty that assumes that without 8,000 servicemen and some passing warships, we shall fall flat on our faces." Referring to Spanish and U.S. colonial rule, Senate president Jovito Solanga concluded, "Today we have finally summoned the political will to end 470 years of foreign military presence." It was, he said, "a day of liberation."[25] For such hard-core anti-base senators, no compensation package, however generous, would have made a difference.

It is uncertain whether the Bush administration, left to its own devices, would have increased the offer. Domestic political realities precluded that step in any case. Critics of the agreement both inside and outside Congress questioned whether the Subic Bay base was needed in a post–Cold War world at any price. Increasing the compensation package would have placed the administration in the untenable position of blatantly sacrificing the interests of American taxpayers.

Instead of offering the carrot of more compensation, Washington implied that it might use the stick of economic retaliation. There were ugly hints that if the Philippine Senate rejected the base agreement, Manila's status as a trading partner might suffer. That was alarming to all Filipinos since the United States was a crucial export market. In particular, the Philippines benefited from rather liberal sugar and textile quotas. Even the partial loss of such preferences would have a serious impact on an economy that had only minimally recovered from the disastrous corruption that had taken place during the long dictatorship of Ferdinand Marcos.

Such hard-ball tactics had some impact on the ratification debate. As the Senate vote drew near, the Aquino government abandoned its low-key approach and tried to rally public opinion in favor of retaining the U.S. presence. Economic motives appeared to be paramount. Not only did the government and its supporters not want to lose the 40,000 jobs provided by the base (losing nearly 30,000 jobs because of the closure of Clark was considered enough of a blow), but the prospect of new protectionist trade barriers was even more alarming.

Although Washington's tactics may have swayed Aquino and a sizable portion of the Filipino population, they did not budge opponents in the Senate. The coalition of senators who insisted on more compensation and those who wanted the U.S. forces out of Subic Bay as a matter of national pride proved to be more than sufficient to defeat the base agreement. When the final vote was taken on September 16, 1991, just hours before the expiration of the existing accord, proponents could muster only 11 votes in the 23-member chamber—far short of the two-thirds majority needed for ratification. Eight of the 12 senators who voted to reject the document appeared to be members of the hard-core faction.

Instead of accepting defeat gracefully, the Bush administration engaged in a variety of transparent diplomatic maneuvers. Washington's initial response was to support the efforts of the Aquino government to overturn the Senate's verdict by a national referendum. The U.S. embassy in Manila immediately issued a statement that the United States stood "fully behind the president in her continuing efforts to put in place the new treaty."[26] When Aquino rescinded the eviction notice that had been issued earlier, the Bush administration took the position that the previous (1947) agreement was still fully in force, despite the rejection of the new treaty. According to Kenneth M. Quinn, deputy assistant secretary of state for Asian and Pacific affairs, Aquino's action meant that "there is now no termination date for the 1947 agreement," although he conceded that the agreement might "in the future" be terminated by mutual agreement or after one year's notice by either party.[27]

The administration's support for Aquino's campaign to overturn the Senate's decision was unwise, for it injected the United States into a bitter domestic constitutional dispute. Many Filipinos were especially sensitive to Washington's taking sides in that fashion because of America's status as the former colonial ruler. It also proved to be unwise from a practical standpoint. Aquino's ploy had little chance of success—a point that became evident when a furious political opposition denounced her actions as unconstitutional. Indeed, she soon conceded that even some pro-bases constituencies refused to back her bid for a referendum.[28] Faced with mounting criticism, she beat a hasty retreat—leaving U.S. officials in the embarrassing position of having supported an unsuccessful power grab.

Nevertheless, the Bush administration still did not abandon all hope of reversing the Senate's decision. It next encouraged Aquino to negotiate an executive agreement that would give the United States three years to withdraw its personnel and equipment from the base, instead of the one year specified in the expired agreement. The underlying hope was that nationwide elections in May 1992 would produce a new Senate willing to reconsider the ratification vote and approve the original 10-year extension.[29] A three-year withdrawal period would give plenty of time for reconsideration, whereas under a one-year deadline, the removal of personnel and equipment would be far advanced by the time a new ratification vote could take place.

The delay strategy did not work much better than backing the referendum proposal had, although Aquino was able to get a majority of the Senate to authorize negotiations for a three-year withdrawal period as part of a compromise to drop the referendum campaign. Bargaining between U.S. and Philippine officials soon bogged down. The principal stumbling block appeared to be the U.S. refusal to commit to a firm withdrawal schedule.[30] Ultimately, the Aquino government, reacting to mounting domestic criticism, gave U.S. officials formal notification that the departure had to be completed by the end of 1992.

Why was the Bush administration so slow to recognize political realities and accept the fact that the long U.S. military presence in the Philippines was drawing to a close? The standard justifications for trying to retain the bases do not stand up to scrutiny. Clark's utility had declined markedly long before the Mount Pinatubo eruption, and a new lease on Subic Bay was a dubious bargain even at the levels of compensation agreed to by U.S. and Philippines negotiators in July. The installation was not essential for the protection of legitimate American security interests even during the Cold War, much less in the post–Cold War era.

Those who wanted the United States to retain the Subic Bay base contended that it would be useful in three possible scenarios:

• It would help contain any expansionist moves by Moscow in East Asia, especially hostile actions directed against U.S. allies in the northwest Pacific.

• It would serve as a staging area for the projection of U.S. force into the southwest Pacific or Southeast Asia and protect the sea lanes in that region in the event of hostilities.

• It would help support U.S. forces deployed in the Indian Ocean and the Persian Gulf regions in peacetime and might be essential for future large-scale deployments during a crisis.[31]

None of those justifications was compelling even in a Cold War security environment in which the United States undertook to contain Soviet (or more generally, communist) power and protect a host of allies and clients in the Pacific Basin and elsewhere. In a post–Cold War setting, the justifications border on the fanciful.

The supposed importance of the Philippine bases as a major component of the effort to contain Soviet military power in East Asia was exaggerated. Given the vast distance of those facilities from the primary U.S. commitments in the northwest Pacific— Japan and South Korea—they played only a limited role in Washington's strategy.[32] Since the commitments themselves had become obsolete, insisting on retaining the Subic Bay base to provide (at most) peripheral support for them was a case of piling folly upon folly.

The base did not have much more utility in deterring China, projecting U.S. power against an adversary in Southeast Asia (i.e., Vietnam), or protecting the sea lanes. As is the case for possible U.S. missions in the northwest Pacific, the scenarios for military action are implausible, and even if one of them were to materialize, the relevance of the Subic Bay installation would be marginal. It is revealing that Subic Bay and Clark played largely ancillary roles in the massive U.S. intervention in Vietnam during the 1960s and early 1970s.[33]

The likelihood of a Philippine naval base's playing a significant role today is even less. There is no prospect of U.S. intervention in Southeast Asia for any reason. One unpleasant and futile crusade in that region was more than enough for the American people. The fall of the noncommunist governments in Indochina was disastrous for the indigenous populations, but it had no discernible impact on the security of the United States—contrary to the alarmist predictions of U.S. officials during the Vietnam War. There are no intrinsic interests in that region that would ever justify a second U.S. intervention. For years the Pentagon and its political allies cited the Soviet forces stationed at the Cam Ranh Bay naval base (originally built by the United States) as a reason for keeping the Subic Bay facility. But Moscow began to withdraw from Cam Ranh in 1990, and the withdrawal was essentially complete before the collapse of the Soviet Union itself.

The emergence of a "Chinese threat" is scarcely more plausible. The notion of an aggressive Chinese navy prowling the western Pacific and threatening the sea lanes belongs in the realm of paranoid fantasy. China's navy is largely configured for coastal defense missions, not distant power projection. Indeed, the alleged need for the United States to protect the sea lanes of the western Pacific from any would-be aggressor is entirely theoretical. There are currently no credible threats to those lanes and none is visible on the horizon. Officials and pundits who contend that vast U.S. naval and air forces must be stationed in that part of the world for such a purpose should be asked to identify the nation or nations that would have the capability and incentive to pose a threat. If none can be cited, then the suspicion grows that the sea lane protection mission is little more than a pretext for maintaining an oversized U.S. force structure.

The primary purpose of the Philippine bases (especially Subic Bay) has been to provide important logistical support to the U.S. military presence in the Indian Ocean and the Persian Gulf regions. But even that role was based on a worst-case scenario—the need for U.S. forces to stage a massive "back-door" intervention in South Asia or the Persian Gulf.[34] That scenario, in turn, assumed that Washington would be countering a full-scale Soviet military effort to dominate the Persian Gulf oil fields or oil routes.

Even if one accepts the dubious arguments of those who insist that the United States has vital interests to defend in the Persian Gulf region,[35] the need for a back-door intervention (always over-stated) has virtually disappeared. As the 1990–91 Persian Gulf crisis demonstrated, threats in the area are now likely to come from small or medium-sized regional powers, not Washington's erstwhile superpower adversary. If they felt menaced by an expansionist rival, other countries in the region would cooperate with the United States as Egypt, Syria, Turkey, and Saudi Arabia did in the campaign against Iraq. U.S. intervention would thus come primarily through the "front door" (i.e., the eastern Mediterranean and its environs). The Subic Bay base would be, at most, marginally relevant.

Moreover, with the collapse of the Soviet expansionist threat, the principal rationale for maintaining a large U.S. military presence in the Indian Ocean and Persian Gulf regions has lost validity. It is highly questionable whether America should assume the costs and risks of policing that volatile part of the world merely to thwart midsized regional powers that can and should be contained by neighboring states. Here again, the security environment is entirely different than it was during the Cold War; it is no longer even arguable that the United States is the only power capable of preventing or repelling aggression. Lesser threats can be met by lesser powers, acting either individually or collectively. There is no reason to maintain a huge naval base in the Philippines to support an unnecessary U.S. military presence in the Indian Ocean and Persian Gulf.

Apparently recognizing that the security justifications for retaining the bases were unconvincing, U.S. proponents increasingly relied on the argument that the facilities made an important contribution to the economic well-being of the Philippines. The overall impact of the U.S. presence was significant; some estimates placed the figure at approximately $1.2 billion each year—nearly 3 percent of the Philippine GNP.[36] The bases also served as the country's largest employer; nearly 70,000 Filipinos were employed—20,000 at highly prized full-time jobs.

Aside from the point that U.S. defense commitments should never be a thinly disguised foreign social welfare program, such arguments ignored the point that the bases had become a serious irritant in U.S.-Philippine relations. In addition to the continuous wrangling over compensation, many Filipinos believed (correctly) that a succession of American presidents supported the corrupt and repressive Marcos regime largely to maintain U.S. access to those facilities.[37] They also considered the bases a symbol of U.S. domination, even a reminder of the colonial era. That perception was reinforced when planes from Clark took to the air to help suppress a military coup against Aquino in December 1989. Even Filipinos who opposed the coup expressed uneasiness about the country's one-time colonial master's intervening in that fashion. During the debate on the base agreement in the Philippine Senate, anti-base senators repeatedly cited the need to cut the colonial apron strings even at the cost of losing economic benefits.

For U.S. officials and other proponents of an extensive military presence in the western Pacific, the prospect of evacuating the Philippine bases is a bitter defeat. They wax nostalgic about the World War II era and the days of close military cooperation between the two countries, and they see no reason to change that relationship. In their view, the defeat of the bases agreement was engineered by "a handful of loudmouth politicos"—left-wing Filipino "Jesse Jacksons."[38] For such Americans, the loss of the Philippine bases symbolizes the end of U.S. dominance in the western Pacific and the erosion of Washington's informal empire.

It is in the best interests of both the Philippine and the American people to end the U.S. military presence. The bases add virtually nothing to the security of the Philippines. Despite Washington's apparent desire to retain the obligation to defend the Philippines contained in the "mutual" security treaty, that country faces no credible external threat. The principal danger comes from the communist New People's Army guerrillas, and the existence of neither

110

U.S. military bases nor the security treaty will have much beneficial impact on that problem.

The Philippine commitment likewise has little relevance to U.S. security. Clark and Subic Bay have become anachronisms in the post–Cold War era. The United States does not need a large military presence in that part of the world to defend its legitimate security interests. A more modest and appropriate naval and air presence further east in the Pacific can be sustained from facilities located in Guam and other American possessions.

Washington does not wish to contemplate a more restrained role, however. Instead, it is seeking to replace the Subic Bay and Clark installations with a more decentralized deployment of forces and the cultivation of more extensive military relationships with other states in the region to guarantee access or transit rights.[39] Discussions are reportedly under way with the governments of Malaysia, Indonesia, and Thailand. Even before the final stages of the Philippine base negotiations began, U.S. officials concluded an agreement with Singapore giving U.S. naval vessels access to that country's port facilities and enabling the United States to rotate squadrons of F-15 and F-16 fighters into a Singaporean air force base for a month at a time from Japan, South Korea, and Alaska. After the vote by the Philippine Senate and the failure to delay the withdrawal of U.S. forces from Subic Bay, the Bush administration concluded an accord shifting the logistics operations command task force of the Seventh Fleet from Subic Bay to Singapore.[40]

That agreement, along with Bush's remarks during his January 1992 East Asian trip, underscored Washington's determination to maintain an extensive military presence in the western Pacific. In his speech to the Australian parliament, Bush conceded that "there is some concern in Asia about America's commitment given our imminent departure from Subic Bay." He then stressed that the United States would remain engaged militarily. "We know that our security is inextricably linked to stability across the Pacific, and we will not put that security and stability at risk. I can assure you that the United States intends to retain the appropriate military presence to protect its allies and to counter threats to peace."[41]

American naval and air units will remain on guard to protect the region from phantom threats and, perhaps more significant, to remind Japan that the United States remains the preeminent power

111

in that part of the world. It was an appropriate symbol of Washington's mindset that the port access agreement was concluded with Singapore, a country that has been one of the most outspoken opponents of a larger Japanese political and military role. The United States may be finally vacating the Philippine bases, but it shows no signs of abandoning the retrograde thinking and imperial pretensions that caused U.S. leaders to cling to those facilities to the bitter end.

5. Pakistan: The Perilous Connection

The U.S. military commitments to ANZUS and the Philippines may be useless from the standpoint of American interests, but they do not create any serious danger to the United States. The same cannot be said for the defense treaty with Pakistan. Not only has the Cold War rationale for military cooperation with Islamabad disappeared, but that association could entangle the United States in conflicts that have nothing to do with the original purposes of the treaty. It may not be as dangerous as the commitment to defend South Korea—primarily because the United States does not have troops stationed in Pakistan—but the alliance is dangerous enough.

A Cold War Relationship

A close security relationship with Pakistan was the cornerstone of U.S. security policy in South Asia throughout most of the Cold War. Beginning with the administration of President Dwight D. Eisenhower, Washington regarded Pakistan, along with Iran, as an essential obstacle to any Soviet expansionist moves toward the Indian Ocean and the oil fields of the Persian Gulf. The relationship was formalized in May 1954 with the signing of a mutual defense assistance agreement. Washington agreed to supply Pakistan's armed forces with modern military equipment, and in exchange Pakistan agreed to cooperate in efforts to strengthen the defense of the region (i.e., help contain Soviet power) and give the United States a reliable base for intelligence-gathering operations.[1] In September 1954 Washington also induced Pakistan to become a founding member of the Southeast Asia Treaty Organization and in February 1955 to sign the Baghdad Pact establishing the Middle East Treaty Organization. Those actions emphasized that the United States regarded Pakistan as a keystone power on the southern perimeter of the USSR and that the "region" Pakistan was expected to help defend was rather large.

U.S.-Pakistani military collaboration gained increasing importance as India established close political and economic ties with

Moscow in the middle and late 1950s and Washington began to view New Delhi as a de facto Soviet ally. It was a measure of the importance Washington attached to the relationship that when the Baghdad Pact collapsed (after a coup against the pro-Western monarchy in Iraq), the United States moved promptly to sign a comprehensive bilateral treaty of military cooperation with Pakistan in March 1959.

Relations between the two allies have not always been smooth, however. Many in Congress and the U.S. foreign policy community found it distasteful for Washington to support a succession of military dictatorships in Pakistan against democratic India. Some of those critics also advanced the more pragmatic argument that India would inevitably become the dominant power on the subcontinent and that the United States was, therefore, supporting the losing side.

Pressure from such pro-India factions impelled President Lyndon B. Johnson to embargo arms aid to Pakistan during the 1965 Indo-Pakistani war, when it became evident that Pakistan had violated restrictions on the assistance by using U.S.-supplied weapons for aggressive purposes. There were even more serious tensions in the relationship during the administration of President Jimmy Carter. Increasing evidence of a surreptitious nuclear weapons program along with incidents of flagrant human rights violations by the military dictatorship of Gen. Mohammed Zia ul-Haq (who had overthrown an elected government in 1977) led to a suspension of U.S. economic and military aid.

Nevertheless, Washington has always been careful not to risk a complete rupture in the security relationship. When war erupted between India and Pakistan in 1971, the administration of President Richard M. Nixon openly backed Pakistan, viewing the crisis as a Soviet-Indian effort to destabilize an important U.S. ally and dominate South Asia.[2] Any inclination to abandon the Pakistan alliance disappeared entirely in 1979 when, in rapid succession, Washington's long-time ally, the shah of Iran, was overthrown by an Islamic fundamentalist revolution and the Soviet Union invaded Afghanistan. The first event eliminated one of the two major surrogates the United States had relied on to maintain a semblance of stability and to contain Soviet power in the Persian Gulf–South Asian region. Pakistan's status as the sole remaining major U.S. ally in the region, therefore, made that country even more important in Washington's strategic calculations. The second event suggested that Moscow was exploiting the new weakness in the anti-Soviet coalition and was perhaps making a bid for regional dominance. It seemed especially alarming to U.S. officials that the invasion of Afghanistan marked the first use of the Red Army outside the East European satellite empire.

The Carter administration promptly muted its criticism of the Zia regime's human rights record, reiterated the 1959 security guarantee, and offered a new military aid package totaling some $400 million.[3] Thereafter, Pakistan resumed its role as a major U.S. political and military outpost in South Asia. Congress authorized a $3.2 billion five-year economic and military aid package in 1981 and an even larger amount when that authorization expired in 1987. In exchange, Pakistan served as a crucial conduit for U.S. military assistance to the Afghan *mujaheddin*, the coalition of insurgent forces that was battling the Soviet army of occupation.

The continuing presence of Soviet troops in Afghanistan securely cemented the U.S.-Pakistani military relationship, despite growing public and congressional apprehension about Islamabad's apparent determination to achieve a nuclear weapons capability. Moscow's agreement in May 1988 to withdraw its forces, and the fulfillment of that agreement in February 1989, however, eliminated the key factor that had sustained U.S.-Pakistani solidarity. Relations between Washington and Islamabad have become increasingly strained, as evidenced by the application in October 1990 of the so-called Pressler Amendment, which cut off military aid because of Pakistan's repeated refusal to give adequate assurances concerning its nuclear program. Indeed, there is a growing perception in U.S. policy circles that Pakistan has become a major threat to the effort to prevent the proliferation of nuclear weapons.

New Rationales

One might assume that given the demise of the Soviet Union and the emergence of tensions over nuclear proliferation, Washington would move to renounce the 1959 defense treaty. There is certainly no need to contain a Soviet expansionist threat in South Asia, which had always been the U.S. rationale for the alliance. Yet, as in the case of America's other alliances, there has been no effort to terminate the connection. To the contrary, the Bush administration has

115

apparently sought to evade the restrictions of the Pressler Amendment by continuing to issue export licenses to U.S. firms that are
supplying arms to Pakistan.[4]

There has even been a half-hearted attempt to come up with
a new justification for the alliance. Predictably, defenders of the
relationship claim that it makes an important contribution to
regional stability. With the volatile Persian Gulf next door, Pakistan
would supposedly be a useful ally in the event of a new gulf crisis.
Pakistan's allegedly secular regime (along with that of Turkey) is
also viewed as an important counterbalance to the power of Iran's
Islamic fundamentalist government and the more amorphous
influence of Islamic fundamentalism as a doctrine. Pakistani officials, searching for ways to justify and preserve the military relationship with the United States, have been quick to cultivate the image
of their country as a crucial secular barrier to a growing "Islamic
fundamentalist threat" in the region.[5]

Such justifications are highly dubious. Pakistan's reliability as an
ally in future gulf crises cannot be assumed. Although Islamabad
officially supported the international coalition against Iraq, the government faced intense domestic opposition to even its limited contributions to the war effort. Public anger at the suffering caused by
the bombing of Iraq remains strong months after the end of the
war. Pakistani support for another military action against a fellow
Islamic country—especially if the issue of aggression were not as
clear as it was in the case of Iraq's invasion and annexation of
Kuwait—would be problematic at best.

The notion of Pakistan as a secular U.S. ally against the menace
of Islamic fundamentalism is even less credible. The Islamic fundamentalist threat is being vastly exaggerated, as discrete developments in diverse portions of the Islamic world are transformed by
nervous (or cynical?) Western policy experts into components of a
grand conspiracy.[6] Those who stress the monolithic quality of the
purported threat ignore numerous factors. For example, the ancient
and bitter doctrinal dispute between the Sunni and Shi'ite factions
of Islam would probably be sufficient by itself to disrupt solidarity.
The "Islamic world" extends from Morocco to Indonesia—a swath
of territory approximately 10,000 miles long. Within that area are
numerous races and cultures with different languages, histories,
governments, and ideologies. The prospect of a monolithic movement uniting such disparate peoples is even less plausible than

116

the concept of Leninist solidarity—a bogeyman that gave earlier generations of Westerners nightmares. Even more than the professed alarm about German or Japanese expansionist ambitions, the "discovery" of the Islamic fundamentalist threat has all the characteristics of threat procurement.

Moreover, even in the unlikely event that the threat of Islamic fundamentalism proved to be genuine, Pakistan would be a poor candidate to counter its influence. Indeed, Westernized Pakistanis complain that the Islamabad regime displays many of the intolerant characteristics associated with the fundamentalist stereotype. Their complaints have some merit. Beginning with the Zia dictatorship in the late 1970s, Pakistani officials have sought to apply strict interpretations of Islamic law to more and more aspects of society, and the current government shows no signs of reversing that trend.

In its policy toward Afghanistan, Islamabad has taken actions that actually strengthened the forces of Islamic fundamentalism, much to the chagrin of U.S. officials. Although the United States and Pakistan cooperated closely in efforts to support the Afghan *mujaheddin,* their policy agendas have not always been compatible. In particular, Washington watched with increased concern as a disproportionate amount of military aid supplied by the CIA was diverted by Pakistan's Inter Services Intelligence Directorate to the most radical *mujaheddin* faction, the Hezb-i-Islami headed by Gulbuddin Hekmatyar.[7]

Troublesome U.S. Obligations

Perpetuating the obsolete alliance with Pakistan poses subtle but serious dangers to the United States. Article 1 of the 1959 defense treaty provides that "in case of aggression against Pakistan," the United States "will take such appropriate action, including the use of armed forces, as may be mutually agreed upon" to "assist the government of Pakistan at its request."[8] Although the article includes the ritual disclaimer that such assistance will be taken "in accordance with the Constitution," that restriction means little given that since World War II U.S. presidents have virtually ignored the war powers of Congress. If President Bush could overthrow the government of Panama without the slightest congressional input and send more than 400,000 military personnel to the Persian Gulf before bothering to ask Congress for a supporting resolution, he or a future chief executive could undoubtedly come to Pakistan's aid on his own volition, regardless of constitutional niceties.

There is one especially noteworthy aspect of the 1959 treaty. Although the United States undoubtedly viewed the arrangement as part of the overall strategy to contain Soviet expansion, the language of the treaty contains no such restriction; the U.S. commitment to provide assistance becomes operative in the event of any act of "aggression" against Pakistan from whatever source. Moreover, Pakistani leaders have long viewed the treaty as a mechanism to activate U.S. protection in response to an attack from India. Pakistani governments have invoked the treaty to request arms on several occasions: after India's takeover of the Portuguese enclave of Goa in 1961, after a clash with India in 1965, and most notably during the bloody war with India in 1971. In the first two cases, U.S. administrations successfully fended off the specific arms requests by providing additional assurances of firm U.S. backing if Pakistan's security or territorial integrity were seriously jeopardized. (The context of those assurances suggested a willingness to employ U.S. forces, if necessary.) During a critical phase of the 1971 crisis, the Nixon administration went considerably further in responding to Pakistan's requests for assistance. Washington dispatched an aircraft carrier task force to the Bay of Bengal, according to National Security Adviser Henry Kissinger, "ostensibly for the evacuation of Americans but in reality to give emphasis to our warnings" to India.[9] Although the principal reason for that action was the administration's perception that the war was part of a Soviet-inspired strategy to destroy Pakistan, Indian officials not surprisingly regarded it as U.S. interference in India's long-standing struggle with its rival on the subcontinent.

The open-ended nature of the treaty language is not the only factor that supports Pakistan's position that the document commits the United States to provide assistance against non-Soviet sources of aggression. At the time of the 1971 war, some members of the State Department contended that the obligation was qualified by its context—the 1958 Eisenhower Doctrine that pledged the United States to "secure the territorial integrity and political independence" of Middle Eastern countries from "any nation controlled by international Communism."[10] The treaty with Pakistan, in their view, thus excluded an Indo-Pakistani war unless there was clear evidence of Soviet involvement.

Kissinger scorned such "legalistic loopholes" and insisted that the treaty was not restricted to meeting a Soviet threat. Furthermore, he noted that "over the decades of our relationship with Pakistan, there had grown up a complex body of communications by the Kennedy and Johnson administrations, going beyond the 1959 pact, some verbal, some in writing, whose plain import was that the United States would come to Pakistan's assistance if she was attacked by India."[11] Those communications included a letter from President Kennedy to Pakistani president Mohammed Ayub Khan dated January 26, 1962; an aide-mémoire presented by the U.S. ambassador to Pakistan on November 5, 1962; a public statement by the State Department on November 17, 1962; and an oral promise from President Johnson to Ayub Khan on December 15, 1965.[12] The Nixon administration's support for Pakistan in the 1971 war adds additional support to the argument that the treaty obligates the United States to help defend its ally against aggression from any source.

Whether the United States would actively assist Pakistan in a conflict with India now that the Soviet factor is no longer relevant is unknown. The pertinent question is, why preserve a treaty that might entail such an obligation? The Cold War notion that India was willing to act as Moscow's surrogate in South Asia was always overdrawn, but it provided at least a plausible thesis that backing Pakistan against a power that was friendly to the USSR served the security interests of the United States. No such argument can be made now. Even if India moves to assert its preeminence in the region—which, given its population, economic resources, and military capabilities, it may well do—that change in the power configuration should matter little to the United States. Preventing Indian dominance is certainly not worth provoking a diplomatic—much less a military—crisis with New Delhi. Maintaining the security alliance with Pakistan creates precisely that danger.

Nuclear Dangers

The possibility of a confrontation with India should concern the American public. The Indian subcontinent will be one of the most dangerous and volatile regions in the world during the post–Cold War era. India and Pakistan have already fought three major wars since partition and independence in 1947 and engaged in dozens of "minor" border clashes. Forces from the two countries continuously skirmish over the disputed province of Kashmir, and Pakistan has stepped up its support (including the supply of weapons) for an increasingly bold force of Kashmiri guerrillas. Relations between Islamabad and New Delhi remain extremely tense, and a new war could break out at any time.

To make matters even more alarming, both nations may already have operational nuclear arsenals. Certainly, they have the capability to produce such arsenals on short notice. India exploded what it described as a "peaceful" nuclear device in 1974, and most experts believe that India is a full-fledged (albeit undeclared) nuclear state. The evidence is less clear with respect to Pakistan, but there is little question that Islamabad has been diligently pursuing a nuclear weapons program for more than a decade.[13]

There has also been nuclear saber rattling on occasion from both capitals. Several senior Indian military leaders have explicitly cited the "Pakistani threat" as a major reason why India needs a nuclear deterrent. One Indian official, Maj. Gen. Satinder Singh, even published an article in the *Indian Defense Journal* providing a detailed scenario for a nuclear war with Pakistan. In his scenario, Singh speculates that Pakistan, encouraged by the turmoil in the Soviet Union, India's one-time protector, decides to pursue its expansionist ambitions by launching a nuclear strike against India, obliterating New Delhi, and exploiting the resulting chaos to occupy Kashmir. Singh assumes that India is able to absorb the sneak attack and responds by launching nuclear reprisals against Islamabad, Lahore, and other major Pakistani cities. Naturally, India routs the nefarious Pakistani aggressors and wins the war. The lesson for India from that nightmare scenario is, according to Singh, "Production of nuclear weapons must not lag behind political threats."[14]

Although generals in all countries are sometimes prone to engage in morbid fantasies, Singh's speculation has some basis in fact. India certainly shows no inclination to give up its nuclear weapons program. Even when Pakistan offered a proposal in June 1991 for discussions among the United States, the USSR, China, India, and Pakistan to explore the idea of establishing a nuclear-free zone in South Asia, Indian officials bluntly rejected the suggestion as "illusory."[15] Indeed, India might well refuse to renounce nuclear weapons even if Pakistan did so, because New Delhi also fears a

120

security threat from China. Jasit Singh, director of the Institute for Defense Studies and Analyses, a quasi-governmental think tank in New Delhi, stated candidly, "Two of our neighbors have nuclear weapons and I'm afraid they're not terribly responsible."[16]

Of course, Pakistan may view the motives of its much larger and more populous adversary as aggressive rather than defensive. Pakistani officials, in turn, see the development of their own nuclear arsenal as the great equalizer, offsetting India's greater conventional military capabilities. That is not an unreasonable thesis. India's armed forces outnumber those of Pakistan by 1.265 million to 565,000, it has 630 combat aircraft to 327, and 45 major combat ships to 19. India spends nearly $9 billion a year (3.9 percent of GDP) on the military compared to Pakistan's $3.19 billion (8.1 percent of GDP).[17] Even with a much larger burden on its economy, Pakistan finds that it cannot match India's conventional forces.

The decisive defeat of Pakistan in the 1971 war underscored its increasingly inferior military position. The fighting not only demonstrated the battlefield dominance of India's larger force, it also had other consequences. The independence of East Pakistan (Bangladesh) as a result of the conflict greatly increased the population gap between India and Pakistan by removing more than one-half of the latter's prewar population from Islamabad's political jurisdiction. It also reduced Pakistan's economic base by more than one-third. In more direct military terms, the emergence of Bangladesh greatly reduced the likelihood that India would have to fight a two-front war in any future showdown with Pakistan, thus simplifying New Delhi's logistics problems.

From Pakistan's perspective, the 1971 war was a watershed event. Since that time, Islamabad has been caught in a conventional arms contest that it cannot win. In the view of Pakistani political and military leaders, a nuclear arsenal offers the one feasible way of preventing India from pressing its growing military advantage to the point of expunging its rival from the map.

Both governments may honestly view their arsenals as defensive, not provocative. In a best-case scenario, the existence of those arsenals might even impose a regional version of the "balance of terror" that prevented a nuclear conflict between the United States and the Soviet Union during the Cold War. Several factors, however, suggest that the Indo-Pakistani nuclear rivalry may be far more dangerous and unstable than the superpower model. An unidentified senior diplomat familiar with South Asia believes that both countries will have not only nuclear weapons but also medium-range ballistic missiles by the mid-1990s.[18] (India, in fact, recently tested its Agni missile, which has a range of 1,550 miles and a payload capacity sufficient to carry a nuclear warhead.)[19] The implications of such a crude first-generation delivery system are disturbing, he contends. "Each side will have to assume the worst of each other. And this is destabilizing because of the hair-trigger nature of these missiles in times of tension."[20]

One of the consequences of pursuing covert weapons programs is that neither country has communicated the nature of its nuclear doctrine—what kinds of provocations might lead to a decision to use nuclear weapons—to its rival. Gen. K. Sundarji, a retired chief of staff of the Indian army, points out that the lack of doctrine is most dangerous. In the event of war with Pakistan, the Indian high command would be under pressure not to go past a certain threshold, but "they cannot be sure of what Pakistan thinks the threshold is. One must go with impressions and guesses."[21] That is a chilling prospect, and one must assume that the Pakistani military leaders face the same dilemma.

The danger entailed in the failure to articulate nuclear doctrines in an environment of habitual confrontation cannot be overstated. It was the gradual realization that such doctrines had to be made explicit—combined with various crisis management agreements such as the establishment of "hot lines" between the Kremlin and the White House—that prevented the Cold War from being even more dangerous than it was. The history of Indo-Pakistani antagonism, the tense state of current relations, and the growing nuclear capabilities of both countries are a potentially deadly combination. With the possible exception of the Korean Peninsula, South Asia is the most likely arena for a nuclear war in the post–Cold War era.

Courting a Confrontation with India

That prospect makes the U.S. determination to maintain a military alliance with Pakistan incomprehensible. The association could involve the United States in a conflict between India and Pakistan that could easily go nuclear. Defenders of the treaty insist that there is no such danger because nothing in the document requires the

United States to send military forces to aid Pakistan. That is technically true, but it misses a larger point. The mere existence of the alliance leads Indian leaders to assume that the United States will assist Pakistan in some fashion in the event of war. Indeed, the treaty legally and morally obligates Washington to render aid if Pakistan is the victim of aggression, and one can be certain of two things: Pakistan will insist that it is the aggrieved party no matter who starts the fighting, and Islamabad will ask for U.S. help in repelling "aggression."

Such a request would create the same dilemma for Washington that similar requests did in 1965 and 1971. Either U.S. policymakers dishonor a solemn treaty obligation, which would raise serious doubts about the credibility of U.S. military commitments in other parts of the world, or Washington provides assistance and thus becomes entangled in a dangerous conflict. The risks posed by U.S. interference could be greater under current conditions than they were in the 1971 crisis. In addition to the added nuclear dimension, in a post–Cold War setting there would be no Soviet patron to either reassure or restrain New Delhi. The latter is an important consideration, since there is intriguing evidence, albeit circumstantial, that without Moscow's realization that the 1971 war was spiraling out of control and threatening the embryonic détente with the United States, India would have continued fighting until it had eliminated Pakistan as a political entity. Certainly, the Nixon administration feared that the government of Prime Minister Indira Gandhi wanted to pursue that objective.

In a new war, India could well decide to finish off its adversary, and the United States, as Pakistan's ally, would be viewed as the principal obstacle to victory. Even sending U.S. weapons to Islamabad would irritate India, and any U.S. military maneuvers (e.g., dispatching a carrier battle group to the Bay of Bengal as Washington did in 1971) would confirm New Delhi's worst suspicions. Such a step could lead to a tragic miscalculation. U.S. policymakers might view a redeployment as merely a gesture of support for Pakistan (Kissinger notes that in the 1971 crisis, "Nixon had no intention of becoming militarily involved, but he was determined that *something* be done"),[22] but there is no guarantee that Indian political leaders— much less Indian military leaders—would necessarily view redeployment in the same way. Unable to rely on Soviet protection to counter a direct U.S. intervention, Indian officials would be understandably jittery about any increase in the U.S. military presence in their region in the midst of a war. The memory of Washington's intervention against Iraq—which began as a build-up to protect Saudi Arabia—could make the Indians even more apprehensive. Under such conditions, a military incident between U.S. and Indian forces is not out of the question.

Even if that danger is not acute, there is no reason the United States should run *any* risk of a clash with India. Yet Washington seems to be taking steps to increase the likelihood of U.S. entanglement if India and Pakistan engage in another military confrontation. A secret intelligence memo from the Pentagon-based National Intelligence Office for Warning, leaked to the press in May 1992, provided an indication of the thinking of some U.S. officials. The memo reportedly urged the Bush administration to define a strategy for American armed forces in the event of hostilities in South Asia. Although the ostensible goal of Washington's policy would be to prevent an escalation of an Indo-Pakistani conflict to a nuclear exchange, the memo clearly envisions active U.S. involvement. A high-level source familiar with the document observed that inaction "would irrevocably damage [the U.S.] position as leader of the free world."[23]

It is unlikely that India would welcome even well intentioned interference on the part of Pakistan's treaty ally. Although Washington might view its role as that of an honest broker trying to head off a regional nuclear catastrophe, nearly four decades of tense Indo-U.S. relations have made the United States unbelievable in a mediating role. Although there had been signs of a cautious rapprochement between Washington and New Delhi after the end of the Cold War, the underlying suspicions resurfaced in May 1992, when the United States imposed sanctions on India's Space Research Organization because it had received sophisticated missile technology from Russia in violation of the guidelines of the International Missile Technology Control Regime. The sanctions provoked an immediate outcry throughout India, as newspapers and even members of parliament accused Washington of interfering in India's affairs and trying to impose its will on other countries.[24] The pervasive atmosphere of mistrust would make any U.S. role in an Indo-Pakistani showdown a matter of extreme concern to New Delhi and would heighten the chances of a miscalculation.[25]

Instead of searching for ways to bolster Pakistan as a regional surrogate and a force for stability, thereby risking a confrontation with India, the United States should move to distance itself as quickly as possible from its Cold War era ally. Indeed, Washington has every reason to cultivate cordial relations with New Delhi. India is likely to become the preeminent power in South Asia (assuming that it can overcome its own internal ethnic and political divisions).[26] Washington would gain no advantage by attempting to influence the outcome one way or the other; a dominant Indian role in the region would not threaten any discernible U.S. interest. Which nation is the leading power in South Asia can be—and should be—a matter of profound indifference to American policymakers. Pakistan may have had some utility as a U.S. political and military outpost during the Cold War, but even then the value to the United States of supporting an autocratic and unstable client was greatly overstated.

Without the Soviet threat, maintaining the alliance with Pakistan is a case of gratuitous interference in purely regional concerns. It would provide the United States with no significant benefits while needlessly making this country a political—and potentially a military—adversary of India. Even without the possibility of a nuclear exchange, the defense pact is a foolish commitment from the standpoint of America's best interests. Given that added danger, it is a reckless obligation—a risky anachronism that should be jettisoned immediately.

6. The Rio Treaty: Disguising U.S. Hegemony

As the United States began to develop a strategy to contain Soviet expansionism in the aftermath of World War II, it needed to secure its own geopolitical "back yard" in the Western Hemisphere.[1] The challenge to the administration of President Harry S Truman was twofold: to create an institutional arrangement that would effectively exclude not only Soviet military power but communist political influence in Latin America and to find a way to disguise the extent of U.S. regional hegemony. The latter requirement was as important as the former. Latin American nations remained wary of Washington's tendency to flex its military muscles and interfere in their internal affairs. Memories of the repeated armed interventions by the United States during the early years of the 20th century were still strong. Most Latin American states had cooperated in the U.S.-led effort against the Axis powers in World War II, but a few (most notably Argentina) had resisted Washington's diplomatic and economic pressure to enlist in that campaign.

A blatant attempt to unilaterally assert U.S. power and underscore Washington's hemispheric hegemony in the embryonic Cold War was certain to provoke further resistance or even outright intransigence. To forestall that problem, U.S. policymakers decided to create a multilateral regional security agreement that would be consistent with the provisions of the charter of the new United Nations.

America's First Cold War Alliance

The Inter-American Treaty of Reciprocal Assistance, signed at Rio de Janeiro in September 1947, and the subsequent pact concluded at Bogotá in April 1948, which established a charter for the Organization of American States (OAS), created an official regional collective security mechanism for the Western Hemisphere. Article 1 of the Rio Treaty specifies that "an armed attack by any state against an

American State shall be considered as an attack against all of the American States," and each of the signatories undertook to help repel such an assault. Article 6 provides further that if the "integrity of the territory or the sovereignty or political independence of any American State should be affected by an aggression which is not an armed attack," the signatories would still consider collective action.[2]

Article 6 clearly refers to a campaign of political subversion by a hostile power—a matter that was already on the minds of U.S. policymakers during the earliest stage of the Cold War. Indeed, attempted subversion was seen as more troublesome and far more probable than armed attack; few people regarded an invasion of a hemispheric country by an external power as a serious danger. An assault from outside the hemisphere would have been an enormous logistical undertaking, and not even the Soviet Union had a fraction of the air- and sea-lift capabilities necessary to mount such an attack.

The provisions of the Rio Treaty were fleshed out in the Bogotá agreement. That accord established the OAS as a "regional agency," as provided for in the UN charter, and made it a vehicle for carrying out the political, economic, and military sanctions outlined in the Rio Treaty. At the insistence of several of the Latin American signatories, however, article 15 was included in the OAS charter. That provision states:

> No State or group of States has the right to intervene, directly or indirectly, for any reason whatever, in the internal or external affairs of any other State. The foregoing principle prohibits not only armed force but also any other form of interference or attempted interference or attempted threat against the personality of the State or against its political, economic and cultural elements.[3]

Article 15 was an unmistakable attempt to prevent a repetition of the U.S. military coercion of other hemispheric nations that had become routine earlier in the century. Although the "right" to intervene had supposedly been abandoned by President Franklin D. Roosevelt as part of his Good Neighbor policy, Latin American countries remained apprehensive and wanted more formal guarantees of noninterference. Article 15, they hoped, would provide at least some additional protection.

As it has turned out, the treaty provision has done little to restrain U.S. actions. Not only has the United States launched three full-scale invasions of Latin American countries—the Dominican Republic (1965), Grenada (1983), and Panama (1989)—but it has engaged in a variety of covert operations to undermine governments (even democratically elected ones) deemed unfriendly to U.S. interests. The most notorious incident was the CIA-orchestrated coup against the elected government of Jacobo Arbenz-Guzmán in Guatemala in 1954.[4] There is also evidence that the United States used covert tactics to destabilize the Marxist regime of President Salvador Allende in Chile during the early 1970s, and Washington may have played a role in the ouster of left-leaning President Juan Bosch of the Dominican Republic a decade earlier.

At the time the Rio and Bogotá agreements were concluded, there were few illusions that an alliance among equals was being established. A more realistic interpretation of U.S. objectives was that the Rio Treaty and the OAS were arrangements to legitimize a dominant U.S. political and military role in the hemisphere. Washington had viewed with alarm the efforts of Italy and Germany to establish networks of political and economic influence throughout Latin America during the years immediately preceding U.S. entry into World War II and had worked feverishly to repel such challenges to U.S. preeminence.[5] In the late 1940s it appeared that the Soviet Union intended to pursue a similar strategy of subversion, and given the "internationalist" appeal of communist ideology, Moscow might prove to be a more formidable adversary. The presence of corrupt and repressive regimes in many Latin American countries gave the Soviets a target-rich environment.

The Rio and Bogotá agreements signified an implicit bargain between the Latin American governments and Washington. The Latin American regimes would cooperate in U.S.-led efforts to exclude Soviet (or more generally, communist) influence from the hemisphere; in exchange, the United States would help its political allies remain in power by providing generous amounts of military and economic aid.[6] Both sides kept their part of the bargain. Throughout the Cold War, the United States gave billions in aid to incumbent hemispheric governments and established close ties with Latin American military establishments. Those regimes used U.S.-supplied arms and training to ruthlessly suppress leftist guerrilla movements whenever they emerged. Unfortunately, in many instances right-wing governments also terrorized civilian political critics, both moderates and radicals. Washington's explicit or tacit support of an assortment of authoritarian clients despite evidence of egregious human rights abuses was a staple of its Cold War policy in the hemisphere. The attitude of U.S. policymakers was typified by Secretary of State Alexander M. Haig, Jr., who admitted that one of the first actions of Ronald Reagan's administration had been to downplay criticism of America's "friends" for such abuses. Even the feeble and inconsistent human rights policy of the Carter years was apparently too much for Haig. "We told Argentina that it had heard its last public lecture from the United States on human rights," he boasted.[7] The Argentine junta that Haig was so eager to cultivate was ultimately responsible for kidnapping and murdering more than 9,000 political opponents.

Both the Rio Treaty and the OAS were products of the Cold War. Venezuela's president, Carlos Andrés Pérez, noted that the OAS was "born imbued with the central concern of the cold war period . . . the need to contain the expansion of communism on a global scale. To the extent that the United States and Latin America shared this ideological and strategic conception, the system of collective security enjoyed acceptance and legitimacy."[8]

Fears about Soviet political penetration of the hemisphere were not entirely unwarranted. Moscow did seek to exploit the social and economic woes of Latin American societies, supported left-wing insurgencies, and hoped for the emergence of potential client regimes. From a geopolitical standpoint, that strategy was quite logical. A proliferation of pro-Soviet forces would create trouble for the United States on its southern flank, cause it to divert military resources from the principal Cold War arenas in Europe and East Asia to neutralize that challenge, and thereby inhibit Washington from effectively prosecuting the Cold War. The emergence of a full-fledged communist regime in Cuba under the leadership of Fidel Castro at the end of the 1950s seemed to validate the fears of U.S. officials, and their apprehension escalated when Moscow and Havana established a military alliance. The danger that could be posed by Soviet clients in the hemisphere became all too apparent when the USSR moved offensive missiles into Cuba in 1962, triggering a crisis that brought the superpowers perilously close to nuclear war.

In addition to the military dangers, during the 1960s incumbent regimes throughout the hemisphere feared that Castro's revolution would spread like an ideological plague. The United States moved to bolster clients in a variety of ways, including creation of a new array of military and economic aid programs, but the fear that Cuba would be merely the first of a series of communist dominoes in Latin America proved to be exaggerated. Moscow was able to establish cordial ties with the Allende government in Chile, but that country never came close to being a Soviet ally, much less an obedient client. The Kremlin came closest to achieving "another Cuba" in Nicaragua after the 1979 Sandinista revolution. Moscow provided extensive military and economic aid to the Sandinista government throughout the succeeding decade, and Soviet officials undoubtedly hoped that other Leninist revolutions would sweep Central America.

Despite the close Soviet-Nicaraguan relationship, however, Managua never became an effective Soviet geopolitical outpost. Leftist insurgencies in El Salvador and Guatemala faltered after promising starts, and the Reagan administration took vigorous action to isolate Nicaragua as Presidents Eisenhower and Kennedy had Cuba two decades earlier. More important, the deepening political and economic troubles in the Soviet Union itself made the pursuit and support of new clients a luxury Moscow could no longer afford. Cuba, Nicaragua, and other Soviet dependents elsewhere in the world created an enormous drain on the already depleted Soviet treasury. Even before the collapse of the government of Soviet president Mikhail Gorbachev and the dismemberment of the USSR, Moscow's political penetration of the Western Hemisphere had become more of an annoyance than a serious threat.

New Missions for the OAS

The end of the Cold War raises serious questions about the need to maintain the Rio Treaty. Its provisions for collective defense against outside military aggression never did have much relevance. The only episode after World War II that qualified as an identifiable military threat to the hemisphere was the Cuban missile crisis, and both the nature of that threat and its resolution suggest that a hemispheric alliance has meager utility. Washington dealt with the crisis in a bilateral eyeball-to-eyeball confrontation with its superpower adversary, and the Latin American allies added little to U.S.

131

power or influence. Indeed, it is almost impossible to imagine a scenario in which the other Rio Treaty signatories would be of significant help in repelling a military threat from outside the hemisphere. It is equally difficult to imagine what the source of such an external threat would be now that the Soviet Union no longer exists.

There is likewise little validity to the argument that the pact might be useful for containing an aggressively expansionist hemispheric power, since there are no regimes that appear to have expansionist agendas. With the exception of Argentina, which seized the Falkland Islands in 1982, the only hemispheric country that has used military force against other states in recent decades has been the United States. And despite the language of the Rio Treaty or the OAS Charter, there is no prospect of collective action against that source of aggression.

The treaty might be more relevant to the nonmilitary "threats" contemplated in article 6, but that kind of mission has an enormous potential for mischief. Washington's desire to prevent the emergence of regimes loyal to a major power outside the hemisphere is not entirely without merit. That is especially true of the Caribbean Basin, a region that constitutes a long-standing security interest of the United States.[9] Indeed, the original goal of the Monroe Doctrine in the 1820s was to prevent the resubjugation of the newly liberated Latin American republics or the establishment of new European clients or colonies in the hemisphere. Either possibility was deemed inimical to American security interests. Applying the same reasoning, a succession of U.S. administrations sought to stymie the political penetration of the hemisphere by the fascist powers in the late 1930s and early 1940s and the USSR thereafter.

It is not the political composition of governments in Latin America but the nature of their political and military relations with outside powers that is properly the concern of the United States. Washington has no security justification for intervening merely because it regards a regime as ideologically unpalatable. America's legitimate security concerns with Cuba and Nicaragua during the Cold War were not based on the repressive nature of those regimes but on the fact that the USSR was attempting (with some success) to use them as strategic outposts. In the post–Cold War period, the danger that a major nonhemispheric power will use surrogates in that fashion is highly remote. There may be some home-grown anti-U.S.

dictatorships or insurgencies (the Maoist Shining Path guerrillas in Peru are an example), but such developments constitute annoyances, not significant security threats, to the United States.

Washington may fall prey to two dangerous temptations in formulating its post–Cold War security policy toward Latin America. The first temptation will be to continue the long history of arrogant military interventions either unilaterally (as in the Dominican Republic and Panama) or with a transparent multilateral facade (as in Grenada). Either approach will create needless friction between the United States and its hemispheric neighbors. Latin American societies recall the repeated U.S. military coercion in the early decades of the 20th century and are hypersensitive to any new manifestation of domination by the "Colossus of the North."[10]

The second danger is more subtle and can arise from Washington's membership in the OAS combined with the goal of creating more credible multilateral vehicles for U.S. military interventions. Proposals to make the OAS an association for rooting out the remaining dictatorships in the hemisphere and preventing the overthrow of existing elected governments—as well as for attaining more nebulous objectives such as waging the drug war and preventing environmental degradation—are proliferating. A resolution passed at the annual OAS meeting in June 1991, the so-called Santiago Declaration, reflected that trend. It created a rapid response mechanism to any "sudden or irregular interruption of the democratic political institutional process or of the legitimate exercise of power by the democratically elected government in any of the Organization's member states."[11] The resolution also stated that the OAS must be willing to take "any measures deemed appropriate" to restore constitutional rule whenever it is overthrown.

The principal catalyst for attempts to strengthen the OAS's military powers was the coup in Haiti that ousted the elected government of Jean-Bertrand Aristide on September 30, 1991. Robert A. Pastor, former director of Latin American and Caribbean affairs for the National Security Council, immediately issued a call to arms, drawing a parallel with the Gulf War. "The United Nations, with the muscle of the U.S.-led forces, demonstrated in the Persian Gulf war that aggression could be reversed. Now that the Organization of American States has voted to reject the coup in Haiti, it should go further and try to prevent other coups in the hemisphere—if necessary with collective military action." Pastor speculated that Haiti's military might "need the threat of an O.A.S. peacekeeping force to persuade it to yield power." The United States should "agree to participate in such a force," although in contrast to the gulf episode, it should not lead the intervention.[12]

Pastor was not alone in advocating that the OAS act militarily to oust the Haitian usurpers. The editors of the *Los Angeles Times* and other publications supported that course, and at least some members of the Bush administration initially seemed sympathetic.[13] The administration soon had second thoughts, however, and confined itself to encouraging the OAS to impose economic sanctions on Haiti. Administration leaders perhaps recalled that the United States had embarked on a "temporary" occupation of Haiti in 1915—and remained there for the next 19 years. That sobering historical record did not deter such enthusiastic interventionists as syndicated columnist Georgie Anne Geyer, who went beyond merely proposing an OAS intervention to restore the Aristide government. "If Haiti is to persist as a nation," she wrote, "it will have to be in some creative way 'recolonized' for a time. Outside countries would have the authority to go in for a period of, say, 10 years, and reorganize and industrialize and educate the population." The military would have to be "neutralized," and the "ambitions of demagogic politicians" would have to be "frozen" during that time.[14]

Suggestions that the United States and other OAS members undertake aggressive nation-building programs have ebbed and flowed as the OAS-imposed economic embargo on Haiti has dragged on and the military rulers have remained in control. The horrendous suffering inflicted on the already destitute Haitian population by the embargo has led some observers to suggest that the sanctions be lifted and the new regime be granted de facto if not de jure recognition. More and more members of the U.S. policy community, however, have been calling for military action to resolve the impasse.[15]

An abortive coup by the Venezuelan army in early February 1992 caused a new flurry of suggestions that the OAS take steps to preserve elected governments. Pastor promptly expanded his earlier proposal, arguing that the most important task for the inter-American system was "to codify a set of automatic, escalatory sanctions that would be implemented if and when the democratic process is interrupted in any member country." Although such sanctions might begin with diplomatic isolation of the offending regime, the cessation of aid programs, and the freezing of financial assets, some situations might require the imposition of a full trade embargo "enforced by the navies of OAS members" and the insertion of "an inter-American peace force to prevent gross human rights violations and oversee the restoration of democracy."[16]

The editors of the *New York Times* proposed an equally ambitious agenda. Citing the events in Haiti and Venezuela and the activities of the Shining Path in Peru, the *Times* insisted that the time had come "to create a new inter-American military force that could intervene to protect democratic governments from hijacking by armed terrorists." Outside intervention was "no longer tantamount to big-power bullying," the editors claimed, although a hemispheric collective security organization would work best if the United States maintained a relatively low profile and political control of the new security force was "shared broadly." Nevertheless, it was urgent that such a military force be established. "With the region's militaries again becoming restive and the Shining Path on the march, there's no time to lose."[17]

To its credit, the Bush administration has not yet adopted such a reckless policy agenda. Missions involving the coercive export of democracy or the protection of existing democratic regimes would be fraught with peril for the United States. Historically, most Latin American countries have experienced cycles of alternating democratic rule and rule by military juntas, and while we may hope that the recent trend toward democracy in the hemisphere will be lasting, there is no guarantee that it will be. At the very least, many of the new democracies are quite fragile and confront daunting economic and social problems. The attempted coup in Venezuela was a sobering reminder of that fragility. Indeed, before the February revolt, Venezuela was considered a mature and stable democratic system, having emerged from its last period of dictatorship more than three decades ago. If disaffected military elements could make a bid for power in that country, they certainly could in nations where elected governments are less entrenched.

That point was confirmed in early April 1992 when Peruvian president Alberto Fujimori, in collaboration with the military, declared a state of emergency and dissolved the national legislature. Fujimori's presidential coup represented a serious test of the new OAS doctrine of guaranteeing the inviolability of democratic governments, and it underscored the problems inherent in such pretensions. OAS leaders faced a serious dilemma. Imposing sanctions on a nation the size of Peru was a substantially more difficult undertaking than isolating tiny Haiti. Moreover, any effort to weaken the incumbent Peruvian regime risked playing into the hands of the Maoist Shining Path. In a worst-case scenario, a comprehensive OAS embargo might destabilize the Fujimori government enough to enable the guerrillas to seize power. Faced with that dilemma, the OAS has dithered, officially criticizing Fujimori's overthrow of the constitutional order but refraining from adopting substantive coercive measures.

One could hope that the sobering Peruvian episode will lead to the demise of proposals to make the OAS the hemispheric guardian of democracy, but it is unlikely that the ardent multilateral interventionists will be so easily dissuaded. If their advice is ever adopted, the OAS—and with it the United States—could find itself in the middle of an assortment of internecine conflicts. There are no compelling reasons for Washington to even consider undertaking democracy-preserving missions. Given the absence of a great power challenger that might seek to use Latin American nations as geopolitical assets against the United States, it does not matter from a security standpoint whether a particular Latin American country has a democratic, authoritarian, or (in the case of Cuba) totalitarian regime. We, of course, hope that democratic capitalist systems will blossom in the hemisphere as elsewhere in the world, but that desire does not warrant the risk of becoming entangled in the internal politics of other nations. It would undoubtedly be a great tragedy for the people of Peru if the Shining Path came to power, for example, but the effect on the security of the United States would be barely detectable. Attempting to prevent the guerrillas' success would certainly not be worth the dangers of enlisting in an OAS "peace-keeping" force.

Even in the Western Hemisphere, alliances represent unprofitable entanglements for the United States. It would be better for the United States to withdraw from the Rio Treaty and the OAS and preserve its freedom of action. That is not to suggest that Washington should continue to practice unilateral intervention at the slightest provocation, as it has done all too often in the past. Instead, U.S. officials should explicitly pledge that there will be no interference in the internal affairs of other hemispheric countries unless a country establishes close political and military ties with an adversary of the United States. Since that is now an extremely remote possibility, the practical effect of such a doctrine of "restrained unilateralism" would be an absence of U.S. interventionist initiatives for the foreseeable future.

A U.S. withdrawal from the OAS—or at least from any military obligations under its charter—would not necessarily lead to the demise of that association. In fact, it might have the opposite effect. Because of its enormous military and economic power, the United States automatically dominates any hemispheric organization. The absence of the United States from OAS councils, or the adoption of de facto associate member status, would enable the Latin American countries to formulate their own policies without fear of U.S. dictation or defiance. If they believed that a regional collective security organization were desirable, they would be free to pursue that objective, adjusting OAS policies in whatever way they thought appropriate. They could even adopt the "democracy protection" mission, if they concluded that it was feasible and worthwhile. In short, an OAS without the suffocating U.S. presence could offer the other nations of the hemisphere ways to emerge from the long shadow of Washington's paternalism.

Whether those countries maintain the OAS, create a new organization with different powers and objectives, or opt for no multilateral security arrangements at all should not unduly concern the United States. There is no serious threat to U.S. security in the hemisphere, nor is one likely to appear in the foreseeable future. Washington does not need to perpetuate a security mechanism that was of little use even during the Cold War and has virtually none in the post–Cold War period.

7. Global Stability and Domestic Vested Interests

The determination to preserve America's Cold War era alliances is largely a reflection of the Bush administration's obsession with preserving international stability. Indeed, the goal of stability is the one consistent, tangible feature of the president's otherwise nebulous "new world order."

There are several reasons the administration and its allies in the foreign policy community have embraced that mission. Many of them—particularly those of Bush's generation—are still haunted by the events of the 1930s and 1940s. In their view, any conflict—no matter how minor or geographically remote—has the potential to lead to a destructive general war that would eventually engulf the United States. America's failure to realize that truth, they believe, encouraged the fascist aggressors and led to a global tragedy. Conversely, the wise statesmen of the Cold War era who recognized that peace is indivisible prevented an even greater tragedy by containing communist expansionism. The need for early and vigorous action against aggression, collective defense arrangements among "peace-loving" nations, and a dominant U.S. leadership role are articles of faith for Bush and much of America's aging foreign policy elite.

Such policy assumptions may be simplistic, excessively rigid, and frequently inapplicable to the post–Cold War international system, but they are the product of decent and genuine desires to promote a more peaceful world.

Unfortunately, more calculating and self-serving motives coexist with that of advancing the cause of peace. Those who stress the alleged virtues of stability equate preserving the global status quo with preeminent status for the United States. Since the end of World War II, two generations of policymakers and nongovernmental experts have derived career benefits and emotional satisfaction from the United States' status as a superpower—indeed, the dominant actor in the international community. Although the Soviet Union

139

mounted a challenge to U.S. dominance, it was a one-dimensional challenge. Moscow had the military might to make a claim to the title of superpower, but the USSR's pervasive economic weakness (brought about by the inherent defects and contradictions of a command economy) could not sustain such pretensions.

With the disintegration of the Soviet Union, U.S. leaders and other advocates of an interventionist foreign policy see the United States as the sole remaining superpower, with the opportunity to exert unprecedented influence on world affairs.[1] U.S. dominance can be sustained, however, only if the Cold War era's secondary powers, especially Japan and the nations of the European Community, continue to follow Washington's leadership. Any movement on their part to adopt more independent policies and to play larger political and military roles would automatically threaten U.S. pre-eminence. In a genuinely multipolar international system, the United States might well be the single most powerful nation, but it would no longer enjoy hegemonic status. Preserving the U.S.-led system of alliances is crucial to smothering the ambitions of those potential rivals and perpetuating Washington's Cold War era dominance.

Emphasizing the need for stability also directly benefits a number of powerful vested interests. The most obvious ones are the U.S. military establishment with its nearly $300 billion a year budget and the network of defense contractors that profit from such generous expenditures. But there are others. The various intelligence agencies, especially the CIA, that were established during the early years of the Cold War and inexorably expanded their authority, personnel, and budgets throughout the long twilight struggle with the Soviet Union have no desire to see their power curtailed. The end of the U.S.-Soviet rivalry poses a serious threat to the health of the intelligence community as well as to other elements of the national security bureaucracy.

Finally, a less obvious but highly influential vested interest threatened by the end of the Cold War is the assortment of consulting firms and think tanks that employ experts on a wide array of Cold War issues. As journalist Tom Bethell observed, "'Board game' conferences to discuss choke points and sea lanes will become harder to find, and those who used to attend them will have to find another line of work."[2] An academic, consultant, or policy analyst who spent his entire career evaluating the capabilities of NATO and Warsaw Pact forces probably views the end of the Cold War in much the same way as the East German border guard who, after his government opened the Berlin Wall, complained: "It's not good. We will lose our jobs." A midlevel NATO official expressed similar sentiments after the Rome summit at which the alliance's new defense doctrines were ratified: "I only hope they last till I retire."[3]

The preservation of Washington's global network of alliances and the adoption of the international stability mission guarantee the continuing power, prestige, and financial health of those various interest groups. Not surprisingly, they have become vocal and potent lobbyists for maintaining an activist political and military leadership role for the United States in the post–Cold War world.

Thus, the enthusiasm for a strongly interventionist foreign policy and the perpetuation of Cold War era alliances is a complex product of sincere (albeit mistaken) assumptions about the international system and crass, self-serving motives. It is unlikely that either one of those factors operating alone would be sufficient to sustain a policy that is so detached from reality and has consequences so contrary to the best interests of most Americans. Acting together, however, the two factors produce a momentum that is exceedingly difficult to reverse.

Washington's Obsession with Stability

For the Bush administration, global stability has become the post–Cold War equivalent of the quest for the Holy Grail. The emphasis on stability has been the underlying theme in the administration's response to numerous situations. That bias impelled Bush to deliver his speech in Kiev in August 1991 in which he sharply criticized secessionist movements in the Soviet Union and endorsed the union treaty engineered by Mikhail Gorbachev.[4] Washington's actions after the abortive Soviet coup confirmed the preference for a unified USSR. The administration's hesitance to recognize the independence of the Baltic republics, its expression of support for the treaties of economic union and political confederation, and the repeated insistence that Soviet military forces remain under the control of the tottering central government were all manifestations of that attitude. Only when it became indisputable that the union could not be preserved and that Gorbachev had no political future

did Washington begin to alter its policy. Even then, the Bush administration had to be dragged kicking and screaming into accepting
the fact that it had to deal with an assortment of independent
republics. It was notable that Washington lagged far behind the
members of the European Community in extending diplomatic
recognition to the Ukraine and the other republics of the former
Soviet Union.

Given that the administration preferred the stability of keeping
the old Cold War adversary intact to the unpredictability that would
accompany disintegration, it is not surprising that it stresses stability in other parts of the world. The fear of fomenting instability
appears to have been a crucial reason for Washington's reluctance
to press Beijing on China's human rights violations. It also was a
motive for the unmistakable policy "tilt" toward the central government in Belgrade during the initial stages of the Yugoslavian crisis.
On the eve of that country's civil war, Secretary of State James A.
Baker III made remarks in Belgrade condemning any unilateral
attempts to withdraw from the federation—sending a clear message
of disapproval to secessionist elements in the breakaway republics
of Slovenia and Croatia.[5] When the two disgruntled republics
ignored Washington's advice and declared their independence
shortly thereafter, the State Department deplored the move. Deputy Secretary of State Lawrence S. Eagleburger insisted that the
actions were "certainly a threat to the stability and well-being of
the people of Yugoslavia." Paraphrasing Ben Franklin, he added,
"In the end the Yugoslavs [must] hang together or they may hang
separately."[6] The Bush administration clung to the fiction of a viable, unified Yugoslavia even as that entity visibly disintegrated.
Months later, the administration opposed Germany's decision to
recognize the independence of Slovenia and Croatia and was miffed
when Bonn failed to honor U.S. wishes.

The obsession with stability has even given the administration's
Persian Gulf policy a perverse consistency. The initial U.S.-led
military intervention was designed to reverse Iraq's takeover of
Kuwait, which Bush and his advisers viewed as a bid by Baghdad
for regional preeminence and, therefore, profoundly destabilizing.
The addition of revenue from Kuwait's oil exports to the large
sums that Iraq derived from its own production could support an
expansion of Saddam Hussein's already large military machine,

give Baghdad a much larger voice in OPEC pricing decisions, and reduce the influence of Washington's moderate Arab allies. From the administration's perspective, the cumulative effect of those trends would threaten the dominant geopolitical position that the United States had attained in the region after World War II and had jealously guarded against all challengers.

The same desire to preserve as much as possible a regional status quo favorable to the United States also explains the subsequent refusal to march on to Baghdad and oust Saddam or to aid the anti-Saddam rebellion launched by Shi'ite and Kurdish insurgents immediately after the end of Operation Desert Storm. That U.S. inaction alternately puzzled and infuriated many Americans who had supported the president's original decision to intervene in the gulf crisis. How, they asked, could Bush let the Iraqi tyrant remain in power?[7] After all, he had repeatedly compared the man to Adolf Hitler, portrayed the international coalition's resistance to his aggression as a crucial test of the new world order, and even called on the Iraqi people to overthrow him.

It was not that the administration necessarily wanted to see Saddam survive politically. U.S. officials would have welcomed an overthrow of his regime by the Iraqi military and the installation of a friendlier government in Baghdad. (Indeed, there were signs throughout the gulf crisis that Washington was pursuing a covert operation to encourage Saddam's officer corps to topple him from power. A new program with the same objective appeared to be in place in early 1992.)[8] Clearly, Washington had no illusions that it could trust Saddam. The United States had supported him in a variety of ways throughout his long war against Iran—most notably by deploying U.S. naval forces in the Persian Gulf in 1987–88 to protect Kuwaiti oil tankers, a major source of the funds Iraq used to wage the war. Saddam had repaid that help by double-crossing Washington and making a greedy bid for regional preeminence. If that were not enough to rupture the relationship between Washington and Baghdad, the devastation of Iraq's military power and civilian infrastructure during Operation Desert Storm was certain to make Saddam an implacable enemy of the United States.

Consequently, Washington would have shed few tears at Saddam's departure from power. U.S. officials were equally concerned, however, about what would replace his regime. A new government drawn from the same Sunni Moslem elite that had spawned Saddam was acceptable to the administration, since that elite was committed to preserving Iraqi unity—no small task given that country's contending ethnic and religious factions—and to opposing the influence of Iran's fundamentalist regime. As columnist William Safire noted with acerbic accuracy, "Mr. Bush has made it known that he wants a military junta to oust Mr. Hussein and continue 'stable' Sunni domination of the other three-fourths of Iraqis."[9] The kind of regime that might emerge from a successful Shi'ite-Kurdish insurgency was a very different matter. Desert Storm commander Gen. Norman Schwarzkopf was more candid than civilian policymakers when he conceded, "Frankly, if Saddam Hussein leaves, I am not too sure who he is going to be replaced with. We might be worse off than we are now."[10]

In particular, Washington could not be confident that either faction would not seek to dismember Iraq, thereby creating enormous regional instability. The Kurds had long sought to establish an independent Kurdistan in the northeast, and although they now disavowed that goal in their public statements, such assurances were unconvincing. U.S. leaders realized that the existence of an independent Kurdish republic—or even an strongly autonomous Kurdish region—would pose severe problems for Turkey, one of Washington's most reliable allies. More than 50 percent of the Kurds live in Turkey, 25 percent live in Iraq, and most of the remainder live in Iran. Ankara had been waging a sporadic campaign against Kurdish Workers party secessionist forces in several southeastern provinces for years. An independent Kurdistan would be an irresistible political magnet for Turkey's Kurdish minority and would, at the least, intensify the ongoing guerrilla campaign. Supporting the Kurdish-Shi'ite insurgency against Saddam, thus, not only risked fragmenting Iraq and creating a dangerous power vacuum, but also risked strengthening secessionist forces in Turkey. That prospect represented instability with a vengeance, to the administration's way of thinking.

Washington's caution was reinforced by its suspicions of the Shi'ites' political agenda. Although it would have been a oversimplification to portray Iraqi Shi'ites as puppets of Tehran, several leaders did have ties with that government. Since the Shi'ites were concentrated in the south of Iraq near the Iranian border, there was the possibility that the insurgents might attempt to establish a separate republic in that region. Even if they were willing to keep Iraq intact, they would undoubtedly attempt to create a Baghdad-Tehran political axis. That was not a prospect that Washington relished. The primary reason the United States had aided Iraq during its war with Iran was precisely to prevent the expansion of Tehran's influence.[11] Furthermore, Washington's ally Saudi Arabia did not welcome the prospect of a radical Shi'ite government on its borders.[12]

Given the Bush administration's fondness of stability, the failure to support the Shi'ite-Kurdish uprising in March and April 1991 was consistent with its overall policy toward the gulf region. With U.S. assistance, that rebellion might have succeeded in toppling Saddam, but it also threatened to fragment Iraq and create greater regional instability.

The preference for stability over competing values is apparent in other administration actions. It was no accident that Bush and Baker repeatedly stressed that one major goal of the U.S.-led intervention in the Persian Gulf crisis was the restoration of Kuwait's "legitimate" government.[13] But as Robert W. Tucker and David C. Hendrickson noted, "However much liberty was taken in defining membership within the 'free world,' it could not be said with candor that Kuwait formed part of it."[14] Even some supporters of the decision to resist Iraqi expansionism found it difficult to swallow the proposition that a medieval autocracy dominated by a single family had any claim to legitimacy. It was entirely in character, however, that the Bush administration rejected suggestions that the United States call for free elections in Kuwait or otherwise distance U.S. policy from the ruling al-Sabah family.

There may have been a certain measure of embarrassment in the American republic's acting as the patron of a reactionary authoritarian regime, but the advent of democracy in Kuwait could have produced unpredictable and perhaps unpleasant outcomes. There was certainly no guarantee that democracy would lead to victory by pro-Western factions. Limited experiments with democratic elections in Jordan and Algeria in 1989 and 1990 had resulted in strong showings by anti-Western Islamic fundamentalist groups. Moreover, even if elections in Kuwait did not lead to victory by radical factions, the mere existence of a democratic Kuwait would have a subversive impact on Saudi Arabia and the other conservative monarchies in the gulf region. None of those regimes would welcome a secular, modernist regime on their borders. In short, democracy in Kuwait threatened to be the source of serious regional instability. The Bush administration opted to support the interests of Washington's conservative, status quo allies—even if that meant pursuing a policy contrary to America's own values.

The same bias toward stability was evident in January 1992 when the first free parliamentary elections in Algeria's history led to a decisive victory by the fundamentalist Islamic Salvation Front in the first round of balloting. Within days, the Algerian military forced the resignation of President Chadli Bendjedid, who had fostered democratic reforms. The military then created an emergency State Security Council and canceled the final round of the elections. The initial public response of the Bush administration seemed at least mildly supportive of the crackdown, and privately U.S. officials were even more supportive.[15]

Again, the reason for Washington's policy was the fear of instability. The emergence of another Islamic fundamentalist regime would have sent political shock waves through the entire Moslem world and would have posed a special threat of contagion to Algeria's neighbor, Tunisia—one of Washington's oldest allies in the region. It also would have threatened to cause a flood of refugees as more secular Algerians fled to southern Europe, especially France, Algeria's former colonial ruler. Aware that France and other European countries were extremely sensitive about the immigration issue (as evidenced by the growing political strength of the xenophobic Jean-Marie le Pen and his allies), Washington preferred an authoritarian military government in Algiers to the turmoil that would be caused by a fundamentalist regime, albeit a democratically elected one.

The pattern of the administration's conduct clearly shows a bias in favor of order and stability (even if it is accompanied by repression) and an aversion to change and instability. It is a reflexive policy, typical of a conservative, status quo power. The administration's insistence on maintaining Washington's Cold War era alliances is merely one manifestation of that larger world view. Washington sees those alliances both as bulwarks against regional instability and as mechanisms for ensuring a dominant U.S. leadership role in the new world order.

146

It is no accident that U.S. officials repeatedly stress that NATO must be maintained to prevent turmoil in Europe or that a continuing U.S. military presence and the preservation of various mutual security treaties are vital to the stability of East Asia. Given the deep-seated policy assumptions of those officials, it would be surprising if that justification did not figure prominently in their arguments.

The Unattainable Objective of Global Stability

Making global stability the lodestar of U.S. foreign policy in the post–Cold War era is dangerously short-sighted. The immediate future is likely to be one of the most turbulent periods in world history.[16] Many regions are still dealing with the legacy of the imperial age. Throughout the Balkans, the Middle East, Sub-Saharan Africa, and South Asia, the European imperial powers carved out colonies or established client states without reference to the wishes of the indigenous inhabitants or long-standing linguistic, cultural, and economic patterns. In some cases, ancient enemies were grouped together in a single jurisdiction; in other instances, ancient cultures were arbitrarily divided.

It is hardly surprising that those imposed political settlements are now being challenged. Iraq's invasion of Kuwait; the effort to create an independent Kurdistan out of portions of Iran, Iraq, and Turkey; the strife in Yugoslavia; the disorders in Zaire, Ethiopia, Sudan, and Somalia; and the disintegration of the last great multinational empire—the Soviet Union—are all harbingers of the post–Cold War era. The wonder is not that such artificial entities as Yugoslavia and the USSR have fragmented, but that they managed to hold together for so long.

The Cold War rivalry obscured and sometimes even dampened ethnic and religious conflicts. Although the United States and the Soviet Union jockeyed for political advantage in various regions, they also had a mutual interest in keeping client states in line. Neither superpower wanted to be placed in a situation that would allow an ambitious client with its own political agenda to drag its patron into a confrontation with nuclear implications. The rivalry, therefore, was pursued within the context of informal but reasonably discernible rules. Furthermore, Moscow kept the lid on ancient disputes throughout the republics of the Soviet Union and the satellite nations of Eastern Europe. Such quarrels were by definition disruptive, threatening the dominant position of the Communist party and even its ability to govern. (The Soviets were not the only ones to firmly repress those conflicts. Long-time Yugoslavian dictator Marshal Josip Broz Tito exhibited a similar intolerance for divisive conduct within his multinational state.)

Although the various regional and internecine disputes were largely suppressed during the Cold War, they were by no means resolved. In fact, one of the most striking (and depressing) features of the initial post–Cold War period is the rapidity with which ancient conflicts and grievances have resurfaced in several parts of the world. Any attempt by Washington to maintain global stability in the face of such powerful trends is almost certain to fail.

The assortment of U.S.-led Cold War era alliances designed to contain Soviet expansionism is ill-suited to dealing with the instability that will convulse various nations and regions. Even assuming that it would be in the best interest of the United States to undertake the mission of preserving global stability, the most important alliances are concentrated in Western Europe and East Asia, two regions that are likely to be relatively stable. In those portions of the world that will see the greatest instability (the Middle East, South Asia, Africa, and Eastern Europe), Washington has few formal security mechanisms. U.S. policymakers thus face the task of either vastly expanding the theaters of operations of its alliances or relying on ad hoc arrangements with "friendly powers" in the pertinent regions.

Attempts to expand the geographic coverage of existing alliances will encounter resistance on the part of other members. Allies who were happy to maintain a security tie with the United States to protect them from Soviet aggression are likely to be less enthusiastic about enlisting in U.S.-led efforts to police other regions. Even in the Persian Gulf crisis, Washington discovered that (with the exception of Britain) it had to exert extraordinary pressure on other major powers to get them to participate in a collective military response—and in the cases of Germany and Japan, such pressure still produced only economic contributions. If cajoling allies to unite against an adversary who seemed to be a Hollywood caricature of an international villain, in a case in which Washington could invoke an allegedly mortal threat to the world's oil supply, proved to be a difficult task during the twilight of the Cold War—when U.S. power and prestige were arguably at their zenith—it will be considerably more difficult in future episodes.

Finally, it is not at all clear that the mere existence of an alliance or the presence of U.S. military forces will have much of a stabilizing impact even in the immediate vicinity. In the months after the fall of the Berlin Wall, it became an article of faith among Atlanticists that keeping U.S. troops on the Continent would discourage blood-letting among the contending ethnic and religious factions in Eastern Europe. The first test of that thesis came in the summer of 1991 in Yugoslavia, and the results indicated that the deterrent effect of U.S. forces was vastly overrated. Indeed, there is no evidence that the Serbs, Croats, and Slovenes paid any attention whatsoever to the deployment of U.S. tank and infantry divisions in Germany when making their respective policy decisions. The onset of fighting in Yugoslavia suggests that neither NATO nor the U.S. troop presence can serve as a "scarecrow" to prevent instability. What is true of NATO is also true of the other alliances. Washington cannot get away with a policy based on a bluff—the hope that revisionist regimes or movements will capitulate because they conclude that the United States will intervene with its forces, thus sparing Washington from actually having to do so. The only way the stability mission has any prospect of success is if U.S. leaders are willing to intervene whenever that bluff is called. Such a strategy, however, would involve the United States in a host of nasty, intractable conflicts and would strain the resources of a much larger and more expensive military force than even the Bush administration has envisaged for the post–Cold War era.

The Unipolar Fallacy

Advocates of a global stability mission also assume that other major international actors will be cooperative junior partners in U.S.-led security efforts. That is an extremely dubious premise based on the notions that the United States as the "sole remaining superpower" can dominate the international system and that other powers have no alternative but to defer to Washington's policy preferences. The most outspoken proponent of that thesis has been neoconservative columnist Charles Krauthammer. In the pages of *Foreign Affairs* he argued: "The immediate post–Cold War world is not multipolar. It is unipolar. The center of world power is the

149

unchallenged superpower, the United States, attended by its Western allies."[17] His use of the term "attended" is most revealing. For Krauthammer and those who subscribe to his "unipolar" thesis, the other Western powers—even such ascendant states as Germany and Japan—are little more than aides to carry out Washington's orders. According to Krauthammer, "America's preeminence is based on the fact that it is the only country with the military, diplomatic, political and economic assets to be a decisive player in any conflict in whatever part of the world it chooses to involve itself." The United States can employ that multidimensional power, "unashamedly laying down the rules of world order and being prepared to enforce them."[18]

Krauthammer and other intellectual cheerleaders for the new world order overstate the ability of the United States to dominate the international system and the willingness of other Western nations to support that effort. The embarrassing gap between Washington's aspirations as a global hegemonic power and the limits of America's ability to play that role became evident during the Persian Gulf War. The military triumph of the U.S.-led coalition did not alter the fact that Washington had to beg its allies to pay for the war effort. Indeed, it is possible that neither Congress nor the American people would have backed the campaign against Iraq if American taxpayers had had to shoulder all or even most of the financial burden. Such a humiliating dependence on the largesse of other countries is hardly consistent with the image of an unchallengeable superpower. What it evokes is the image of a military giant with economic feet of clay.

The actions of various participants in the international system also contradict Krauthammer's unipolar thesis. Other nations—even America's Cold War era allies—are already beginning to resent and resist Washington's global hegemonic pretensions. Opinion-making elites in nations as diverse as Japan, India, the Philippines, and France have expressed alarm about America's exploitation of its position as the sole remaining superpower, and they openly advocate measures to counterbalance U.S. influence.[19] Aides to French president François Mitterrand contend that the passing of the bipolar world has "exacerbated the arrogance" of American officials, leading the Bush administration to believe that it can now impose its views on the rest of the world.[20] Instead of being intimidated by America's "sole remaining superpower" status, French officials have become more resistant to U.S. demands and seemingly are seeking opportunities to exhibit greater policy independence. The same pattern is evident in the conduct of Germany, Japan, and other regional powers.

The belief that other Western nations will continue to follow Washington's leadership as they did throughout the Cold War is erroneous. International relations theory (as well as international relations history) would predict the gradual dissolution of Cold War era Western solidarity now that there is no longer a credible common threat to promote cohesion among allies. One of the most enduring features of the international system is the tendency of midsized powers to coalesce to counterbalance the strength of a would-be hegemonic power. Unless they have no alternative, such nations do not join or "bandwagon" with the dominant power.[21]

Enthusiasts for U.S. global military leadership occasionally acknowledge that historically the international system has behaved in that way, but they argue that attempts to balance U.S. power will not take place. Why? Because the United States would be a benign hegemonic power whose policies would benefit not only America but the other major nations of the world community. President Bush stated that thesis explicitly in his January 1992 State of the Union Address.

> A world once divided into two armed camps now recognizes one sole and preeminent superpower: the United States of America. And they regard this with no dread. For the world trusts us with power—and the world is right. They trust us to be fair, and restrained; they trust us to be on the side of decency. They trust us to do what's right.[22]

The supposed absence of an incentive to oppose Washington's leadership is enhanced because all the other major powers (except China) are democracies, and according to the conventional wisdom, democracies do not pursue belligerent policies, especially toward other democracies. However, the belief that Japan, the leading European powers, India, China, and other international actors will obediently defer to Washington is, at best, naive. Americans might assume that U.S. hegemony is inherently benign, but other governments and populations will not necessarily agree. Nor can we count on democratic solidarity to prevent a falling out among the erstwhile Cold War era allies. The absence of intramural conflict among the leading democracies during most of the 20th century has led some observers to the conclusion that such conflicts are impossible. There is, however, a more likely explanation. Throughout that period, the democratic nations faced dangerous threats from totalitarian powers. Not surprisingly, the democracies submerged their own differences and banded together to meet that danger, realizing that infighting would be suicidal. It is a leap of logic to conclude that such democratic solidarity will endure in the absence of a common totalitarian threat. U.S. leaders cannot assume that the diplomatic, economic, and military agendas of other Western nations will always coincide with our own—much less that those nations will routinely be Washington's junior partners. The notion that the United States can transform its Cold War network of alliances into a concert of great powers to preserve global stability is a fantasy.

Administration actions also suggest that policymakers do not believe their own brave rhetoric about the willingness of other nations to accept America's benign hegemony. Any doubts on that score were erased when a draft of the Pentagon's defense planning guidance document for 1994–99 was leaked to the media in March 1992. Concern that Washington's Cold War era allies might challenge U.S. global primacy pervaded that document, and various strategies were outlined to keep those allies subservient. Among other things, the planning document stressed that the United States "must seek to prevent the emergence of European-only security organizations," since they might undermine NATO, the principal channel for U.S. influence in European affairs. Similarly, the draft warned of unspecified dangers if either Japan or South Korea sought to play larger regional roles in East Asia. The overall U.S. strategy, according to the document, should be to discourage the emergence of any political-military competitors.[23]

It is proving to be a difficult psychological adjustment for U.S. officials to accept other powers' playing larger and more independent roles. Nevertheless, it is predictable that major European powers, acting either collectively through the European Community or individually, will adopt more assertive positions in that part of the world. Similarly, Japan is likely to eventually play a political and military role in East Asia commensurate with its status as an economic great power. India, China, and other regional powers will also emerge as increasingly important international actors. The bipolar system is dead, and the current unipolar configuration is little more than a momentary phenomenon.

Washington's strategy fails to comprehend the significance of the changes that have taken place in the post–Cold War international system. Washington would not only preserve useless Cold War era alliances but add a variety of open-ended commitments to America's already onerous security burdens. The new world order would have the United States continue spending far more on the military than does any other Western country—and would apparently do so in perpetuity. The much-touted "peace dividend" from the end of the Cold War would be a mirage. Indeed, Bush administration officials have openly boasted that it will be. According to Defense Secretary Richard B. Cheney, "The peace dividend is peace." President Bush has expressed similar sentiments, asserting that the peace dividend cannot be measured in financial terms.[24]

Intellectual Vested Interests

Such a response is due in part to ossified thinking, but there are other motives as well. The U.S. foreign policy community has grown accustomed to the United States' being the acknowledged leader of the free world throughout the Cold War and they have no desire to see that status diminish. Indeed, with the disintegration of the Soviet Union they now see the United States as the unchallenged leader of the *entire* world. To them, America's global leadership status is not merely a matter of national pride—although there is a good element of that. They also view it as a reflection of their own importance. American policymakers and nongovernmental experts have long been treated with the respect, even deference, due representatives (official or unofficial) of a superpower with worldwide commitments. A more circumscribed role for the United States, therefore, threatens their professional status and, perhaps, even their self-image. That sense of loss may explain why so many prominent foreign policy professionals react with uncharacteristic emotion to suggestions that American power is in relative decline or that the United States should adopt a less ambitious security strategy.

The threat to influence, status, and professional identity also helps to explain the frantic search for new missions for the United States in the post–Cold War world. At times those efforts are so wide ranging as to constitute a campaign of threat procurement. There are many examples of that behavior in addition to the ongoing efforts to find new rationales for NATO and the other Cold War alliances. When the military of Haiti overthrew the elected government of president Jean-Bertrand Aristide, some activists not only urged the administration to impose economic sanctions but pressed the United States to orchestrate a military intervention by the Organization of American States.[25] Proponents of action rarely even addressed the question of what relevance the political composition of the Haitian government had to the security interests of the United States. (Haiti has been ruled by dictatorial regimes throughout most of its history without any discernible adverse impact on the United States.) Nor did armchair interventionists respond to objections that the United States had dominated Haiti's political affairs earlier in this century without any lasting beneficial effect. They seemed to believe that the United States, as the "global leader," had an automatic obligation to correct an injustice—the overthrow of an elected government.

Similar suggestions were made about U.S. intervention in Liberia's civil war, despite the fact that it was not even clear which of the contending factions had a moral claim to U.S. assistance. Adventurous types also urged the United States to lead a NATO intervention on behalf of the beleaguered Croats in Yugoslavia's civil war. The conservative Center for Security Policy, directed by former assistant secretary of defense Frank Gaffney, asserted that not only must NATO expel all Serbian forces from Bosnia and Croatia, but "NATO's mission should not be considered complete until [Serbian president] Slobodan Milosevic is brought to justice for crimes against humanity."[26] At times, one had to wonder if, according to the logic of interventionists, there was any conflict anywhere in the world that did not merit U.S. involvement.

The appearance of a book in early 1992 by Monteagle Stearns, a former U.S. ambassador to Greece and a prominent scholar at the Council on Foreign Relations, illustrates that point. In his study, *Entangled Allies: U.S. Policy toward Greece, Turkey, and Cyprus,* Stearns argues that the deteriorating relations among those three countries demand U.S. action.[27] Although the proximate cause of the danger is the continuing division of Cyprus into de facto Turkish and Greek ministates, Stearns contends that there will be no solution to the Cyprus problem until there is significant improvement in relations between Greece and Turkey. Such progress requires reconciling differences over a bewildering array of issues including the exploration and exploitation of the mineral resources of the Aegean shelf, territorial disputes involving a number of Aegean islands, and tense face-offs between Turkish and Greek military forces.

The United States, of course, must take the lead in solving all those troubles—an activist policy that seemed to appeal to some members of the Bush administration even before the appearance of Stearns's book.[28] To those who would ask why the parochial quarrels of two midsized states in a distant part of the world should matter a whit to America, Stearns responds with three justifications for U.S. involvement. Washington, he insists, must take steps to prevent an armed clash between two NATO allies, and he notes that the United States stepped in on three previous occasions (1964, 1967, and 1974) to avert that danger. Because Greece and Turkey border the volatile Balkans, Stearns maintains that they can play a stabilizing role there—if their own conflicts do not hobble them. Finally, he argues that the Gulf War showed that Greece and Turkey are important stepping stones to the Middle East and are therefore important to U.S. commitments in that region.

The first two rationales are textbook examples of the circular reasoning that frequently characterizes arguments for perpetuating Washington's global interventionist strategy. The most prominent reason that NATO supporters invoke for retaining the alliance is that it is an essential arrangement for preventing instability. Yet in this case, the reverse argument is used: the United States must deal with the instability engendered by the quarrel between Greece and Turkey to preserve the unity and effectiveness of NATO. (We need an alliance because of instability, and we need to prevent instability because of our alliance.) Stearns's third justification is an example of the "piggyback" reasoning used to justify U.S. commitments. The United States must keep Greece and Turkey pacified because they are relevant to other U.S. policy objectives in the Middle East. Greco-Turkish problems, however, would become far less important if the United States were not entangled in the various Middle East conflicts. Stearns's reasoning is typical of global interventionists—each component of America's far flung network of obligations is used to justify some other component. In the same manner, proponents of keeping the Philippine bases or revitalizing ANZUS frequently cite the relevance of those ties to U.S. military missions in the Persian Gulf.

Stearns's book also demonstrates that the search for alternative rationales for a global interventionist policy is limited only by the imaginations of its proponents. Indeed, there are several competitors to the global stability mission embraced by the Bush administration and its allies. Sen. John Glenn (D-Ohio), for example, has stated that stopping the spread of weapons of mass destruction is "America's new manifest destiny."[29] Others in the foreign policy community have also urged the United States to adopt a strategy of coercive nonproliferation, either alone or in concert with the UN Security Council, to prevent "outlaw" nations from acquiring nuclear arsenals.[30]

An increasingly popular alternative mission for the United States is the campaign against international narcotics trafficking, an effort that would require the U.S. military to play a significant role. The Pentagon's spending for anti-drug missions has soared from $380 million in FY 1989 to $1.25 billion in FY 1992. It is an interesting "coincidence" that the drug war mission first became prominent just as the Cold War was beginning to wind down.[31]

An even more widely discussed candidate for Washington's post–Cold War mission is the "export" of democracy throughout the world. A number of journalists, pundits, and think tank scholars have urged the United States to lead a "second global democratic revolution."[32] Achieving that objective would require the expansion of the grant-making authority of the National Endowment for Democracy, a willingness to impose economic sanctions on a variety of recalcitrant authoritarian regimes, a generous application of foreign aid to help sustain new democratic governments, and at least occasional use of U.S. military power to defeat dictators and install democracies. Not surprisingly, proponents of a global democracy mission were among the most outspoken advocates of extensive U.S. intervention in such places as Haiti and Iraq.

A crusade to export democracy has one feature in common with its international stability competitor: it is unattainable. For those who want to perpetuate a global interventionist policy, that is not a liability but an asset. There is little prospect that all of the more than 180 nations in the world are going to become democracies in the foreseeable future, and thus a continuing need for U.S. activism is ensured. There will always be dictatorships to undermine and freedom fighters to support. The unlimited time horizon for the policy also guarantees that foreign aid and military budgets will remain large and that there will be plenty of "problems" for policymakers and outside experts to address. In that respect, either the international stability or the global democracy mission is better than the Cold War for the interests of the national security bureaucracy and its allies. Even during the darkest days of the Cold War, there was always the possibility that the U.S.-Soviet conflict would come to an end—as it ultimately did. There is no comparable danger that either the stability or the democracy mission might suddenly become obsolete.

Proponents of alternative missions for the United States in the post–Cold War world often have acrimonious disputes about what that mission should be. The one point they agree on, however, is that the United States must maintain its existing military alliances. Indeed, they uniformly regard the alliances as the essential foundation of U.S. foreign policy.

Political and Institutional Motives

The search for alternative missions is the intellectual response of vested interests that are threatened by the end of the Cold War. For beleaguered members of the foreign policy community, it is a happy coincidence that the new ways in which the United States can continue to exercise global political and military dominance also benefit their own careers or institutions. Although the fondness for interventionism is not necessarily evidence of hypocrisy, there are examples of brazen career- or budget-motivated justifications. Indeed, some of the alternative missions being proposed are so farfetched that it would be hard to fathom any other motive. A prime example was the argument made by Vice Admiral Roger Bacon, commander of the Navy's Atlantic submarine fleet, that ballistic missile submarines would be useful in helping to combat international drug trafficking.[33] Unless he contemplated launching nuclear warheads at the coca fields in Peru, it is difficult to imagine what he had in mind.

The most obvious evidence of crass political and institutional agendas is the tendency of executive branch officials and members of Congress to view the defense budget as a large federal jobs program. An unusually candid admission of that motive was made by Rep. G. V. (Sonny) Montgomery, an influential conservative Democrat from Mississippi. "We're cutting the military too much," he complained in the autumn of 1991. "When you spend money for defense, you get two things, a good defense . . . and secondly you get people jobs. That's the name of the game out here, keeping people working."[34] Montgomery and his colleagues, of course, understand quite well the political benefits to incumbents of delivering and sustaining such jobs—and the potential adverse political consequences of base closings or the loss of military contracts to firms in their districts.

Secretary of Defense Cheney has also resorted to the jobs rationale to discourage more aggressive cuts in the Pentagon's budget. "If you're interested in the economic impact, especially the consequences for the economy over the next year or two, further dramatic cuts now will do more damage than any good you might do with the resources that are freed up," Cheney insisted in an interview with the *San Diego Union*. Cuts in defense spending, the cancellation of weapons, and the planned closing of bases were already "having an impact on the economy, slowing the recovery from the recession," he contended.[35]

It is not just the view of the nation's defense budget as a militarized federal public works program that makes the statements of Montgomery and Cheney so offensive. It is also the underlying cynicism—the willingness to exploit almost any argument to justify large military budgets. Chairman of the Joint Chiefs of Staff Gen. Colin Powell typified that cynicism when he observed: "I'm running out of demons. I'm running out of villains. I'm down to Castro and Kim Il Sung."[36] On another occasion, when touring the Soviet Union, he commiserated with a Soviet general about budget cuts imposed on the military establishments by their respective governments. When an embarrassed Powell looked around and discovered several journalists in the vicinity, he cautioned his Soviet colleague to be more discreet. "The reporters are hearing us complain about whose budget is less."[37]

Parochial motives are also evident in the way specific components of the military budget are inserted or removed. The annual battles between Congress and the executive branch over specific weapons systems frequently have little to do with the performance of the weapons and even less with strategic considerations. Instead, the determining factors appear to be which companies in which states or congressional districts have the contracts. During the rapid military build-up of the Reagan years, such conflicts were muted. As journalist Rowan Scarborough noted: "Those cash-flush days kept both Capitol Hill and the Pentagon happy. Billions of dollars for such projects as the B-1B bomber and the Strategic Defense Initiative were spread out among congressional districts across the country."[38]

As public pressures for lower defense spending have mounted, executive-congressional squabbles (and even congressional battles between delegations from different states and regions) have intensified. In the 1992 budget, for example, Cheney advocated halting production of the Army's M1 tank and eliminating plans to build the V-22 Osprey (a revolutionary tilt-rotor aircraft—a hybrid of helicopter and airplane) for the Marine Corps. Instead, he favored allocating resources to the next generation of high-tech weapons such as the B-2 bomber and the F-22 fighter. Congress responded by halting production of the B-2 at 15 planes while fully funding the production of the first three Ospreys at a cost of $625 million. Not only did Congress order the Army to buy 60 new M1-A2 tanks, but it also mandated the start-up of a new program to turn older M-1s into M-1A2s, over the Pentagon's objections. The decision to build more tanks was an especially egregious example of congressional use of the military budget for pork-barrel purposes. The M-1 was designed for massive tank battles on the plains of Europe in the event of a Warsaw Pact invasion. One could scarcely imagine a less relevant weapon for the post–Cold War world. The Army does not need the number of tanks that it has now, much less additional ones. But the M-1 is built in Michigan and Ohio, two states with powerful congressional delegations controlled by senior leaders of the majority party in Congress. Efforts by Congress in 1992 to continue the construction of the Seawolf submarine—a weapon system predicated on the need to wage a conflict against the most sophisticated elements of the Soviet navy—over administration objections reflected similar political considerations.

Another major struggle occurred between the administration and Congress over the status of reserve forces. Cheney proposed cutting the National Guard and reserve forces by 107,526 personnel as a cost-saving measure and relying to a greater degree on active duty units. The legislation that emerged from the House of Representatives actually increased the authorized strength of the guard and reserves—at a cost of $645 million.[39] Senate defenders of the reserves also came to the defense of the besieged institution. When the Illinois Army Guard was targeted for a cut of 58 percent— substantially more than the national average in the Pentagon's plan—Sen. Alan Dixon (D-Ill.), chairman of the Subcommittee on Preparedness of the Senate Armed Services Committee, won approval for a requirement that any guard reductions be spread evenly among the states.[40]

The congressional solicitude for the budget and personnel levels of the guard and other components of the reserve forces is not difficult to comprehend. Don M. Snider of the Center for Strategic and International Studies noted that many in Congress consider the reserves a jobs program.

> After all, more than 1.1 million men and women are in the various armed forces reserves. Unlike regular soldiers they are older volunteers with roots in their states and communities. They are likely to vote. They enjoy reserve duty and the extra money and civic fulfillment it brings. Having an Army Reserve or National Guard unit can bring a district an armory, civilian jobs and other Federal benefits. It is understandable that legislators listen to the reservists as they would to other special interest groups.[41]

Even some members of Congress who complain about unnecessary alliance commitments and advocate defense budget reductions in the abstract adopt strikingly different positions when proposed reductions involve contractors or bases in their states or districts.[42] Rep. Patricia Schroeder (D-Colo.), a long-time critic of excessive military spending, nevertheless led a group of mostly liberal Democratic representatives in protesting plans by the independent Base Closure and Realignment Commission to close 34 domestic military bases. There was a lengthy parade of complaints by representatives whose districts would be adversely affected. "Our experience with this process could be visited upon you and your constituents," warned Rep. Olympia Snowe (R-Maine), whose state was slated to lose Loring Air Force Base and nearly 4,200 jobs. "The process was

160

supposed to be fair and was supposed to be objective," protested Rep. Thomas M. Foglietta (D-Pa.), "but it was neither fair nor objective." Coincidentally, Foglietta's district was to lose the Philadelphia Naval Shipyard and its almost 7,000 jobs.[43] The bases earmarked by the commission were actually only a small fraction of the facilities that even the Pentagon concedes are not needed for national defense.

Public Choice Factors

Such self-serving activities on the part of the national security bureaucracy and its allies in Congress and the foreign policy community are textbook examples of the processes described in public choice economic theories. The foremost public choice theorists, Nobel laureate James M. Buchanan and his colleague Gordon Tullock, observe that interest group activity "is a direct function of the 'profits'" those groups expect "from the political process."[44] Proponents of government programs seek to secure concentrated benefits for chosen constituencies, while dispersing the costs as widely as possible (and whenever possible, disguising those costs).

Gradually, policy networks or "iron triangles"—three-way interactions involving the permanent bureaucracy, members of Congress (especially key committee and subcommittee chairmen), and special interest lobbies—emerge to promote larger agency budgets and the distribution of concentrated benefits to members of the triangle. Those benefits are both tangible (government contracts to favored corporations and political advantages to senators and representatives who can take credit for new projects in their states or districts) and intangible (a greater sense of importance and prestige among members of the bureaucracy and associated consulting firms or think tanks). The latter also form the core of issue networks (shared-knowledge groups) interested in some aspect or problem of public policy.[45] Issue networks help policy triangles disseminate ideologically charged information that legitimizes policies and enables the triangles to dominate the public debate on a particular topic. The fact that they are not overtly affiliated with the government creates an aura of independence and gives their studies, news stories, and speeches a credibility that official government pronouncements might not have.

The nearly $300 billion a year military budget is a massive source of profits and other benefits. The size of that budget is, in turn,

heavily dependent on the ability of interest groups and the bureaucracy itself to articulate missions and identify security threats
to justify the expenditures. Not surprisingly, during the Cold War
a powerful foreign policy iron triangle developed linking the Pentagon, the State Department, and the intelligence agencies; military
contractors and subcontractors; and members of Congress—especially those sitting on the armed services and appropriations
committees. All three factions had an interest in promoting and
sustaining a global interventionist foreign policy and the large military and intelligence budgets that it required. They were supported,
in turn, by an aggressive and vocal issue network that lobbied for
an activist U.S. military role in the world and a comprehensive,
long-term effort to contain the Soviet Union.

Most of the time, it did not prove too difficult to generate public
support for such a policy; a large, nuclear-armed adversary was a
credible threat to the security of the United States in the view of a
majority of Americans. Nevertheless, whenever the public seemed
complacent about the Soviet threat, or showed signs of questioning
the need for massive military expenditures, the foreign policy iron
triangle "hyped" the threat in a variety of ways.[46] Cynics noted
early on in the Cold War that Soviet submarines seemed to be
sighted off the U.S. coast every time the Pentagon's budget was
pending in Congress. On a more subtle level, officials appear to
have repeatedly exaggerated Soviet economic and military capabilities. As late as 1989 the CIA produced estimates that the Soviet
economy was more than two-thirds the size of the U.S. economy
(making it larger than Japan's) and that the USSR was closing the
gap. The Soviet economy was actually less than half the size of
the CIA estimate—putting the USSR in approximately the same
economic league as Italy or France. Such an egregious error—which
was made continuously for nearly four decades—can only be attrib-
utable to monumental incompetence or deliberate deception. "For
a generation," Sen. Daniel Patrick Moynihan (D-N.Y.) noted during
the confirmation debate on the appointment of CIA director Robert
Gates, "the Central Intelligence Agency told successive Presidents
everything there was to know about the Soviet Union, except that
it was about to fall apart, principally from internal failures and
contradictions."[47]

The fact that the CIA's error conveniently served to magnify
Soviet strength—especially the ability of the USSR to sustain a

huge military establishment—makes the possibility of deliberate deception at least plausible. As columnist Tom Wicker observed, the CIA "became part of, and helped sustain, the commitment of successive administrations to meeting the 'Soviet threat' far past the point where the actual threat posed the myriad and fearful dangers so often proclaimed." Equally important, "The Soviet threat also justified the CIA itself—its budget, its derring-do . . . its very existence."[48] The agency, in short, had a huge institutional incentive to portray the Soviet threat in the most dire terms.

Although there are frequently divisions and shifting coalitions within any issue network, the various factions have a common interest in preserving and expanding the issue-area in which they operate. Any development that makes the issue-area seem less urgent threatens the interests of all participants. That is why the sudden end of the Cold War was so disconcerting to members of the national security network. Within a matter of months, the principal justification for an interventionist policy and large military budgets, which had been used with great success for more than four decades, disappeared. The American public, having borne great risks and financial burdens throughout that period, could be expected to conclude that the United States was now able to scale back its security obligations and make substantial cuts in the military budget. Indeed, that is precisely what happened. By the spring and summer of 1990, there was growing sentiment for a "peace dividend"—a trend in public opinion that was only interrupted, not reversed, by the Persian Gulf conflict and the attendant patriotic fervor.[49]

If the Soviet threat had gradually ebbed rather than collapsed, proponents of interventionism might have had more time to adjust and create a new justification—perhaps by identifying a new "necessary enemy"—in an orderly fashion. Instead, they foundered, desperately casting about for new missions to legitimize existing policies and spending levels. The best they have been able to come up with on short notice is the need to keep the bulk of Washington's security commitments intact to guard against instability, unpredictability, and uncertainty. Such vague "threats" obviously lack the visceral impact or credibility of a large expansionist enemy such as the Soviet Union. "There is no obvious, predictable threat out there any more," Gen. Merrill McPeak, the Air Force chief of staff,

163

observed ruefully in an interview. "What we have now is general-ized uncertainty," something that is very hard to sell to a skeptical populace.[50] Even as he defended the Pentagon's proposed FY 1993 budget, Cheney conceded to the Senate Armed Services Commit-tee, "The threats have become remote, so remote that they are difficult to discern."[51] Because of the absence of a credible serious menace to the security of the United States, the national security network finds its policy rationale seriously challenged for the first time in more than half a century.

Members of the foreign policy triangle and its allies in the issue network have a vested interest in regarding the preservation of U.S. political and military dominance as an end in itself. As former congressman Otis Pike observed: "What is going on in Washington is not so much hypothetical shooting wars as very real turf wars." The leaders of the national security bureaucracy "are all ambitious or they would not have risen to their present role or rank. They see their turf threatened and their stature shrunk if the end of the Cold War reduces the size of the establishments they head, if tax dollars flow out of defense and into education or health or agriculture or drugs or crime or the other bureaucratic fiefdoms that handle other issues and make up the power structure of our nation. They are fighting for money and power as well as defense."[52]

Even the modest reductions in military spending proposed by the Bush administration have been made grudgingly, and only to forestall assaults by critics demanding deeper cuts. Without pres-sure from the public and from a minority in Congress and the foreign policy community who fear that the United States can no longer afford to bear the global military burdens that it did through-out the Cold War, even those limited reductions would probably never have been suggested. An unidentified high-level Navy offi-cial tacitly conceded that point when he explained why he opposed reducing the number of aircraft carrier battle groups from 15 to 10 (rather than the 12 proposed by Cheney in April 1990). "We urgently need 12 carriers," the official insisted, *"although if you asked anyone their real feelings, they'd still push for 15 flattops."*[53]

Maintaining an array of needlessly risky and costly commitments may serve the interests of the foreign policy triangle, but it does not benefit the American people. Polls taken in late 1991 indicated that more than 40 percent of the public favored cutting the military budget in half by the end of the 1990s.[54] Unless U.S. forces are stretched dangerously thin, however, that result can only be achieved if the United States eliminates its obligations to defend an array of allies—although advocates of so-called selective engagement invariably try to evade that problem.[55] Achieving meaningful reductions in military spending means moving beyond the ossified thinking and entrenched interests that have governed Washington's initial post–Cold War policy and developing a new security doctrine for the United States—one of strategic independence.

8. Declaring America's Strategic Independence

Instead of preserving obsolete Cold War alliances and embarking on an expensive and dangerous campaign for global stability, the United States should view the collapse of Soviet power as an opportunity to adopt a less interventionist policy. For the first time in 50 years, there is no powerful threat to U.S. security such as Nazi Germany or the Soviet Union, nor is there a potential new threat of that magnitude on the horizon.

The importance of that change in the international system cannot be overstated. During the Cold War, it at least could be argued that what appeared to be minor regional or internal conflicts had larger implications since they typically involved allies or surrogates of the rival superpower. In a starkly bipolar world—one without geopolitical peripheries—a plausible case could be made that a victory for a Soviet client state or a pro-Soviet political movement automatically represented a loss for the U.S.-led "free world." Indeed, Washington's policy of surrounding the USSR with anti-Soviet alliances was designed to prevent such losses in regions that were deemed important to America's security or economic well-being. The thesis that aggression anywhere automatically concerned the United States greatly oversimplified a complex geopolitical environment even at the height of the Cold War. In a multipolar post–Cold War international system, that thesis has lost what meager validity it may once have had.

As noted in Chapter 7, the post–Cold War world is likely to be a disorderly place for a variety of reasons, but without a hegemonic rival to exploit the turmoil, most of the conflicts and quarrels will be irrelevant to America's own security interests. The United States can, therefore, afford to view them with detachment, intervening only as a balancer of last resort if a conflict cannot be contained by powers in the affected region and is expanding to the point where America's security is threatened. The vastly changed international system means that Washington's network of Cold War era alliances is an expensive anachronism. It also means that assuming a global policing role to prevent disorders in the Third World would be unnecessary as well as imprudent.

Instead of viewing the changes in the international system as a tremendous opportunity for the United States to shed security burdens and reduce its oversized military budget, however, Washington stubbornly clings to its Cold War era commitments. Officials search for new rationales and new interventionist missions to justify the perpetuation of old alliances.

The nature of those rationales is evident in the provisions of a 70-page classified Pentagon planning document leaked to the press in February 1992.[1] A select group of Department of Defense planners working under the direction of David E. Jeremiah, vice chairman of the Joint Chiefs of Staff, came up with the following scenarios, which were described as "illustrative" of the kinds of threats the United States would confront in the post–Cold War world.

- Iraq recovers from the devastation wrought by Operation Desert Storm and invades Kuwait and Saudi Arabia.
- North Korea, which is assumed to have a limited nuclear weapons capability, launches an invasion of South Korea.
- The Iraqi and North Korean invasions take place at the same time.
- A military coup in the Philippines leads to chaotic fighting among contending factions, thereby threatening the safety of Americans living in that country.
- An alliance of right-wing military elements and Colombian drug lords threatens the security of the Panama canal.
- Russia and Belarus attack Lithuania.
- Around the turn of the century, a new anti-democratic, expansionist superpower emerges to challenge the United States, requiring total U.S. mobilization for global war.

What is so striking about all of those scenarios is that there is no inclination to ask why such events should require a military response—and in most cases, a sizable one—on the part of the United States. Only the last example would pose a serious threat to America's security, but the Pentagon planners blithely assume that all of the adverse developments would affect vital U.S. interests. Their reasoning is highly suspect. Take, for example, the scenario in which Russia and Belarus invade Lithuania, triggering a U.S.-led NATO counterattack that ultimately involves more than 7 American combat divisions, 45 fighter squadrons, 4 heavy bomber squadrons, 6 aircraft carrier battle groups, and a Marine expeditionary force. It is certainly appropriate to ask why the United States should engage in such a dangerous enterprise. Lithuania was under Soviet domination for more than half a century before it regained its independence in 1991. Although the occupation was certainly tragic for the Lithuanian people, in all that time not a single U.S. administration believed that a sufficiently important American interest was at stake to risk a major war to expel the Soviets. Those who argue that Lithuanian independence is now worth a confrontation with a nuclear-armed Russian republic must explain how and why that issue has become so crucial. There is nothing in the Pentagon's planning document to suggest that that question was addressed at all.

It is conceivable that the war scenario exercise was nothing more than a cynical attempt to justify a large force structure and high levels of military spending. After all, the conclusion was that the U.S. military must be prepared to fight two major regional wars simultaneously and, at the same time, be able to assist the European allies in preventing a resurgent Russia from pursuing an expansionist agenda. Given that reasoning, it would be exceedingly difficult to cut the military budget below the levels proposed by the Bush administration.

There appears to be a deeper problem, however: an inability (or, perhaps, an unwillingness) to formulate a rational definition of American security interests in a post–Cold War world. Administration policymakers habitually fail to distinguish between what Earl Ravenal terms the "what" questions (the nature of specific developments) and the "so what" questions (why those developments should matter to the United States).[2] Indeed, most of the administration's congressional critics fall into that trap. Rep. Les Aspin (D-Wis.), for example, while contending that it is possible to cut another $50 billion to $100 billion from the military budget over a five-year period, accepts virtually all the administration's assumptions about the need for the U.S. military to play a hyperactive global role. Pentagon spokesman Pete Williams's description of Aspin's alternative budget as, "Let's see if we can come up with a number that's lower than theirs," and his observation that Aspin "does not say what capability can be dispensed with," were devastatingly accurate indictments.[3]

Some members of Congress even chided the Pentagon for omitting plausible war scenarios from its list. Sen. J. James Exon (D-Neb.) wanted to know why the possibility of another Indo-Pakistani war was not mentioned.[4] It evidently never occurred to Senator Exon to reflect on why it would be in the interest of the United States to become militarily involved in a conflict on the Indian subcontinent.

The distinction between "what" and "so what" factors is crucial. Even the most ardent interventionists cannot assume that the United States will be able to intervene in every case of aggression or instability. American lives and resources are finite. A defense strategy must be based on a coherent concept of American security interests and an assessment of the most effective means of protecting those interests. The failure of the administration and most of its establishment critics to address those fundamental issues is a confession of intellectual bankruptcy.

A new U.S. policy of strategic independence would start with a consideration of such factors. Strategic independence would have three guiding principles: a more rigorous definition of vital interests, the preservation of U.S. decisionmaking autonomy, and an avoidance of grandiose international "milieu" goals.

Determining Vital Security Interests

A more rational definition of America's security interests recognizes that there is a discernible hierarchy. In particular, policymakers must adopt a narrower definition of *vital security interests* than the vague and casual one used throughout the Cold War. U.S. officials have repeatedly labeled lesser interests as vital—in part to generate domestic support for dubious commitments and interventionist enterprises. Policymakers have sometimes even transformed largely irrelevant matters into vital ones, in the process putting America's prestige on the line. The massive Vietnam commitment, which vastly exceeded the intrinsic stakes, is the quintessential example. President Lyndon Johnson's assertion that the United States had entered the Vietnam conflict "because there are great stakes in the balance" illustrated the underlying thinking.

Johnson went so far as to equate the rationale for the U.S. effort with "the principle for which our ancestors fought in the valleys of Pennsylvania."[5]

Incantations about vital interests cannot disguise the fact that some interests clearly matter more than others, which makes it essential to establish a hierarchy of concerns. Unfortunately, U.S. leaders have rarely done so—at least on an explicit, systematic basis. Historian Melvyn P. Leffler's observation that policymakers during the Truman administration "projected American interests everywhere," applies with equal or greater force to later administrations. As Leffler notes, an important lesson to be learned from the mistakes of that era is "the need to differentiate among interests, refrain from ideological crusades, and avoid the temptation to define all major interests as national security imperatives justifying the use of force."[6]

A vital interest ought to have a direct, immediate, and substantial connection with America's physical survival, political independence, or domestic liberty. The requirement that an interest have a "direct" connection would negate the tendency of interventionists to engage in "daisy chain" assertions about vital interests. An extreme but revealing example of that process was Dwight D. Eisenhower's formulation of the so-called domino theory to justify a U.S. role in South Vietnam. Eisenhower warned that the communization of Vietnam would have far-reaching implications. "You have a row of dominoes set up, you knock over the first one, and what will happen to the last one is a certainty that it will go over very quickly. So you could have a beginning of a disintegration that would have the most profound influences." He warned that the abandonment of Vietnam would lead to the loss of all of Indochina, then Burma, then Thailand, then Malaya, then Indonesia. Nor was that all. The toppling dominoes would move on to threaten the Philippines, Australia, New Zealand, and the principal geopolitical prize in East Asia, Japan. He concluded that "the possible consequences of the loss [of Vietnam] are just incalculable to the free world."[7]

The implicit premise was that maintaining the integrity of the "island defense chain" (Japan, the Philippines, and the ANZUS allies) was a vital U.S. interest. Eisenhower's secondary premise was that the spread of communist influence throughout Southeast Asia and the southwestern Pacific would threaten those nations, and that the security of Thailand, Malaya, and neighboring countries, therefore, also became a vital U.S. interest. Moreover, since the loss of Indochina would undermine the security of other Southeast Asian nations, Indochina was a vital U.S. interest. Finally, because Vietnam was the linchpin of Indochina, Vietnam was a vital U.S. interest.

That is a classic example of daisy chain reasoning leading to the absurd conclusion that the preservation of a friendly regime in a small Southeast Asian nation (actually, one-half of that nation) was imperative to the United States. Even if one accepted the premise that Japan and the other members of the "island defense chain" constituted vital U.S. interests, it should at least have been necessary for interventionists to demonstrate that those countries faced a serious, credible threat to their security. Instead, improbable scenario was piled on top of improbable scenario to justify an enormous military commitment to a nation that had, at most, meager relevance to Washington's principal East Asian allies—and even less relevance to the United States.

Unfortunately, the faulty logic of Eisenhower's domino theory has not entirely gone out of fashion, despite the Vietnam debacle. Proponents of a U.S.-led intervention in Yugoslavia employ similar reasoning. They begin with the premise that Western Europe is indisputably a vital U.S. interest; move on to assume that if the conflict in Yugoslavia spilled over the borders, it would pose a threat to Western Europe; and then conclude that stopping the existing fighting (which has not yet gone beyond the borders of Yugoslavia) is a vital interest of the United States.[8]

Insisting that a vital interest have a direct relationship to America's security would greatly reduce the chances of confusing minor stakes with essential ones. So would insisting on a clear temporal connection (the "immediate" standard). Interventionists are constantly coming up with nightmare scenarios in which a vital interest may be at risk sometime in the future, if immediate action is not taken. A contemporary example of that argument is the purported need to prevent "unstable" or "outlaw" regimes from acquiring nuclear weapons—by launching preemptive military strikes if necessary.

Deterring a nuclear attack on the United States is undoubtedly a vital interest, but it is not at all clear that adopting a strategy of coercive nonproliferation to neutralize theoretical future threats is a reasonable way of defending a vital interest.[9] Unless the danger is both clear and immediate, it is often better to adopt hedging strategies and seek to buy time. Much can happen in intervening years. A hostile regime may be overthrown, a nuclear weapons development program may prove to be too expensive, the incumbent regime may decide that there are more political disadvantages (e.g., starting a regional arms race) than advantages to acquiring such an arsenal, or it may determine that cordial relations with the United States are advantageous. Robert W. Tucker and David C. Hendrickson rightly chastise proponents of coercive nonproliferation for being too hasty. "It should be remembered that the same temptation arose during the cold war when first the Soviet Union and then China developed nuclear weapons. It was said in the early 1950s about the Soviet Union, just as it was later said in the early to mid-1960s about China, that it would be impossible to enter into a deterrent relationship with either regime." They note that had America acted on those panicky impulses, "the 'long peace' associated with the cold war would have been considerably shorter than it was."[10]

The policy of patience paid off. Today the Soviet Union is no more, and its successor states show every sign of wanting friendly relations with the United States. The relationship with China, although more difficult, has become one of coexistence, and few people would argue that Beijing poses a serious threat to important U.S. interests.

A vital interest must also have a substantial connection to America's security. It is not enough that the preservation of the status quo would prevent an economic inconvenience or an ideological annoyance. The standard should be much higher. It would undoubtedly be an economic benefit to the United States if the Persian Gulf oil supply were to remain in friendly hands. The price of that important commodity would probably be lower and the chances of a supply disruption would certainly be less than if a hostile power or combination of powers controlled the flow. Nevertheless, as discussed hereafter, the economic impact of greater turmoil or the emergence of an anti-U.S. regional hegemonic power would hardly be catastrophic. To describe the protection of Persian Gulf oil as a vital U.S. interest is to indulge in wildly inflated rhetoric.

173

Protecting a favorable set of conditions may well be desirable in the abstract, but the pertinent question is whether the American republic can accept the consequences of a less congenial situation. The United States is a strong power and can put up with a good many inconveniences or annoyances. Very few interests are so essential that their defense warrants the costs and risks of military intervention.

That point is especially relevant because, in addition to the conceptual definition of a vital interest, there is an important operational one. A vital interest is one for which the nation must be willing to fight a major war, if necessary. A threat to a vital interest would automatically involve the very survival of America as a free society, and repelling such a threat would justify all but suicidal exertions. That sobering realization alone should inhibit policymakers from using the concept promiscuously.

Establishing a Hierarchy of Interests

Deterring a military attack on U.S. territory is the clearest example of a vital security interest, but preventing other, less cataclysmic events can also be included in that category. For example, the United States does not want to find itself subjected to credible nuclear blackmail by another power. That development might pose only a potential threat to the republic's physical survival, but it would involve the compromise of its political independence and, conceivably, the liberties of the American people.

For similar reasons, preventing the emergence of another global superpower military challenger could reach the level of a vital interest. That is why it is imperative that U.S. policymakers constantly monitor the international system and not assume that a specific set of policies is appropriate for all time. There is no need for the United States to intervene merely because a regional power somewhere in the world is growing stronger militarily, but at some point an expansionist state might be able to disrupt the global geopolitical balance to such an extent that it would pose a serious threat to America's own security. It is a vital U.S. interest to prevent any hostile country from attaining that degree of power.

Two important factors enter into the assessment of possible threats to vital interests. First, the definition of vital interests is partially but not primarily—much less exclusively—geographic. In general, the more distant a region, the less likely it is that developments there will be germane to America's security, but U.S. leaders must not fall into the trap of drawing arbitrary lines to delineate a sphere of influence. Given the nature of modern weaponry, even distant threats can sometimes be serious. Conversely, some events in the immediate international neighborhood may be little more than annoyances.

More important than geography is the convergence of two characteristics in another state: extensive, modern military capabilities—especially the acquisition of weapons of mass destruction and delivery systems capable of reaching American territory—and the manifestation of implacable hostility toward the United States. Both characteristics are essential. A regime may be intensely anti-American, but if it does not possess a first-class military force, any threat it could pose will be marginal. Similarly, there is no reason for undue alarm even if another country has significant military power, provided it has maintained a consistent record of friendly relations with the United States—although a substantial military build-up would justify close monitoring.

Some defense experts dispute the relevance of assessing intentions. Indeed, there is a venerable defense policy cliché that one must always focus on other nations' capabilities, not their intentions, which are sometimes said to be unknowable. But an assessment of capabilities without reference to probable intentions is an inherently futile exercise. It also has insidious policy implications, for it would logically require the United States to be prepared to combat any conceivable threat to its interests, no matter how improbable. Yet even those who advocate an interventionist foreign policy rarely adopt such an extreme position. For example, it is doubtful that U.S. policymakers spend a microsecond worrying about a British military threat—even though Britain has a nuclear arsenal. If a more hostile power, say Iran, had an identical military capability, far greater apprehension would exist—and be warranted. The determining factor in the contrasting responses to those two situations is the assessment, not of military capabilities, but of intentions.

The second factor relevant to repelling threats to vital interests is that a narrow definition of those interests does not mean that the

United States must wait until missile warheads are falling on American cities to take action. U.S. leaders have an obligation to constantly monitor the international geostrategic environment and to determine whether an emerging threat may soon pose a lethal danger and, if it does, take steps to contain or neutralize it. That standard should not, of course, become a pretext for launching preemptive military strikes or for intervening in every minor conflict because there is a remote possibility that an expansionist regional power might someday pose a threat to the United States. It does mean, however, that the United States must maintain state-of-the-art military forces adequate to defend vital American security interests. The strategy pursued by the United States throughout the 19th century (and to a some degree in the 20th century until World War II) of waiting until an attack had taken place to raise the necessary forces and weaponry is not feasible given the requirements and characteristics of modern warfare.

Below the level of vital interests is that of *conditional* or *secondary interests.* In that category are assets that are pertinent but not indispensable to preserving America's physical integrity, independence, and domestic liberties. Preventing the domination of either Western Europe or East Asia by a power hostile to the United States would be a prime example of a conditional interest. The economic capabilities and technological sophistication of the societies in those two regions make them relevant security factors. Any power that could subdue those societies and effectively use their populations and resources would be well on its way to posing a serious threat to America's security.

Indeed, that was the prospect that Washington feared when Nazi Germany and Imperial Japan embarked on their expansionist campaigns in the late 1930s. For a brief time in the late 1940s and early 1950s, an even greater nightmare—the domination of *both* regions by a single movement, Soviet-led international communism—seemed a possibility. In retrospect, it is easy to see that the monolithic nature of communism was more apparent than real and that the danger of Moscow's being able to extend its sway over all of Eurasia was vastly exaggerated. But in fairness to the architects of America's Cold War strategy, it was not so clear at the time. There were indications of fissures in the Leninist facade when Yugoslavia's communist dictator Marshal Tito broke with Moscow in 1948, but not until the onset of the acrimonious Sino-Soviet split at the end of the 1950s was the notion of a monolithic communist movement decisively refuted. U.S. policymakers in the initial decade of the Cold War may have overreacted to the USSR's expansionist abilities and intentions, and in the process bequeathed to later generations of Americans a needlessly burdensome and entangling network of military alliances, but their apprehension about the adverse geopolitical trends in Europe and East Asia was understandable.

Nonetheless, the importance of Western Europe and East Asia to the security of the United States, while significant, does not generally reach the level of a vital interest. The United States will certainly be more comfortable if the nations in those regions are capitalist, democratic, and reasonably friendly toward it, but such conditions are not indispensable. In most cases, however, the United States could survive the emergence of a more hostile geopolitical environment in either area. The possibility of a "Finlandized" (pro-Moscow) Western Europe—a prominent concern of alarmist types in the West before the collapse of the Soviet empire—was an example of a development that might have threatened a secondary, but not a vital, U.S. interest.

Although the protection of secondary security interests justifies some U.S. action, it does not warrant extraordinary exertions. For example, the possibility that the USSR had the military strength to intimidate (if not actually conquer) the war-weakened nations of Western Europe in the late 1940s was a reasonable argument for some security cooperation between the United States and the members of the Brussels Pact, including assisting the European powers to rebuild their defense capabilities. It might also have warranted a temporary Monroe Doctrine–style declaration that the United States would consider a Soviet attempt to dominate Western Europe militarily as a threat to America's security. (Even such an outspoken opponent of NATO and other manifestations of a global interventionist strategy as Sen. Robert Taft [R-Ohio] favored such a declaration.) Adopting such measures would have been a more limited and prudent response than creating a vast, long-term military alliance for the entire North Atlantic region. It would have avoided making Western Europe a permanent security dependent of the United States, with all the burdens and problems that relationship has entailed. In short, NATO was an excessive commitment—in both extent and duration—for the protection of a secondary interest.

The lowest category of security concerns is *peripheral interests.* Those consist of assets that marginally enhance America's security but whose loss would constitute more of an annoyance than a serious setback. The emergence of new radical leftist regimes in Central America, the subjugation of a midsized trading partner such as South Korea, and the control of the Persian Gulf oil supply by a regional power hostile to the United States are examples of events that would impinge on peripheral American security interests.

Washington can usually afford to ignore such developments, and any action that is taken is justified only if it involves minimal cost and risk to the United States. For example, when Iraq invaded Kuwait in August 1990, it would have been reasonable for the Bush administration to have pursued diplomatic efforts to encourage Turkey, Syria, Saudi Arabia, Egypt, and other powers in the region who had a security interest in containing Iraqi expansion to form an alliance to block further aggression by Baghdad. Easing the restrictions on arms exports by U.S. manufacturers to some of those countries might also have been warranted. None of those steps would have imposed additional burdens on U.S. taxpayers, nor would they have posed a serious risk of war. The administration, of course, went far beyond the kinds of limited actions that were appropriate for dealing with a threat to a peripheral interest. Although Washington got away with its gamble in the narrow military sense (the long-term policy consequences of disrupting the region so completely may be another matter entirely), it was an imprudent and excessive response given the limited stakes.

Most developments in the international system do not even reach the threshold of peripheral security interests. Which political faction rules in Angola, Burma, Fiji, Estonia, or Liberia need not be of burning concern to U.S. officials. Even if a threat should emerge to the independence of Lithuania, New Zealand, or Botswana, it would not pose a measurable danger to America's security. It is a pertinent lesson that, despite the dire warnings of those who contended that U.S. intervention in Vietnam was essential to prevent a domino effect that would topple noncommunist governments throughout an arc from India to Japan, Hanoi's victory barely created a geostrategic ripple beyond Indochina. It certainly did not jeopardize the security of the American republic.

The ordering of security interests is, of course, inherently subjective. There is no magic formula that will determine with precision which developments constitute threats to which categories of interests. Ultimately, that judgment must be made by policymakers on a case-by-case basis. Nevertheless, it is essential to have an analytical framework within which to examine specific cases. Security interests, moreover, should be narrowly defined, and those who insist that an alliance commitment is necessary or that U.S. forces must intervene to prevent an undesirable result ought to have the burden of proof placed squarely on their shoulders. Their policy preferences automatically create tangible costs and risks to the American people (as opposed to the entirely theoretical costs and risks of declining to take action), and it is right to demand that they present a compelling reason for their policy prescriptions. That requirement would help to discourage the tendency to define virtually everything as a vital interest.

Maximizing Decisionmaking Autonomy

The second principle guiding a policy of strategic independence would be an emphasis on U.S. decisionmaking autonomy. Washington should avoid collective defense or collective security arrangements, since they inevitably limit America's options and can entangle America in conflicts that are of little relevance to its own security. As a matter of general principle, the United States should not only phase out its obsolete Cold War era alliances; it should be wary of entering new ones except in the most extraordinary circumstances. Alliances tend to lock the United States into commitments that might make sense under one set of conditions but become undesirable, counterproductive, or even dangerous when those conditions change.

The NATO obligation is a case in point. When the United States first signed the treaty, there were solid arguments for helping to protect a weak Western Europe from a militarily powerful and apparently aggressive Soviet Union. America's great economic strength made the commitment seem affordable and its monopoly of nuclear weapons made the level of risk appear acceptable. By the 1960s, however, the situation was markedly different. The West

179

European nations had recovered economically and could afford to provide the forces needed for their own defense. At the same time, the risk to the United States of continuing to shield its European allies had greatly increased, because the Soviet Union had acquired a sizable arsenal of nuclear weapons and a delivery system capable of reaching the United States. Washington, therefore, confronted an increasingly unappealing combination: wealthy allies who were content to free ride on the U.S. security guarantee and the danger that protecting those allies could put America's survival at risk. During the 1970s and 1980s, both the expense and the danger inherent in the alliance became even more pronounced.

A Taft-style informal declaration would at least have made it easier for the United States to extricate itself from the obligation to help defend Western Europe when the circumstances changed. Conversely, formal alliances attract an assortment of vested interests that make it difficult to terminate the arrangement even when the original reason for the commitment has disappeared. The creative new missions to justify the continuation of NATO in the post–Cold War era illustrate the point.

Although it is usually advantageous to retain America's decision-making autonomy, it would be going too far to argue that the United States must never enter into an alliance with another state. Even George Washington in his Farewell Address, one of the intellectual canons of traditional noninterventionist foreign policy doctrine, conceded that it might be necessary to have "temporary alliances for extraordinary emergencies."[11] The operative terms are "temporary" and "extraordinary." Even in those rare instances in which it might become necessary to enter into a security relationship with another country, the commitment should be kept as narrow as possible and retained only as long as needed to neutralize the common threat. Treaties with broad obligations (such as most of America's Cold War alliances) and no discernible termination point are precisely the kinds of entanglements that should be avoided.

The desirability of maintaining a maximum amount of flexibility and decisionmaking autonomy also makes it ill-advised for the United States to support proposals to strengthen the peace-keeping and enforcement powers of the United Nations.[12] An interventionist policy within a global collective security arrangement may be the worst of all possible policy alternatives for the United States. Unilateral interventionism at least leaves U.S. officials the latitude to determine when, where, and under what conditions to use the nation's armed forces. Working through the UN Security Council to reach such decisions reduces that flexibility and creates another layer of risk. That is certainly true if Washington is serious about collaborating in genuine collective security operations and does not merely seek to use the United Nations as a multilateral facade for U.S. policy objectives. U.S. officials have frequently exploited the United Nations or regional security bodies to give U.S. initiatives a multilateral patina.[13] That was the case as far back as the Korean War. The commander of "UN" forces in that conflict was always an American, and the United States provided nearly 90 percent of the troops and weaponry. Crucial decisions, such as whether to cross the 38th parallel and liberate North Korea, were made in the Pentagon and White House, not UN headquarters.

The Persian Gulf intervention was only marginally more a bona fide collective security partnership. President Bush was content to work through the United Nations as long as the Security Council members—and other members of the international coalition arrayed against Saddam Hussein—were willing to endorse Washington's policy preferences. The military decisionmaking authority and the composition of the command structure, however, were overwhelmingly American, just as they had been in Korea. Washington was more subtle in creating a multilateral facade for the Persian Gulf intervention than for the Korean "police action," but it was still a facade.

Some U.S. policymakers apparently believe that the Persian Gulf model can be used for future peace-keeping operations in the name of global stability, but that is highly improbable. Other key international actors acquiesced to a dominant U.S. role because of several factors peculiar to the gulf crisis. Even those powers who harbored doubts about the course charted by Washington realized that the cost of opposing U.S. policy would be high. China, for example, knew that opposition would probably mean the end of its Most Favored Nation trading status. Moscow understood that any interference would doom hopes for a much sought aid package to salvage its crumbling economy. Neither government viewed the protection of Saddam as important enough to risk U.S. anger and retaliation.

181

It will not always be so. Other powers are likely to insist on far more policy input—a genuinely collaborative decisionmaking process—as the price of their cooperation in future interventionist enterprises, and collaboration would automatically mean a dilution of U.S. decisionmaking autonomy. That could be undesirable in two ways. America could encounter interference from other Security Council members and be inhibited from taking action in cases where genuine U.S. security interests were at risk. At the very least, getting the cooperation of other key actors creates an element of delay, which can sometimes prove damaging or even deadly.

The danger that the United States might be inhibited from taking necessary action is matched by the risk that it could be drawn into collective security enterprises that were not in its interests at all. U.S. leaders will not be able to use the United Nations only when it is convenient for Washington. The other permanent members of the Security Council will have their own security priorities for which they want UN support, and they will insist upon quid pro quos from the United States. That problem is further complicated by the fact that there will be increasing pressures to expand the roster of permanent members. Japan and Germany are certain to seek that status to more accurately reflect their political and economic influence in the world arena, and such regional powers as India, Brazil, and Nigeria also have membership ambitions. Accommodating the wishes of the four other current permanent members would be difficult enough for Washington, but trying to placate eight or nine colleagues would be far more so. That is perhaps one reason the Bush administration has deflected proposals to expand the permanent membership of the council—contending that such suggestions are "premature."

The differing security agendas of the principal international actors create an enormous potential for diplomatic "log rolling" in the Security Council. UN partisans invariably argue that there is no danger that the United States will be drawn into peace-keeping or peace-enforcement operations against its will, since all permanent members have veto power. That is an excessively structuralist interpretation, and it ignores the role of incentives and other aspects of how a political organization such as the United Nations operates in practice. Theoretically, Washington could, of course, veto any action that might entangle it in an unpalatable collective security venture. But the "go along to get along" incentives that exist in all legislative bodies will be increasingly present in UN deliberations. If the United States wants UN support for operations that further U.S. policy objectives, it will find itself under enormous pressure to support operations that other council members deem important—even if those ventures are irrelevant to U.S. interests or are potentially dangerous.

The mounting pressure for UN military action in Yugoslavia—coming increasingly from the apprehensive members of the European Community—may be the first example of that process. Despite the Bush administration's reluctance to be drawn into the conflict, U.S. forces are almost certain to be part of a UN operation. Refusal to participate in the operation would be condemned as a shirking of Washington's "duty" as a leader of the international community.[14]

There is no compelling reason for the United States to risk that sort of entanglement. Instead of encouraging the expansion of the United Nations' security powers, U.S. officials should make it clear that we intend to remain aloof from collective security operations. Although there is no urgent need to withdraw from the United Nations (the organization plays a marginally beneficial role as a forum for airing grievances and as a mediator of disputes), the United States ought to view its Security Council membership and the veto power it confers primarily as an insurance policy to prevent any adversary from mobilizing the council to adopt policies contrary to U.S. interests.

Maximizing decisionmaking autonomy must be an important feature of post–Cold War U.S. security strategy, which should be designed to achieve what Senator Taft once referred to as the "policy of the free hand"—the goal of keeping America's policy options open to the greatest extent possible.[15] Avoiding alliances and other entanglements does not necessarily mean that the United States will automatically refrain from intervening. There may well be instances in which intervention is advisable or even imperative to protect vital security interests. The point is that the United States should always make such fateful decisions for itself; they should not be dictated or influenced by elaborate treaty obligations.

Avoiding New World Order Fantasies

The final principle would be to resist pursuing ambitious international "milieu" goals. America would undoubtedly be happier in a world of peaceful democratic states, but such a world is unattainable—or at least it is not attainable at an acceptable level of cost and risk. Moreover, although such a transformation of the international system might be desirable, it is not essential to America's security.

Interventionists have repeatedly oversold the importance of an activist U.S. policy for making the international system more stable and democratic (often not even realizing that there is a certain tension between those two goals). Without U.S. "leadership" to achieve those objectives, it is argued, America's own liberty and safety cannot be secure. Conversely, a U.S.-led crusade to create a stable, democratic world will lead to an era of peace and prosperity for all. That objective echoes the assertion of Woodrow Wilson when he presented his 14 Points to a war-weary world, and that is no accident; many advocates of post–Cold War U.S. activism are unabashed admirers of Wilson.

The most popular version of the thesis holds that, with the collapse of Leninist systems around the globe, the United States should seek to make democracy a universal system.[16] Proponents advance several reasons for making that goal the centerpiece of Washington's foreign policy. Such a mission, they contend, is not only consistent with America's heritage and values but virtually mandated by them: a new manifest destiny. Second, because democracies are inherently nonaggressive—and they especially do not go to war against other democracies—a proliferation of democratic regimes would make the world a more peaceful place, thereby serving America's security interests. Finally, it is argued that democratic regimes are likely to be pro-American and thus create a more congenial international political environment for the United States.

Each of those assertions has a kernel of truth, and the promotion of democratic political values and market economic principles should be an important part of Washington's diplomatic agenda. But most crusaders for global democracy want to go far beyond diplomatic initiatives. They advocate funding "friendly" overseas political factions through the National Endowment for Democracy (NED), using foreign aid to encourage democratic reforms, and imposing economic sanctions on recalcitrant regimes. More militant types want to employ the CIA for covert operations to destabilize authoritarian governments and even see the Grenada and Panama military interventions as models for ousting dictatorships. It all adds up to an extremely crowded and ambitious agenda for the United States.

There are two sets of objections to going down that path. At the most basic level, the methods proposed by the global democracy crowd are inadequate, counterproductive, or dangerous. Increasing the number of Voice of America broadcasts, for example, will hardly be sufficient to implement a global democratic revolution. Expanding the NED budget is likewise a tepid strategy for achieving such a grandiose goal.

In the case of the NED, moreover, U.S. meddling in the political affairs of other nations may do more harm than good. One need only recall the scandal of NED money channeled to opponents of Costa Rican president Oscar Arias Sanchez because he had the temerity to oppose U.S. policy toward Nicaragua. The spectacle of the NED trying to interfere in the affairs of the only long-standing stable democratic system in Central America was tragicomic. Soviet dissident Vladimir Bukovsky's caustic assessment that the NED "floundered, at best doing little, and at worst doing damage," during the final months of the Soviet Union's existence is another example.[17]

Foreign aid programs are even more counterproductive. By their very nature government-to-government aid transfers strengthen the public sector, which is about the last thing most nations need. Moreover, the record of foreign aid programs since the 1950s demonstrates that they tend to foster command economies and corrupt political structures, not democracy. We have no reason to assume that the results would be different in the future.

Using CIA covert operations or military intervention to impose democracy is excessively dangerous as well as potentially counterproductive. The fiasco of the U.S.-led multinational intervention in Lebanon in 1982–83 to back the elected government of Amin Gemayel, which resulted in the deaths of more than 250 U.S. military personnel, is an example of how such operations can go wrong. Even when "success" is achieved, as in the December 1989 invasion of Panama to oust dictator Manuel Noriega and install the government that had been elected the previous May, there can be serious lingering problems. The rising level of violence directed against U.S. forces stationed in Panama is only the most obvious manifestation.

Even if the global democracy enthusiasts were to realize their goal, they would probably be disappointed in the results, for the "peaceful democracies" thesis is greatly overstated. Democracies have often been aggressive and expansionist. The United States engaged in at least two wars of conquest: the Mexican War in the 1840s, which amputated nearly 50 percent of Mexico's territory, and the Spanish-American War in 1898, which was a flagrant move to acquire overseas colonies.

The U.S. experience is hardly unique. Britain's commitment to democracy did not prevent it from greatly expanding its imperial holdings in the late 1800s—including waging the brutal Boer War. France under the Third Republic pursued aggressive imperial designs in Asia and Africa, as did several other democratic European powers. More recently, India did not hesitate to launch an attack on Pakistan in 1971 when New Delhi saw an opportunity to weaken its long-time adversary by supporting the secessionist movement in East Pakistan (now Bangladesh).

Even the contention that democracies do not go to war against other democracies is open to question. Since democratic regimes have attacked nondemocratic states, one should at least be cautious about assuming that they would never attack a sister democracy. Moreover, there have been at least two cases of interdemocratic bloodletting. One was the American Civil War, in which two democratic governments engaged in enthusiastic slaughter for more than four years. The other was World War I, in which the full-fledged democracies of Britain and France fought against largely democratic Wilhelmine Germany. Although some may contend that Germany was not "a real democracy" in 1914, it had competing political parties, an elected parliament with significant powers, and a relatively free press. Wilhelmine Germany, in short, was at least as democratic as many of the nations (e.g., South Korea and Pakistan) and more democratic than some (e.g., the Potemkin democracies of Central America) that partisans of the new world order cite as evidence of a worldwide democratic tide.

It is true that there have been no recent cases of interdemocratic warfare, but as noted in Chapter 7, there is an explanation of that lack of conflict that is more probable than the supposed inherently peaceful nature of democratic states. From the 1930s to the late 1980s, Western democratic nations confronted a series of dangerous

186

expansionist totalitarian powers. Faced with those common threats, they submerged their differences and banded together. One cannot assume that democratic solidarity would automatically exist in the absence of such threats.

There is also little evidence that democratic nations would always be pro-American. Even during the Cold War, when democracies had every incentive to gravitate to the United States for protection against the Soviet Union, not all did so. Other political or geostrategic considerations sometimes intruded. For example, India, the world's most populous democracy, maintained a de facto alliance with Moscow beginning in the mid-1950s. Apprehension about two hostile neighbors, China and Pakistan, impelled New Delhi to seek ties with the Soviet Union to offset those threats. The lack of democratic solidarity operated in the other direction as well; Washington opted for an alliance with a succession of dictatorships in Pakistan rather than cultivate close ties with India.

It is also a mistake to assume that democratic regimes are incapable of oppressive conduct. American interventionists habitually view international politics as a morality play in which Washington should support "the good guys." Reality is usually far more ambiguous. Although political factions may use the rhetoric of democracy, that does not necessarily mean that they embrace the tenets of limited government and inalienable rights. The repressive (but duly elected) governments of Zviad Gamsakhurdia in the republic of Georgia, Franjo Tudjman in Croatia, and Jean-Bertrand Aristide in Haiti provide only the most recent confirmation. Many of the political and military struggles that will take place in the post–Cold War world will not be between "good guys" and "bad guys" but between factions that differ only marginally in corruption and brutality.

An activist policy to impose democracy shares one important feature with its chief competitor, the drive to preserve global stability. Both are arrogant social engineering schemes on an international scale. They assume that U.S. officials can carefully calibrate policies to achieve the desired result. But because policymakers must deal with complex alien cultures that they understand imperfectly, if at all, such confidence is unwarranted. Indeed, the potential for disastrous unintended consequences is enormous.

Instead of pursuing such expensive, dangerous, and quixotic missions, the United States should concentrate on protecting its

187

own essential security interests and adopt the more realistic strategy of being the *balancer of last resort*. That approach is based on the realization that neutralizing serious security threats before they reach lethal levels also means monitoring the health and effectiveness of regional balances of power or more formal regional security organizations. In most cases, regional balances will tend to form of their own accord. The anarchic nature of the international system means that competing powers have political and security incentives to prevent any of their number from achieving a hegemonic position. That is not to say that regional balances never shift or even occasionally break down, but nations threatened by the emergence of an aggressively expansionist power typically move to counter that power, not tamely submit to it.[18] In other words, a country with global hegemonic aspirations would usually find its expansionist agenda blocked (or at least contained) by nations in its immediate region who felt that their own security was endangered.

Occasionally, the nations in a particular region may conclude that they have enough security interests in common to move beyond an implicit or explicit balance of power and create a regional collective security organization. The Western European Union is an example of such an effort. (Unfortunately, as the existence of NATO demonstrates all too well, the concept of a region—and hence a regional security organization—can be stretched beyond any rational definition. The notion of a "North Atlantic" region that encompasses territory from Hawaii to Turkey would baffle even the most flexible geographer.) Unless a multilateral security organization is merely a facade for domination by a regional hegemonic power, there are several crucial prerequisites. They include a substantial and prolonged convergence of the security interests of virtually all the pertinent states, the absence of an aggressively expansionist power in the region, and a consistent willingness to resolve intraregional disputes by peaceful means. Only rarely will all of those conditions be present, which is why less comprehensive alliances and informal balances of power are likely to be the norm in most areas of the world. Nevertheless, where they do emerge, the United States should encourage regional collective security organizations since they reduce the prospect of large "breakout" aggressive powers that could threaten vital U.S. interests.

A restrained approach to defending America's security is not inconsistent with a desire to promote the values of limited government and individual rights. The distinction is that such promotional efforts ought to be confined to diplomacy and the power of example. The impact of the American model can be potent. Many of the demonstrators in the streets of East European cities and Tiananmen Square looked to the American Revolution and the American political and economic system (or at least their idealized version of that system) for inspiration. The source of that inspiration, however, was America's reputation as a haven for the values of freedom, not Washington's bloated military budget and its global network of alliances and military bases. Indeed, insofar as an interventionist foreign policy leads the United States to make common cause with repressive allies or to interfere in the affairs of other societies, the appeal of the American example is diminished.

The most crucial point is that the United States need not remake the world to protect the security and the liberty of the American people. Such an objective probably cannot be attained in any case, and the mere pursuit of the goal will entangle the United States in a array of costly and dangerous commitments. Nearly two centuries ago, Secretary of State John Quincy Adams put it this way: "America goes not abroad in search of monsters to destroy. She is the well-wisher to the freedom and independence of all. She is the champion and vindicator only of her own."[19] That distinction should guide U.S. foreign policy in the post–Cold War era.

The Isolationist Canard

It must be emphasized that strategic independence is not isolationism. The United States can and should maintain extensive diplomatic, cultural, and economic ties with the rest of the world. Washington must also maintain sizable and capable military forces and be prepared to take decisive action if a serious threat to American security does emerge. There is no reason to conclude that the elimination of America's military alliances will inevitably lead to the establishment of an isolated nation besieged by a hostile world.

That is an elementary distinction that seems to elude the Bush administration and a sizable portion of the foreign policy establishment. Whenever critics of America's Cold War era alliances or of the concept of a new world order dare suggest that the United

States can adopt a radically different security strategy, advocates of the status quo respond with Pavlovian cries of "isolationism." President Bush has led that chorus on numerous occasions—most notably during a speech in Hawaii on the 50th anniversary of the Japanese attack on Pearl Harbor. According to Bush, the doctrine of isolationism "flew escort for the very bombers that attacked our men 50 years ago." With that in mind "we must learn and this time avoid the dangers of today's isolationism and its economic accomplice, protectionism. To do otherwise, to believe that turning our backs on the world would improve our lot here at home is to ignore the tragic lessons of the 20th century."[20]

Those who resort to the isolationist epithet habitually rely on such absurd and emotionally charged phrases as "turning our backs on the world." Sen. David Boren (D-Okla.), for example, warns that a new wave of isolationists is telling Americans "not to answer the bell, not to rush out to meet the rest of the world, but rather to slam the door shut. To build a wall around ourselves."[21] In an equally sophisticated vein, NATO commander John Galvin insisted that the only alternative to a continuing U.S. troop presence in Europe "is Fortress America."[22]

One might be tempted to dismiss such caricatures as manifestations of historical ignorance and simplistic thinking, but they occur too frequently, even among scholars who should know better.[23] Something else seems to be at work. Alan Tonelson observes that the mounting criticism of Washington's interventionist global strategy "is terrifying our foreign policy establishment. Commonsensical proposals such as a post-Soviet shift of national priorities to long-neglected domestic needs are automatically smeared as isolationism." He asks, with good reason, "What is the establishment so afraid of?" The mudslinging, Tonelson suspects, "betrays a deeper fear—that the opposition is right."[24]

Christopher Layne offers a similar analysis of the incessant barrage of slurs about isolationism. "By portraying his critics as 'isolationists,'" Layne contends, referring to the Pearl Harbor speech, "President Bush is attempting to evade the real issues" in the debate about America's post–Cold War role and the balance between domestic and foreign policy.

> Bush is dredging up the isolationist specter to counter pressures for a badly needed review of U.S. foreign policy and

a reassessment of national priorities. That dialogue would not be about isolationism. It is nowhere proposed that America dispense with foreign policy, totally disarm or sever its diplomatic and economic ties with the rest of the world. The questions at issue go to the heart of national policy: What are America's vital interests? What military forces are needed to defend those interests? How much can America afford to spend on security without endangering its economic health? Those questions must be addressed.[25]

Occasionally, more substantive objections to eliminating America's alliances surface along with the isolationist canard. One of the most popular is the argument that we live in an increasingly interdependent world, and, therefore, an "isolationist" policy—while it may have been feasible in the 19th century—is now impractical. Typically, that argument focuses on economic interdependence, but it also frequently cites environmental problems, AIDS, and the like.[26] In its crudest form, the global economic interdependence thesis is indistinguishable from the argument that the United States must maintain its alliances to have economic "leverage" with its allies. The more sophisticated version, however, contains a element of truth: U.S. withdrawal from the global marketplace to pursue an agenda of economic nationalism would be a loss for everyone concerned.

But such a step is not inevitable merely because the United States jettisons obsolete security commitments. Those who stress the importance of economic interdependence as a justification for maintaining military alliances seem to assume that Americans cannot have productive commercial relations with nations in other regions unless Washington occupies those regions with its armed forces. That is a faulty assumption. The United States enjoyed a vigorous overseas trade throughout the 19th and early 20 centuries without being the planetary gendarme. Economic relations occur because both parties to a transaction expect to benefit. Those expectations among the United States and its principal trading partners are not going to suddenly collapse because Washington decides that it will no longer subsidize the defense of wealthy allies.

The other major component of the economic interdependence argument as a justification for keeping the alliance system and a capacity for intervention in regional conflicts—America's alleged resource dependency—has even less validity. That thesis achieved great prominence during the 1990–91 Persian Gulf crisis. Early in the confrontation with Baghdad, Secretary of State Baker warned that Iraq's control of Kuwaiti oil would give Saddam Hussein "a stranglehold" on America's economic lifeline, and President Bush asserted that "our jobs, our way of life, our own freedom" would suffer "if control of the world's great oil reserves falls into the hands of Saddam Hussein."[27] Those comments were quite restrained compared with Bush's retrospective view. In a January 1992 campaign speech in New Hampshire, the president insisted that if the United States had not gone to war against Iraq, Saddam would now be controlling Saudi Arabia as well as Kuwait, and American motorists would "be paying $20 a gallon for gasoline."[28]

Bush's New Hampshire remark sets a new standard for silliness. No reputable energy expert, even projecting a worst-case scenario, ever maintained that gasoline prices would have come anywhere near the $20-a-gallon mark. The underlying assumptions about America's resource dependency, however, are worth examining. Indeed, the "oil issue" in the Persian Gulf crisis constitutes the best case that can be made for that proposition. If the arguments do not hold up there, they will not do so anywhere.

Those who supported the gulf war emphasized that if Iraq had moved to conquer Saudi Arabia as well as Kuwait, it would have controlled approximately half of the world's proven oil reserves. The argument contains an assortment of shaky assumptions: (1) that Iraq would have moved into Saudi Arabia (there is still no evidence that Baghdad had such plans), (2) that other regional powers that had much to fear from Iraqi expansion would simply have stood by while such a conquest took place, and (3) that Baghdad's army—which performed so pathetically in the gulf war—would have had the logistical capability to conquer and occupy a territory a vast as Saudi Arabia.

For the sake of argument, however, let us concede that Baghdad both harbored and could have achieved the goal of absorbing Saudi Arabia. Would that really have given Saddam a "stranglehold" on the economies of the West? Merely controlling a large percentage of world oil reserves would not have translated into such power. Indeed, the whole concept of oil reserves is not terribly meaningful, especially in the short term. "Proven reserves" is simply a term used to describe oil deposits that it would be economical to pump under current conditions. Such reserves are not a static quantity; changes in various factors (the discovery of new deposits, the emergence of new extraction technologies, even changes in the market price of oil) can cause major shifts in the amount of proven reserves. Those reserves, in fact, soared from 700 billion barrels in 1985 to nearly 1 trillion barrels in 1990.[29] Moreover, oil reserves include a great deal of oil that no one would contemplate pumping for 40 or 50 years—long after Saddam will have become nothing more than a bad memory.

The pertinent issue—and the one that the administration and other supporters of the war understandably evaded—was how much control Iraq could have gained over current oil *production.* Even a worst-case scenario never supported the administration's panicky assessments. Iraq's annexation of Kuwait gave Baghdad control of 7 percent of global production (compared to 4 percent in Iraq alone). Subsequent subjugation of Saudi Arabia would have raised the total to 16 percent, and even the domination of all the gulf emirates would have brought it to only 22 percent.

David R. Henderson, senior economist for energy on President Reagan's Council of Economic Advisers, estimated that Iraqi control of 22 percent of world production would have been sufficient only to boost world oil prices to about $30 a barrel from the preinvasion price of $20. (Henderson's conclusions were also supported by economists of various political persuasions, including Nobel laureates Milton Friedman and James Tobin.)[30] The total cost to the U.S. economy would have been approximately $29 billion a year. As Henderson observed: "Twenty-nine billion dollars is not small change. But put that number into perspective. It is only about one-half of 1 percent of our $5.4 trillion economy."[31] The effect on the price of gasoline would have been about 24 cents a gallon—bringing the total price to about $1.30 or $1.35, a far cry from Bush's nightmare of $20 a gallon.

Events since Henderson made his analysis have served to confirm his arguments. The world oil market was deprived of both Iraqi and Kuwaiti oil for nearly a year (indeed, it is still largely without Iraqi supplies), and yet the market price continued to hover around preinvasion levels. Some of that price stability was due to the willingness of Saudi Arabia to boost production—which obviously could not have been counted on if Saddam controlled that country—but Saudi action was hardly the only factor. Other producing countries, for example, never reached anything close to 100 percent of pumping capacity, and additional production from those sources could at least partially have offset the loss of Saudi oil. The relative absence of supply dislocations during the gulf crisis was primarily a testimony to the willingness of consuming countries to let the market work. That action (and the positive results) stood in sharp contrast to the policies pursued by the United States during the 1970s—the imposition of price controls, the creation of a government-directed allocation system, and the enactment of a windfall profits tax—that created lengthy lines at service stations and other manifestations of chaos.

The oil justification for the Gulf War simply does not hold up under scrutiny.[32] Henderson was right. "The vaunted oil weapon is a dud." And if the United States does not have to maintain military alliances and be willing to police unstable regions to protect the flow of oil, it certainly does not have to do so to guarantee reliable supplies of other resources. As various scholars have shown, the whole concept of America's resource dependence is vastly overblown.[33] Moreover, in the rare instances in which a dependence exists, not only could the United States easily counter a potential embargo through stockpiling programs, but the supplying country could engage in extortion only if it were willing to suffer the economic consequences of withholding a lucrative export from the market.

Such masochistic behavior is improbable even on the part of stridently anti-American regimes. Economic realities more often than not transcend political differences, and there have been rather extreme examples of that phenomenon. Britain maintained some trade with China during the Korean War, even as British troops were fighting Chinese forces. Although the Reagan administration was busily engaged in trying to subvert the Marxist government of Angola during the 1980s, the United States remained Angola's second largest trading partner and Angolan government military units diligently guarded the installations of Gulf Oil Corporation.

Most other nations benefit from extensive commercial ties with the United States, which is often the principal market for their exports and an important source of development capital. It is notable that throughout the Cold War communist regimes rarely cut off economic relations with the United States; in the vast majority of cases in which a severance occurred, it was at Washington's initiative. In a post–Cold War setting, without the influence of Leninist prejudices, other nations are even less likely to exclude themselves from the benefits of economic ties with the United States.

The notion that America must maintain extensive security commitments because of economic interdependence is unfounded. Moreover, members of the foreign policy establishment who equate strategic independence with economic insularity betray either ignorance or malice. The two doctrines are entirely separable. It is true that some advocates of eliminating alliances have unfortunately embraced policies of economic nationalism and trade protectionism. Patrick J. Buchanan is the best known of those who promote an "America First" strategy with those characteristics, although even Buchanan and his allies do not seek to impose economic autarchy and wall off America from the global trading system.[34] He has, however, given ammunition to those who want to smear all proponents of military retrenchment as isolationists.

There is no contradiction in embracing a policy of free trade and a general attitude of openness to the rest of the world while defining security interests narrowly. Thomas Jefferson, one of the earliest prominent advocates of a noninterventionist foreign policy, stressed that America's policy should be "peace, commerce, and honest friendship with all nations, entangling alliances with none."[35] Some of the most outspoken British opponents of war and imperialism were also strong supporters of free trade. Indeed, that combination was a trademark of Richard Cobden and the other members of the so-called Manchester school who successfully ended Britain's mercantilist policies in the 1830s and 1840s. A large percentage of American "isolationists" in the 20th century were likewise partisans of an open global commercial system.

A system of alliances and an elephantine military budget are not prerequisites for economic relations and cultural ties. Nor are they required for an active and vigorous diplomacy. It is entirely appropriate for the United States to use its good offices to help bring about peaceful resolutions to international disputes whenever possible. Strategic independence would involve an aggressive pruning of security commitments, not the creation of a hermit republic.

195

Nuclear Weapons

Many of the same people who level the isolationist charge also contend that alliances are essential because America cannot find security on its own. Their favorite argument is that the existence of nuclear weapons makes a policy of strategic independence impossible.[36] The world is a much smaller place because of technological advances, they insist, and American territory is no longer immune to attack as it was in the 19th century when the two "oceanic moats" enabled this country to avoid foreign entanglements.

The development of nuclear weapons is assuredly the most important military innovation of modern times, but their existence in no way establishes the need for a global network of military alliances. Indeed, in one respect, nuclear weapons—along with America's geographic advantages—actually enhance U.S. invulnerability, for they virtually eliminate the possibility of a conventional attack on U.S. territory. Given the sizable U.S. nuclear arsenal, an invasion armada could be vaporized long before it approached our shores. Knowing that, only the most irrational power would even make such an attempt. Supporters of the "smaller world" thesis should remember that the most sustained and invasive attack on American territory did not occur in modern times but during the War of 1812 when Washington, D.C., was sacked and burned by British troops.

It is true, of course, that an adversary's possession of nuclear weapons poses a serious potential threat to American security. Moreover, given the trend toward greater proliferation of such weapons, the danger is likely to become more acute in the coming decades.[37] That is an excellent argument for maintaining a credible strategic deterrent and for developing state-of-the-art air defenses and anti-ballistic missile (ABM) systems.

It does not follow, however, that an assortment of U.S.-led alliances reduces the threat posed by nuclear weapons. To the contrary, as the membership of the global nuclear club expands, alliances are dangerous arrangements that can needlessly entangle the United States in conflicts that might go nuclear. Washington's emphasis on the virtues of nonproliferation, symbolized by the 1968 Nuclear Nonproliferation Treaty (NPT), and its continued adherence to the doctrine of extended deterrence may be creating an especially deadly combination.

The nonproliferation system is beginning to produce a perverse result: the regimes that seem the most determined to acquire nuclear weapons are in most cases the same ones the United States and the rest of the international community would least like to see possess them. An analogy with an unintended consequence of domestic gun control laws is applicable. Those laws are fairly effective at taking guns out of the hands of people who would never use them for aggressive purposes but do little to prevent hardened criminals from obtaining them. The NPT—at least in recent years— is leading to a similar outcome. It does an excellent job of persuading the Germanys, Japans, and South Koreas of the world not to pursue nuclear programs. Unfortunately, it is becoming progressively ineffective in dissuading the Irans, Libyas, and North Koreas of the world from doing so.

If U.S. policy does not change, the United States will find itself having to shield an assortment of nonnuclear allies from a rogues' gallery of nuclear-armed adversaries. That would be a more difficult and ultimately a more dangerous mission than protecting those allies from Soviet aggression during the Cold War. Washington always operated on the assumption that although the Kremlin leadership might be ruthless and brutal, it was rational and not unduly reckless. That proved to be a valid, albeit extremely risky, assumption.

U.S. leaders cannot assume the rationality of an adversary with anything approaching the same level of confidence if the U.S. arsenal must deter the likes of Muammar Qadaffi, Kim Il Sung, or Iran's Shi'ite fundamentalist government. That is especially true if the attack to be deterred is on an ideological or a religious enemy. Even the most unstable rulers would probably realize that an attack on the United States itself would lead to a devastating counterstroke, but would they necessarily conclude that the U.S. leaders would risk the consequences of nuclear war to protect third parties?

By continuing to discourage its Cold War era allies from acquiring independent deterrents while preserving the doctrine of extended deterrence and an array of alliance obligations, the United States is placing itself on the front lines of regional disputes that could escalate to nuclear exchanges. True, the consequences of failing to deter a small nuclear-armed state might not be as catastrophic as those of failing to deter the USSR would have been during the Cold

War. Nevertheless, the consequences would be bad enough, and the probability of stumbling into a nuclear conflict would be far greater.

Those who contend that the advent of nuclear weapons makes it essential that the United States protect its security with alliances have it exactly wrong. The nuclear factor—especially the proliferation of nuclear weapons—has made alliances a dangerous luxury for the United States.

A Significant Peace Dividend

A decision to phase out Washington's globe-girdling system of alliances would enable the United States to protect its own security with a much smaller and less expensive military establishment. If it was not obligated to protect the West European nations, Japan, South Korea, and the other allies, the United States could make cuts in its force structure and military budget that would far exceed those contemplated by the Bush administration or even its congressional critics. An alternative force structure based on the doctrine of strategic independence would have the following characteristics.

General Purpose Forces

Since the United States would rarely intervene to affect political outcomes in remote regions, active duty ground forces would have extremely limited utility. The primary purpose of such forces would be to serve as a core around which additional units could be built in the unlikely event that a need for large ground force capability should again arise. A secondary purpose would be to execute rescue operations involving U.S. citizens who were at risk in a country afflicted by acute political turmoil. A new structure combining relevant units of the Army and the Marines need total no more than 250,000 active duty personnel.

Although the United States needs to maintain a significant tactical air power capability, substantial reductions can be made. The number of tactical air wings should be reduced to 16 (9 Air Force, 2 Marine, and 5 Navy). That level should be adequate to handle contingencies requiring rapid response.

The number of aircraft carrier battle groups should be reduced from the current 14 (the administration has proposed 12 by 1997) to 6. That would still enable the United States to deploy 1 battle group in the Atlantic or Caribbean and 2 or 3 in the Pacific at all times, with the others in port on a rotational basis. In the improbable event that a more distant mission were in the security interests of the United States, at least 3 battle groups could be dispatched for such operations. The total number of Navy surface ships should be reduced to approximately 220 (plus 8 or 9 Trident submarines and 40 tactical submarines).

Such a scaled-down conventional force structure would still leave the United States with military capabilities superior to those of any other nation. In particular, Washington's air and naval power would be entirely sufficient in most cases to punish an aggressor that trespassed on vital American security interests. There would be no need to resort to the nuclear option. The conventional force levels contemplated under a regime of strategic independence would not be large enough for the United States to police unstable regions or to protect a network of allies and clients. They would, however, be more than adequate for the defense of America's security. It would be an appropriate military establishment for a nation that pursued a strategy of being the balancer of last resort in the international system.

Strategic Forces

The elimination of obsolete and unnecessary commitments has major implications for America's strategic deterrent as well as its general purpose forces. Washington should move away from extended deterrence and concentrate instead on primary or finite deterrence—discouraging an attack on the United States.

With finite deterrence, the U.S. strategic arsenal can be substantially smaller than it is now, and even smaller than the 3,500 warheads agreed to by President Bush and Russian president Boris Yeltsin at the June 1992 Washington summit. Indeed, the United States should accept Yeltsin's original proposal to cut the U.S. and CIS arsenals to approximately 2,000 warheads each. At the same time, it is essential for the United States to keep a sufficiently large arsenal to deter an attack on American territory by all except the most irrational regimes. Beyond a certain point, fewer is not necessarily better when it comes to nuclear weapons. An excessively small arsenal might tempt an aggressive state to assume that it could "take out" the U.S. retaliatory force with a carefully coordinated attack. Even if the assumption proved wrong—as it probably

199

would—it would be small comfort to Americans after a nuclear exchange. The proposal advanced by former secretary of defense Robert S. McNamara and others to reduce the U.S. arsenal to 1,000 weapons—much less suggestions for even lower levels—could lead to a tragic miscalculation.[38]

A potential aggressor must have no doubt that the U.S. arsenal would be able to survive. To maximize survivability, reductions in the strategic deterrent should be made predominantly in the fleet of land-based intercontinental ballistic missiles (ICBMs), which have always been both provocative (because of their first-strike capabilities) and vulnerable (to an adversary's first strike). The backbone of the new deterrent should be submarine-launched ballistic missiles (SLBMs), since most nations that may develop nuclear weapons will have even less ability than the Soviet Union did to detect missile-armed submarines in the world's vast oceans. With the end of the Cold War, there is no compelling need to retain the venerable strategic triad of bombers, SLBMs, and ICBMs. The danger to America's physical security is no longer that of an all-out assault by a large state-of-the-art nuclear force such as that possessed by the Soviet Union. Guaranteeing the survivability of the deterrent from threats posed by smaller and less technologically sophisticated nuclear powers is, therefore, considerably easier. A scaled-down strategic dyad consisting of 8 or 9 Trident missile submarines and a small bomber fleet (50 or so B1Bs and B2s) would be sufficient.

Strategic Defenses

Maintaining an adequate strategic deterrent would minimize the prospect of a premeditated attack on U.S. territory, but two significant sources of danger would remain. One would be the accidental or unauthorized launch of nuclear weapons, a risk that is likely to mount with the increase in the number of states with nuclear weapons. Many of the new nuclear powers will have neither the financial resources nor the technological capabilities to establish the elaborate command and control systems that were developed by the United States and the Soviet Union.

A second source of danger is the occasional undeterrable leader or regime—the so-called crazy state phenomenon. The entire theory of deterrence is based on the assumption of rational behavior by an adversary; if that premise proves faulty, the theory becomes inapplicable. Although there has been a tendency among policy experts in Western democratic nations to exaggerate the irrational qualities of some mercurial dictators, the crazy state scenario cannot be ignored.

It is essential that the United States augment its deterrent with effective air and missile defenses. The development of an ABM system does not necessarily require the creation of President Reagan's ambitious Strategic Defense Initiative. It was always questionable whether the goal of building an impenetrable defense against an onslaught by the entire Soviet missile fleet was feasible, and the cost might well have been prohibitive. But defending against such an attack is now an extremely improbable mission. At the same time, even a "thin layer" ABM system could offer crucial protection in the case of an accidental or unauthorized launch of a few dozen missiles. The same would be true of a deliberate attack by a new nuclear power that possessed a limited arsenal.

Many of the nations that are seeking to acquire nuclear weapons also have serious programs to build ballistic missile fleets. It is true, as some critics of ABM systems have argued, that there is little chance that any of those states will have ICBMs by the end of this decade. The initial goal of most existing programs appears to be confined to the development of short- or medium-range missiles capable of reaching regional adversaries. Therefore, the critics contend, the United States should delay efforts to build a defensive shield until a credible ICBM threat to American territory emerges.[39]

That conclusion is dangerously naive. First of all, it ignores the problem of an accidental launch of existing CIS intercontinental missiles. Moreover, it is not all that great a technological leap from shorter range missiles to an ICBM capability. None of the emerging nuclear states may have an ICBM fleet in the 1990s, but one cannot be as sanguine about the following decade. Missile defenses cannot be built overnight. Even the single ABM installation in North Dakota, authorized by Congress in late 1991, will not be operational until 1996—at the earliest. Building a nationwide system would take considerably longer. We cannot wait until hostile powers have fully operational ICBM fleets to build adequate defenses.

The other objection raised by critics—that ABM systems offer no protection against alternative delivery methods that enemy governments or terrorist movements might use—also misses the point. True, hostile forces might find other ways of delivering nuclear weapons—small aircraft or smuggling in "satchel bombs"—but the crucial difference is the magnitude of the potential damage. It is unlikely, for example, that a smuggling operation could successfully deploy devices in more than a few population centers. Although the detonation of such weapons would undoubtedly cause extensive damage and loss of life, America could probably recover. (The Soviet Union was able to survive the loss of 10 percent of its population and the destruction of many of its major cities in World War II.) Conversely, the detonation of numerous larger, more destructive missile warheads could devastate American civilization beyond any hope of recovery.

Even an imperfect shield would protect the vast majority of American population centers from that kind of massive damage. As a collateral benefit, it would reduce the likelihood of nuclear blackmail. In a world in which nuclear weapons are proliferating, basic prudence dictates that U.S. leaders not leave the American people defenseless against a missile attack.

Benefits to American Taxpayers

Guided by a policy of strategic independence, the United States would be able to meet its legitimate security needs with a defense force of approximately 875,000 active duty personnel instead of the current level of 2 million or the Bush administration's projection of 1.64 million in FY 1997. At the end of a five-year transition period, the military budget would be $125 billion (measured in FY 1993 dollars). By contrast, the administration proposes spending more than $250 billion in FY 1997 (measured in FY 1993 dollars), and it is probable that military budgets will be even higher thereafter.[40]

The cumulative savings to be gained by moving to a posture of strategic independence over a five-year transition period would be approximately $400 billion. Thereafter, the savings would be at least $125 billion *each year*—a sizable peace dividend by any definition. That figure is approximately the same as the annual cost of Washington's NATO and East Asian alliance commitments.

If returned to the long-beleaguered American taxpayers in the form of tax reductions, such a peace dividend would have an enormously beneficial effect on the economy. The yearly expense of just the major alliance commitments amounts to some $500 for every person in America, or $2,000 for a family of four. Instead of subsidizing the defense of the Europeans, Japanese, and South Koreans, that money could be available for consumer spending, savings, or investment. One suspects that the average American family could find more productive uses for $2,000 a year than funding the Bush administration's pretentious new world order. Government spending at all levels in the United States now consumes more than 43 percent of the national income. With the end of the Cold War, Washington can afford—indeed, it has a moral obligation to provide—a rebate to the taxpayers in the form of a peace dividend.

The Bush administration insists that it is already making significant cuts in the military budget and that further reductions would endanger America's security. Both contentions are false. The much-touted reductions are typically calculated either from Pentagon spending projections made in previous years (which are nothing more than wish lists) or by using the FY 1987 budget as a starting point. The latter tactic is especially disingenuous, because the 1987 budget was the culmination of a spending orgy that had boosted military spending from $146 billion in 1980 to $293.6 billion seven years later. Modest reductions from such stratospheric levels are not terribly meaningful. Despite the administration's rhetoric, the Pentagon's projected budgets in the mid-1990s would be virtually the same in real terms as the median spending levels during the Cold War.

Perhaps the most maddening feature of the administration's plans is that they would have the United States continue spending seven times as much as any other member of the G-7 industrial powers, and 60 percent more than all of them combined. American taxpayers had to pay $287 billion for the Department of Defense in 1991. Meanwhile, Germany spent $34 billion, France $37 billion, and Japan $33 billion.[41] Such a disparity in military burdens was unjustified in a Cold War setting; it makes no sense whatsoever in the post–Cold War world. If the administration has its way, however, that gap will continue indefinitely.

A Defense Policy for a Republic, Not an Empire

A policy of strategic independence is based on a more modest and sustainable security role for the United States and a realistic assessment of the post–Cold War international system. It takes into account the fundamental changes that have occurred in the world in recent years and seeks to position the United States to benefit from an emerging multipolar political, economic, and military environment. Those who advocate perpetuating Washington's Cold War era alliances and conceive of grandiose missions to implement a "new world order" fail to comprehend the significance of the changes in the international system and seem to regard the preservation of U.S. political and military dominance as an end in itself. They show little inclination to ask how a promiscuously interventionist strategy actually benefits the American people.

For those who are serious about preserving the values of a free society, the latter consideration is especially important. The lives, freedoms, and financial resources of the American people are not—or at least should not be—available for whatever foreign policy objectives suit the whims of the national political leaders.[42] The U.S. government has a fiduciary responsibility to protect the security and liberty of the American republic. It does not have a moral or constitutional writ to implement the political elite's conception of good deeds internationally any more than it has a writ to do so domestically.

It is time for Americans to insist on a more rigorous and rational definition of the republic's vital security interests and to reserve the use of U.S. military power for the defense of those interests. American lives and resources are too precious to waste in a search for new enemies to justify old policies.

Notes

Chapter 1

1. White House, Office of the Press Secretary, Press Conference by the President, November 8, 1991, transcript, p. 1.

2. "Rome Declaration on Peace and Cooperation," NATO Press Communiqué S-1 (91) 86, November 8, 1991, p. 2.

3. Quoted in Stephen E. Ambrose, *Eisenhower: Soldier, General of the Army, President-Elect, 1890–1952* (New York: Simon & Schuster, 1983), p. 506.

4. Robert D. Hormats, "Redefining the Atlantic Link," *Foreign Affairs* 68 (Fall 1989): 86.

5. David M. Abshire, "Don't Muster Out NATO Yet: Its Job Is Far from Done," *Wall Street Journal*, December 1, 1989, p. A14.

6. Karen Elliott House, "Atlanticist Aid: Using NATO to Feed Russia," *Wall Street Journal*, November 6, 1991, p. A18. The Bush administration ultimately implemented an extremely limited version of that proposal.

7. Daniel Graham, "NATO and the Spread of Ballistic Missiles," *Washington Times*, November 16, 1991, p. D8.

8. In strikingly similar language, the editors of *The Economist* noted that the Soviet threat of a massive attack on Western Europe had disappeared. "So what is left for NATO to worry about? The answer is: uncertainties." "Life after Threat," *The Economist*, November 2, 1991, p. 46.

9. White House, p. 4.

10. Quoted in Rosemary Sawyer, "Rome Summit Will Unveil 'New NATO,'" *European Stars and Stripes*, November 6, 1991, p. 1. Emphasis added.

11. Quoted in William Drozdiak, "NATO Seeks New Identity in Europe," *Washington Post*, October 4, 1991, p. A19. Woerner is not alone in viewing NATO as a peace-keeping organization for the volatile East European region. A *New York Times* editorial suggested that a NATO rapid deployment force could be used to "contain" conflicts in Eastern Europe, noting that "it's not impossible to imagine a multinational NATO force serving a useful peacekeeping role, separating warring parties and supervising ceasefires." "NATO in Search of a Mission," *New York Times*, June 1, 1991, p. A22.

12. "Rome Declaration on Peace and Cooperation," pp. 4–5.

13. John M. Goshko, "NATO Pledges Increased Cooperation with Countries of Eastern Europe," *Washington Post*, June 7, 1991, p. A17. Various Atlanticist policy experts had suggested such a de facto extension of NATO's security sphere even before the foreign ministers' meeting. See, for example, Peter W. Rodman, "Defending Eastern Europe," *National Review*, May 27, 1991, pp. 31–32.

14. Craig R. Whitney, "NATO Sees a Role with Peacekeepers from Eastern Europe," *New York Times*, June 5, 1992, p. A1; and William Drozdiak, "NATO Widens Mandate on Forces," *Washington Post*, June 5, 1992, p. A41.

15. "State of the World in the 1990s," U.S. Institute of Peace *Journal*, February 1991, p. 3.

16. Alan Riding, "U.S., Wary of European Corps, Seeks Assurance on NATO Role," *New York Times*, October 20, 1991, p. A12; and R. Jeffrey Smith, "NATO's Outlook Clouded by French-German Plan," *Washington Post*, October 19, 1991, p. A20.

17. William Drozdiak and Ann Devroy, "Bush Challenges Europeans to Define U.S. Role," *Washington Post*, November 8, 1991, p. A1.

18. Martin H. Folly, "Breaking the Vicious Circle: Britain, the United States, and the Genesis of the North Atlantic Treaty," *Diplomatic History* 12 (Winter 1988): 63.

19. Don Cook, *Forging the Alliance* (New York: Arbor House, 1989), pp. 114–16.

20. U.S. Senate, Committee on Foreign Relations, *The Vandenberg Resolution and North Atlantic Treaty: Hearings Held in Executive Session on S. Res. 239 and Executive L*, 80th Cong., 2d sess.; 81st Cong., 1st sess. (Historical series, 1973), p. 221. Emphasis added.

21. Ibid., p. 236.

22. Ibid., pp. 123–24, 153.

23. Ibid., p. 228.

24. U.S. Senate, Committee on Foreign Relations, *North Atlantic Treaty Hearings before the Committee on Foreign Relations on Executive L*, 81st Cong., 1st sess., 1949, p. 47.

25. Ibid., p. 321.

26. *Foreign Relations of the United States, 1950*, vol. 3: *Western Europe* (Washington: U.S. Government Printing Office, 1977), p. 273.

27. Ibid., p. 274.

28. Ibid., p. 277.

29. *Public Papers of the Presidents of the United States: Harry S Truman, 1950* (Washington: U.S. Government Printing Office, 1965), p. 626.

30. Memorandum of conversation with Sir Oliver Franks, October 25, 1950, Dean Acheson Papers, box 65, "Memoranda of Conversations, 1950—October" folder, Harry S Truman Library, Independence, Mo.

31. Even the Truman administration's supposedly temporary expansion of U.S. obligations did not go unchallenged. A diverse coalition that included Sen. Robert Taft, former president Herbert Hoover, and former ambassador Joseph P. Kennedy attacked the president's actions and ignited the "Great Debate" of 1950–51. The outcome, however, was an anemic nonbinding Senate resolution admonishing Truman not to send additional troops (beyond the four divisions already planned) without congressional consent. For discussions of the Great Debate, see Ted Galen Carpenter, "United States' NATO Policy at the Crossroads: The 'Great Debate' of 1950–1951," *International History Review* 8 (August 1986): 389–415; and David R. Kepley, "The Senate and the Great Debate of 1951," *Prologue* 14 (Winter 1982): 213–26.

32. Even after he left the presidency, Eisenhower continued to favor a substantial reduction in U.S. forces stationed on the Continent. Dwight D. Eisenhower, "Let's Be Honest with Ourselves," *Saturday Evening Post*, October 26, 1963, p. 26; and Benjamin Welles, "Eisenhower Calls for Drastic Amendment of Nation's Atomic Laws," *New York Times*, May 22, 1966, p. A17. For a discussion of the policy factors that led Eisenhower to preserve a troop presence that he privately opposed, see Ted Galen Carpenter, "Competing Agendas: America, Europe, and a Troubled NATO Partnership," in *NATO at 40: Confronting a Changing World*, ed. Ted Galen Carpenter (Lexington, Mass.: Lexington Books, 1990), pp. 37–40.

33. On de Gaulle's motives for wanting an independent nuclear force, see Jean Lacouture, *De Gaulle: The Ruler, 1945–1970*, trans. Alan Sheridan (New York: W. W. Norton, 1991), pp. 368–69. Even Eisenhower conceded that there was logic to de Gaulle's position.

34. See, for example, Lyndon B. Johnson, *Vantage Point: Perspectives of the Presidency, 1963–1969* (New York: Holt, Rinehart and Winston, 1971), pp. 306–7; and W. W. Rostow, *The Diffusion of Power, 1957–1972* (New York: Macmillan, 1972), pp. 404, 406.

35. Johnson, p. 309.

36. Rostow, p. 396.

37. Ibid., p. 594.

38. Henry A. Kissinger, *White House Years* (Boston: Little, Brown, 1979), p. 948.

39. U.S. Congress, House Committee on Armed Services, *Report of the Defense Burdensharing Panel*, 100th Cong., 2d sess., August 1988, Committee Print 23.

40. Examples of such arguments can be found in Irving Kristol, "What's Wrong with NATO," *New York Times Magazine*, September 23, 1983; and Melvyn Krauss, *How NATO Weakens the West* (New York: Simon & Schuster, 1986).

41. Examples include Earl C. Ravenal, "Europe without America," *Foreign Affairs* 63 (Summer 1985): 1020–35; Christopher Layne, "Atlanticism without NATO," *Foreign Policy* 67 (Summer 1987): 22–45; and David P. Calleo, *Beyond American Hegemony: The Future of the Western Alliance* (New York: Basic Books, 1987).

42. In traditional NATO usage, out-of-area operations referred to possible coordinated measures outside Europe. It did not contemplate operations in Eastern Europe or the Soviet Union, since, by definition, that would have meant war with the Warsaw Pact. With the collapse of the Soviet empire, the out-of-area concept has become somewhat blurred. I have chosen to use the traditional definition. The prospect of NATO actions in Eastern Europe or the former USSR is discussed as part of the new stability mission.

43. Richard Nixon, *Seize the Moment: America's Challenge in a One-Superpower World* (New York: Simon & Schuster, 1992), pp. 142–43.

44. Peter Riddell, "A European View on the Gulf Crisis," in *America Entangled: The Persian Gulf Crisis and Its Consequences*, ed. Ted Galen Carpenter (Washington: Cato Institute, 1991), pp. 33–38.

45. A rare exception is Hudson Institute fellow Mark Helprin, who warns that a militarily resurgent Russia might "attempt to regain strategic depth lost under Mikhail Gorbachev." Mark Helprin, "The Power of Russia Alone," *Wall Street Journal*, December 27, 1991, p. A10.

46. The agreement reached at the June 1992 summit meeting between George Bush and Russian president Boris Yeltsin to reduce the strategic arsenals of both countries to 3,000 or 3,500 bombs and warheads over the next 11 years is an important step toward alleviating the nuclear threat. Again, however, NATO played no substantive role. It will merely bless the outcome.

47. Marian Leighton, "Toward a 'Common European Home': What's in It for Us?" *Global Affairs* 6 (Spring 1991): 80. Some Europeans have advanced similar arguments. See Josef Joffe, *The Limited Partnership: Europe, America and the Burdens of Alliance* (Cambridge: Ballinger, 1987); Josef Joffe, "America's European Pacifier," *Foreign Policy* 54 (Spring 1984): 64–82; and Josef Joffe, "NATO and the Limits of Devolution," in *NATO at 40*, pp. 59–74.

48. John Lewis Gaddis, "Coping with Victory," *Atlantic*, May 1990, pp. 49–60.

207

49. Coral Bell, "Why Russia Should Join NATO," *National Interest* 22 (Winter 1990–91): 37–47. Richard Nixon has openly advocated interim NATO security guarantees and ultimately full alliance membership for the East European nations. Nixon, pp. 129–31. Former U.S. ambassador to the United Nations Jeane Kirkpatrick has put forth a similar policy prescription. Jeane Kirkpatrick, "A NATO Umbrella for Eastern Europe," *Washington Post,* June 8, 1992, p. A18.

50. John J. Mearsheimer presents a broad stability justification. Without the United States' playing the role of continental stabilizer, he contends, all of Europe—West as well as East—is likely to revert to the pattern of destructive rivalries that existed before 1945. John J. Mearsheimer, "Back to the Future: Instability in Europe after the Cold War," *International Security* 15 (Summer 1990): 5–56.

51. Manfred Woerner and Coral Bell are not the only ones to have specifically proposed direct NATO involvement in the security affairs of the former Soviet republics. The editors of the *Wall Street Journal,* for example, contend that the United States and other NATO members should help the Central Asian republics resolve their problems. Referring to the bloody dispute between Azerbaijan and Armenia over the enclave of Norgorno-Karabakh, the editors insist, "This region needs all the stabilizing influences that can be mustered." They then conclude, "If Central Asians are worried about their security, there is no reason why NATO, through Turkey, shouldn't take an interest too." "The Bosporous Bridgehead," editorial, *Wall Street Journal,* February 24, 1992, p. A14.

52. Robert D. Kaplan, "History's Cauldron," *Atlantic,* June 1991, pp. 93–104.

53. For a brief but depressing discussion of the many possibilities for conflict, see Daniel N. Nelson, "Europe's Unstable East," *Foreign Policy* 82 (Spring 1991): 137–58.

54. Unfortunately, even some perceptive critics of the folly of attempting to preserve NATO in the long term frequently want to involve the United States in pan-European peace-keeping missions through the CSCE or similar organizations. The Carnegie Endowment's Jennone Walker, for example, observes that there is no longer any justification for maintaining more than token U.S. forces in Germany, but she nevertheless outlines an ambitious blueprint for Washington to use to help shape political and security developments in Eastern Europe. Jennone Walker, "Keeping America in Europe," *Foreign Policy* 83 (Summer 1991): 128–42.

55. George Wilson, "U.S. Begins Revamping the Military," *Washington Post,* November 26, 1989, p. A12.

56. James Chace, "Answering the 'German Question,'" *New Republic,* December 11, 1989, p. 20. Chace has moderated that view slightly, if at all. See James Chace, *Consequences of the Peace: The New Internationalism and American Foreign Policy* (New York: Oxford University Press, 1992), pp. 68–69.

57. William E. Odom, "The German Problem: Only Ties to America Provide the Answer," *Orbis* 34 (Fall 1990): 483–504. Odom's advocacy of a U.S.-German "partnership" leaves no doubt about which country would be the senior partner. Indeed, the relationship would be more akin to that of parole officer and parolee.

58. Leslie H. Gelb, "Power in Europe," *New York Times,* October 20, 1991, p. E15.

59. Richard Cohen, "Renaissance of Racism," *Washington Post,* November 20, 1991, p. A23.

60. "Galvin Rebukes a U.S. General over Interview," *International Herald Tribune,* October 22, 1991, p. 2.

61. Kenneth Adelman, "New Revelations Raising Old Fears," *Washington Times,* December 11, 1991, p. F3.

62. "The German Question," *The Economist*, October 12, 1991, pp. 18–19.

63. Quoted in Gregory F. Treverton, *America, Germany, and the Future of Europe* (Princeton, N.J.: Princeton University Press, 1992), p. 153. Wolfram F. Hanrieder accurately termed the U.S. and NATO strategy one of double containment. Wolfram F. Hanrieder, *Germany, America, Europe: Forty Years of German Foreign Policy* (New Haven, Conn.: Yale University Press, 1989), pp. 6–11, 142–43, 157.

64. For a discussion of allied ambivalence, if not hostility, toward the prospect of German reunification during the period immediately after the opening of the Berlin Wall, see Christopher Layne, "Germany and America in Post–Cold War Europe: From Double Containment to Single Containment?" Paper presented to the Consortium for Atlantic Studies Symposium "The United States and a United Germany," Arizona State University, September 27–30, 1990. British reaction to the likelihood of a larger, stronger Germany was especially negative. Craig R. Whitney, "Sizing Up Germans: A Thatcher Symposium," *New York Times*, July 16, 1990, p. A6.

65. For a discussion of that prospect, see Jeffrey E. Garten, *A Cold Peace: America, Japan, Germany and the Struggle for Supremacy* (New York: Times Books, 1992). Garten sometimes exaggerates the extent of conflicting interests among those three powers, but his appraisal of the competitive nature of the international system is more realistic than the assessments of most experts.

66. David Binder, "Bonn's Yugoslav Plan Faces More Flak," *New York Times*, December 14, 1991, p. A3; and William Drozdiak, "Europeans' Balkan Stance Attests to Rising German Influence," *Washington Post*, December 18, 1991, p. A25.

67. "Poll Says Germans Want U.S. Troops Out," *Baltimore Sun*, May 13, 1992, p. 6.

68. For a perceptive critique of that tendency, see Michael Lind, "German Fate and Allied Fears," *National Interest* 19 (Spring 1990): 34–44.

69. For a discussion of Washington's ambivalence on the issue of a strong Europe, see Christopher Layne, "Ambivalent Past, Uncertain Future: America's Role in Post–Cold War Europe," in *NATO at 40*, pp. 239–61.

70. Ronald Steel, "NATO's Afterlife," *New Republic*, December 2, 1991, p. 18.

71. A perceptive discussion of the diverging French and U.S. perspectives on European security is Theodore R. Posner, *Current French Security Policy: The Gaullist Legacy* (Westport, Conn.: Greenwood, 1991).

72. Caspar W. Weinberger, "The European Community's New Army," *Forbes*, November 25, 1991, p. 33. The Franco-German goal of greater defense cooperation— and greater independence from the United States—is not a sudden phenomenon. Both trends were quite visible even before the end of the Cold War. See David Garnham, *The Politics of European Defense Cooperation: Germany, France, Britain, and America* (Cambridge, Mass.: Ballinger, 1988).

73. "Rome Declaration on Peace and Cooperation," pp. 2–3.

74. Robert Mauthner, "Common Defence Policy Relies on WEU," *Financial Times*, December 12, 1991, p. 2.

75. Alan Tonelson, "What Is the National Interest?" *Atlantic*, July 1991, pp. 45–48.

76. Quoted in Thomas L. Friedman, "Allies' Yugoslav Spat," *New York Times*, May 30, 1992, p. A3.

77. Steel, "NATO's Afterlife."

78. Quoted in R. W. Apple, Jr., "Bush's Fragile Battalions in Europe," *New York Times*, February 2, 1990, p. A10.

79. "U.S. Is Committed to Presence in Europe, NATO's Top Commander Asserts," *Baltimore Sun*, November 24, p. 6. Various foreign policy scholars have

offered slightly more sophisticated versions of the leverage argument. See Robert J. Art, "A Defensible Defense: America's Grand Strategy after the Cold War," *International Security* 15 (Spring 1991): 31–41; and Stephen Van Evera, "Why Europe Matters, Why the Third World Doesn't: American Grand Strategy after the Cold War," *Journal of Strategic Studies* 13 (June 1990): 10–11.

80. Lugar and Quayle are quoted in Marc Fisher, "Europeans Told of U.S. Isolationism," *Washington Post,* February 10, 1992, p. A1.

81. See Calleo, *Beyond American Hegemony*; and Alan Tonelson, "The Economics of NATO," in *NATO at 40,* pp. 93–107.

82. Paul Blustein, "Europe's Rebuff on Soviet Aid Challenges U.S.," *Washington Post,* October 15, 1991, p. D1; and Hobart Rowen, "The Lesson from Bangkok: U.S. Losing Clout," *Washington Post,* October 27, 1991, p. H1.

83. Rowland Evans and Robert Novak, "Germany's Europe," *Washington Post,* December 20, 1991, p. A27.

84. Quoted in Fisher, "Europeans Told of U.S. Isolationism."

85. Jeane Kirkpatrick, "An Active Europe, a Passive United States," *Washington Post,* November 25, 1991, p. A21.

86. International Institute for Strategic Studies, *The Military Balance, 1991–1992* (London: Brassey's, 1991), pp. 51, 53, 55, 58, 61, 63, 66, 69, 71, 75, 89.

87. See, for example, Walker, "Keeping America in Europe"; and Hugh De Santis, "The Graying of NATO," *Washington Quarterly* 14 (Autumn 1991): 51–65.

Chapter 2

1. International Institute for Strategic Studies, *The Military Balance, 1991–1992* (London: Brassey's, 1991), p. 27.

2. Earl C. Ravenal, *Designing Defense for a New World Order: The Military Budget in 1992 and Beyond* (Washington: Cato Institute, 1991), p. 51; and Ted Galen Carpenter and Rosemary Fiscarelli, "America's Peace Dividend," Cato Institute White Paper, August 7, 1990, pp. 22–25, 46–48.

3. Robert E. Osgood, *The Weary and the Wary: U.S. and Japanese Security Policies in Transition* (Baltimore: Johns Hopkins University Press, 1972).

4. Richard Fisher, "Why Asia Is Not Ready for Arms Control," Heritage Foundation Asian Studies Center Backgrounder no. 113, May 25, 1991. Similar sentiments were expressed in Perry L. Wood, "No 'Peace Dividend' in Southeast Asia," Hudson Institute Briefing Paper no. 118, March 29, 1990.

5. A. James Gregor, "East Asian Security in the Gorbachev Era," in *The U.S.–South Korean Alliance: Time for a Change,* ed. Doug Bandow and Ted Galen Carpenter (New Brunswick, N.J.: Transaction, 1992), pp. 160, 175. Gregor expressed similar views in the initial months of the post–Cold War period. See A. James Gregor, "The Balance of Power Conflicts of Eurasia," *Global Affairs* 5 (Spring 1990): 45–70.

6. William J. Crowe, Jr., and Alan D. Romberg, "Rethinking Security in the Pacific," *Foreign Affairs* 70 (Spring 1991): 124.

7. Winston Lord, "America and the Pacific: Mission Accomplished?" Address delivered at Institute of Public Affairs and Pacific Security Research Institute seminar, July 18, 1990, p. 26.

8. "The President's Report on the U.S. Military Presence in East Asia," Hearings before the Senate Committee on Armed Services, 101st. Cong., 2d sess., April 19, 1990, p. 6.

9. Quoted in Bruce Stokes, "Japan's Asian Edge," *National Journal*, June 29, 1991, p. 1622.

10. Gregor explicitly cites the prospect of a Chinese expansionist threat as a justification for preserving the U.S. presence. See, for example, "East Asian Security in the Gorbachev Era."

11. International Institute for Strategic Studies, *The Military Balance, 1988–1989* (London: IISS, 1988), p. 147; and International Institute for Strategic Studies, *The Military Balance, 1991–1992*, p. 150.

12. China's navy, for example, has no aircraft carriers and only one submarine armed with ballistic missiles. Plans for the development of a second Xia class submarine have apparently been abandoned. The most significant addition in recent years has been some 80 coastal minesweepers, hardly an indication of an intent to increase power-projection capabilities. International Institute for Strategic Studies, *The Military Balance, 1991–1992*, pp. 149, 152.

13. Ibid., p. 165.

14. Douglas MacArthur, *Reminiscences* (New York: McGraw Hill, 1964), p. 304.

15. Amos Jenkins Peaslee, *Constitutions of Nations* (Boston: Martinus Nijhoff, 1985), p. 415.

16. Text of treaty in *The Major International Treaties since 1945*, ed. J. A. S. Grenville and Bernard Wasserstein (London: Methuen, 1987), pp. 118–19.

17. Allen J. Lenz, *Beyond Blue Economic Horizons: U.S. Trade Performance and International Competitiveness in the 1990s* (New York: Praeger, 1991), pp. 34–35. For discussions of the economic consequences of the diversion of research and development funds and talent to the military, see Lloyd Jeffry Dumas, *The Overburdened Economy* (Berkeley: University of California Press, 1986), pp. 207–17; and Graeme Browning, "The R&D Gap," *National Journal*, April 4, 1992, pp. 804–9.

18. MacArthur, p. 304.

19. Ibid.

20. For a discussion of the U.S. objective of incorporating some Japanese military power as part of an anti-Soviet strategy, see John Welfield, *An Empire in Decline: Japan in the Postwar American Alliance System* (Atlantic Highlands, N.J.: Athlone, 1988).

21. James Fallows, "Let Them Defend Themselves," *Atlantic*, April 1989, p. 22.

22. For a discussion of the evolution of Japan's defense policy during the late 1970s and early 1980s, see Masashi Nishihara, "Expanding Japan's Credible Defense Role," *International Security* 8 (Winter 1983–84): 180–205.

23. International Institute for Strategic Studies, *The Military Balance, 1991–1992*, pp. 165–66.

24. Ibid., pp. 55, 58, 75.

25. Japan International Cooperation Agency, *Official Development Assistance Report, 1989* (Tokyo: Ministry of Foreign Affairs, 1990). For a comprehensive discussion of the complex motives for Japan's foreign aid program, see Robert Orr, *The Emergence of Japan's Foreign Aid Power* (New York: Columbia University Press, 1990). On the desire for a more active, but nonmilitary, role in international affairs, see Reinhard Drifte, *Japan's Foreign Policy* (New York: Council on Foreign Relations Press, 1990).

26. David E. Sanger, "Tired of Relying on U.S., Japan Seeks to Expand Its Own Intelligence Efforts," *New York Times*, January 1, 1992, p. A6.

27. "Defence Balloon," *Far Eastern Economic Review*, January 30, 1992, p. 7.

28. David E. Sanger, "Japan Cautioned on Plan to Store Tons of Plutonium," *New York Times*, April 13, 1992, p. A2.

29. T. R. Reid, "Kaifu Abandons Bill to Send Troops to the Gulf," *Washington Post*, November 8, 1990, p. A60.

30. Steven R. Weisman, "Plan by Tokyo for Troop Role with UN Fails," *New York Times*, December 11, 1991, p. A1.

31. David E. Sanger, "Japan's Parliament Votes to End Ban on Sending Troops Abroad," *New York Times*, June 16, 1992, p. A1.

32. For discussions of how the gulf crisis experience has contributed to a reassessment of Japan's foreign and defense policies, see Yoichi Funabashi, "Japan and the New World Order," *Foreign Affairs* 70 (Winter 1991–92): 58–74; Richard Holbrooke, "Japan and the United States: The Unequal Partnership," *Foreign Affairs* 70 (Winter 1991–92): 50–52; and International Institute for Strategic Studies, *Strategic Survey, 1990–1991* (London: Brassey's, 1991), pp. 192–94.

33. Funabashi, p. 58.

34. James Haskell, "Charting a Military Role for Japan," *Washington Times*, August 15, 1991, p. G4.

35. Christopher A. Preble, "U.S.-Japanese Security Relations: Adjusting to Change," Cato Institute Foreign Policy Briefing no. 7, March 14, 1991.

36. Kenneth Hunt, "Japan's Security Policy," *Survival* 31 (May/June 1989): 203.

37. James A. Baker III, "The U.S. and Japan: Global Partners in a Pacific Community," Address before the Japan Institute for International Affairs, Tokyo, Japan, November 11, 1991, *U.S. Department of State Dispatch*, November 18, 1991, p. 842.

38. John Lancaster, "Japan's Political Profile Should Rise, Cheney Says," *Washington Post*, November 23, 1991, p. A18.

39. Quoted in Philip Shenon, "Baker Asks Asians to Move Warily on New Pacts," *New York Times*, July 25, 1991, p. A14.

40. Lancaster.

41. Baker, p. 842.

42. Holbrooke, p. 53.

43. U.S. House of Representatives, *Report of the Burdensharing Panel of the Committee on Armed Services*, 100th Cong., 2d sess., August 1988, p. 66. Yet it is a measure of the ambivalence displayed by U.S. officialdom about a greater Japanese military role that the same report stated, "The Panel does not believe that a large-scale Japanese military build-up would be in the best interests of the United States, Japan, its East Asian neighbors or the rest of the world" (p. 62).

44. Edward A. Olsen, "U.S.-Japan Security Relations after Nakasone: The Case for a Strategic Fairness Doctrine," in *Collective Defense or Strategic Independence? Alternative Strategies for the Future*, ed. Ted Galen Carpenter (Lexington, Mass.: Lexington Books, 1989), p. 74.

45. Melvyn Krauss, *How NATO Weakens the West* (New York: Simon & Schuster, 1986), p. 157.

46. Quoted in Preble, p. 1.

47. T. R. Reid and John Burgess, "U.S. Critics Not Satisfied with Japan's $4 Billion Contribution," *Washington Post*, October 6, 1990, p. A24.

48. Paul Blustein, "Japan to Pay More Costs of GIs Stationed There," *Washington Post*, December 21, 1990, p. A30.

49. Baker, p. 842.

50. Preble, p. 6.

51. The book, initially published only in Japanese, did not attract much attention in the United States until a bootlegged English-language version (rumored to have

been funded by Japan-bashers in the U.S. government) began to circulate. Morita apparently had second thoughts about the wisdom of his coauthorship and withdrew from the project before an official English version of the book was published outside Japan.

52. For an analysis of Ishihara's arguments and their significance, see Andrew Goble and James C. Carlson, "Japan's America-Bashers," *Orbis* 34 (Winter 1990): 83–102. The authorized English edition of Ishihara's book was published in 1991. Shintaro Ishihara, *The Japan That Can Say No* (New York: Simon & Schuster, 1991).

53. Quoted in Bill Powell and Hideko Takayama, "The Japan That Can Take Credit," *Newsweek*, July 25, 1991, p. 27.

54. Steven R. Weisman, "Japanese Coin a Word for New Feeling about U.S.," *New York Times*, October 16, 1991, p. A21. See also T. R. Reid and Paul Blustein, "Japanese View U.S. with New Negativity," *Washington Post* March 1, 1992, p. A1.

55. "Senator Jokes of Hiroshima Attack," *New York Times*, March 4, 1992, p. A12.

56. Kan Ito, "Trans-Pacific Anger," *Foreign Policy* 78 (Spring 1990): 133.

57. Quoted in Jim Hoagland, "Jitters in Bonn and Tokyo," *Washington Post*, March 21, 1991, p. A21.

58. Urban C. Lehner, "More Japanese See a 'Fearsome' U.S. after Gulf Victory," *Wall Street Journal*, March 14, 1991, p. A15.

59. Aurelia George, "Japan's America Problem: The Japanese Response to U.S. Pressure," *Washington Quarterly* 14 (Summer 1991): 18.

60. Quoted in Fred Hiatt, "Marine General: U.S. Troops Must Stay in Japan," *Washington Post*, March 27, 1990, pp. A14, 20.

61. Rochester Institute of Technology, "Japan 2000," Preliminary draft, February 11, 1991, p. 145.

62. "Excerpts from Pentagon's Plan: Prevent the Emergence of a New Rival," *New York Times*, March 8, 1992, p. A14.

63. Takashi Inoguchi, "Japan's Role in International Affairs," *Survival* 34 (Summer 1992): 76.

64. An extreme version of that thesis is that a U.S.-Japanese war is likely at some point. George Friedman and Meredith Lebard, *The Coming War with Japan* (New York: St. Martin's, 1991). Friedman and Lebard tend to overemphasize the factors that divide Japan and America and underestimate important common interests, but their thesis that the two countries are on a collision course must be taken seriously. A milder version of the U.S.-Japanese rivalry thesis is found in Jeffrey E. Garten, *A Cold Peace: America, Japan, Germany, and the Struggle for Supremacy* (New York: Times Books, 1992).

65. Richard V. Allen, "Fifty Years after Pearl Harbor: The Future of U.S.-Japan Relations," Heritage Foundation Lecture no. 356, December 3, 1991, p. 3.

66. Richard Nixon, *Seize the Moment: America's Challenge in a One-Superpower World* (New York: Simon & Schuster, 1992), p. 193. See also Douglas M. Johnston, "Instability in the Asia-Pacific Region," *Washington Quarterly* 15 (Summer 1992): 103–12.

67. Quoted in Karen Elliott House, "Asia's Stability Depends on Relationship of Japan and U.S., Singapore's Lee Says," *Wall Street Journal*, May 18, 1989, p. A13.

68. Damon Darlin, "South Korea, Fearing Japan's Military, Wants U.S. to Remain as Peace Keeper," *Wall Street Journal*, November 20, 1991, p. A12.

69. See, for example, Toshiki Kaifu, "Japan and ASEAN: Seeking a New Partnership for the New Age," Speech in Singapore, May 3, 1991, transcript, p. 6.

70. Marcus Corbin, "After the Cold War in Asia: Time for U.S. Troops in Japan to Come Home," *Defense Monitor* 19, no. 6 (1990): 1–8.

71. Quoted in Kenneth B. Pyle, "The Japanese Question," in *Japan and the World: Considerations for U.S. Policymakers* (Seattle: National Bureau of Asian and Soviet Research, 1990), p. 7.

72. Allen, p. 3.

73. See, for example, the vague and vapid proposals by Secretary of State Baker. James A. Baker III, "America in Asia," *Foreign Affairs* 70 (Winter 1991–92): 9–11.

74. George, p. 18.

Chapter 3

1. Text of the treaty, in *The Major International Treaties Since 1945*, ed. J. A. S. Grenville and Bernard Wasserstein (London: Mathuen, 1987), pp. 119–20.

2. For a concise discussion of the background of the U.S.–South Korean relationship, see Edward A. Olsen, *U.S. Policy and the Two Koreas* (Boulder, Colo.: Westview, 1988), pp. 1–14.

3. Kenneth J. Conboy et al., comps., *U.S. and Asia Statistical Handbook* (Washington: Heritage Foundation, 1991), p. 47.

4. For a discussion of NSC 48/2 and its significance, see Joseph C. Goulden, *Korea: The Untold Story of the War* (New York: McGraw-Hill, 1982), pp. 29–30.

5. For Connally's comments, see "World Policy and Bipartisanship: An Interview with Senator Tom Connally," *U.S. News & World Report*, May 5, 1950, p. 30. For Acheson's remarks, see "Crisis in Asia—An Examination of U.S. Policy," *Department of State Bulletin*, January 23, 1950, pp. 111–18.

6. International Institute for Strategic Studies, *Strategic Survey 1989–1990* (London: Brassey's, 1990), p. 147; and Marcus Corbin et al., "Mission Accomplished in Korea: Bringing U.S. Troops Home," *Defense Monitor* 19, no. 2 (1990): 5.

7. Eugene Moss, "Soviet Fleet Rusts in Vladivostok," *Washington Times*, October 3, 1991; and Kensuke Ebata, "Soviets to Scrap 29 Pacific SSNs," *Jane's Defence Weekly*, October 5, 1991, p. 586.

8. Eric Schmitt, "Russia Is Said to Plan for Smaller Armed Force," *New York Times*, April 2, 1992, p. A10.

9. China's navy consists primarily of small coastal patrol craft. Its supposed deepwater navy has 94 submarines, 19 destroyers, and 37 frigates, many of which are antiquated and of little use except for coastal defense. Most notably, the PRC has no aircraft carriers or heavy cruisers. International Institute for Strategic Studies, *Military Balance, 1991–1992* (London: Brassey's, 1991), p. 152.

10. Olsen, p. 15.

11. Quoted in Corbin, p. 7.

12. Ibid.

13. For a discussion of the costs of the general purpose forces component of the U.S. military establishment, see Ted Galen Carpenter and Rosemary Fiscarelli, "America's Peace Dividend," Cato Institute White Paper, August 7, 1990. Other estimates of the U.S. military presence in Korea are as low as $3 billion per year. See Stephen D. Goose, "U.S. Forces in Korea: Assessing a Reduction," in *Collective Defense or Strategic Independence? Alternative Strategies for the Future*, ed. Ted Galen Carpenter (Lexington, Mass: Lexington Books, 1989), pp. 89–90.

There is less to the ROK's offset of U.S. costs than meets the eye. Approximately $1.5 billion of the most frequently cited $1.8 billion figure consists of "rent-free" real estate for U.S. military installations. Since American forces are there to protect South

Korea, the notion that Seoul is doing American taxpayers a great favor by not forcing them to pay rent for the privilege borders on the perverse.

14. Conboy et al., pp. 45, 47.

15. For discussions of South Korea's economic, technological, and population advantages over North Korea, see Doug Bandow, "Leaving Korea," *Foreign Policy* 77 (Winter 1989–90): 77–93; and Doug Bandow, "Unfreezing Korea," *National Interest* 25 (Fall 1991): 51–58.

16. International Institute for Strategic Studies, *The Military Balance, 1991–1992*, pp. 167, 169.

17. William J. Taylor, Jr., "The Military Balance on the Korean Peninsula: Trends, Linkages, and the Dangers of Premature Judgments," in *The U.S.–South Korean Alliance: Time for a Change*, ed. Doug Bandow and Ted Galen Carpenter (New Brunswick, N.J.: Transaction, 1992), p. 20. For similar arguments, see A. James Gregor, *Land of the Morning Calm: Korea and American Security* (Washington: Ethics and Public Policy Center, 1990), pp. 72–77.

18. See, for example, Tom Marks, "Iraq's Not-So-Tough Army," *Wall Street Journal*, August 21, 1990, p. A14. Marks had studied the Iraqi military as an analyst for U.S. intelligence agencies.

19. Stephen D. Goose, "The Comparative Capabilities of North Korean and South Korean Forces," in *The U.S.–South Korean Alliance*, p. 41.

20. Quoted in Bandow, "Unfreezing Korea," pp. 55–56.

21. Bandow, "Leaving Korea," p. 90.

22. Richard H. Solomon, "The Last Glacier: The Korean Peninsula and the Post–Cold War Era," *U.S. Department of State Dispatch*, February 11, 1991, p. 6.

23. John Lancaster, "U.S. Troop Cut Halted over N. Korea Arms," *Washington Post*, November 21, 1991, p. A1.

24. Edward Neilan, "U.S. Advised to Stay in Korea," *Washington Times*, November 15, 1991, p. A8. Mark T. Fitzpatrick, a senior political officer in the Tokyo embassy, produced a study openly advocating that course. Fitzpatrick noted that U.S. troops have stayed on in Germany after reunification.

25. David E. Sanger, "Shaping a Role in South Korea," *New York Times*, July 2, 1991. Washington has already agreed to have an ROK general command the combined ground forces.

26. James Sterngold, "Seoul Says It Now Has No Nuclear Arms," *New York Times*, December 19, 1991, p. A3. Washington did not formally state that it was withdrawing its arsenal. Indeed, consistent with the long-standing "neither confirm nor deny" policy with respect to nuclear weapons, U.S. officials had never officially acknowledged that such weapons were deployed in the ROK.

27. Pyongyang's drive to acquire an independent nuclear arsenal may also have been intensified by the apparent decision of both Beijing and Moscow to withdraw the protection of their nuclear umbrellas. Robert C. Toth, "'Undeterrables' May Soon Have Nuclear Arms," *Los Angeles Times*, November 4, 1991, p. A1.

28. "Visit to Asia," *Department of State Bulletin*, May 1989, p. 16.

29. "U.S. Relations with Korea," *Department of State Bulletin*, October 1989, p. 30.

30. Solomon, "The Last Glacier," p. 106.

31. Making U.S. troop withdrawals dependent on overall conditions on the Korean Peninsula and throughout East Asia was one crucial defect in President Jimmy Carter's proposal in the late 1970s. See Earl C. Ravenal, "The Way Out of Korea," *Inquiry*, December 5, 1977, pp. 15–18.

32. Damon Darlin, "South Korea, Fearing Japan's Military, Wants U.S. to Remain as Peace Keeper," *Wall Street Journal*, November 20, 1991, p. A12.

33. Ibid. Even the "radical" opposition leader Kim Dae Jung is enthusiastic about retaining a U.S. military presence to guard against Japan and China as well as the threat from North Korea. Kim Dae Jung, "The Once and Future Korea," *Foreign Policy* 86 (Spring 1992): 40–55.

34. For discussions of North Korea's nuclear weapons program, see Andrew Mack, "North Korea and the Bomb," *Foreign Policy* 83 (Summer 1991): 87–104; International Institute for Strategic Studies, *Strategic Survey*, p. 149; and Leonard S. Spector with Jacqueline R. Smith, *Nuclear Ambitions: The Spread of Nuclear Weapons, 1989–1990* (Boulder, Colo.: Westview, 1990), pp. 118–40. See also the reports in *Arms Control Reporter*, 1990, 457.B.31; Don Oberdorfer, "N. Korea Seen Closer to A-Bomb," *Washington Post*, February 23, 1992, p. A1; and Elaine Sciolino, "CIA Chief Says North Koreans Plan to Make Secret Atom Arms," *New York Times*, February 26, 1992, p. A1.

35. T. R. Reid, "Two Koreas Reach Accord Banning Nuclear Weapons," *Washington Post*, December 31, 1991, p. A1.

36. Useful discussions of the cautious thaw in relations between the two Koreas include Bandow, "Unfreezing Korea," and Selig S. Harrison, "A Chance for Detente in Korea," *World Policy Journal* 8 (Fall 1991): 599–631.

37. Don Oberdorfer, "North Korea Releases Extensive Data on Nuclear Effort," *Washington Post*, May 6, 1992, p. A11.

38. For a cautiously optimistic interpretation of North Korean intentions, see "Preliminary Report, Carnegie Endowment Delegation Visit to Pyongyang, Democratic People's Republic of Korea," April 28–May 4, 1992, pp. 1–6.

39. See, for example, Stephen Chapman, "A Nuclear North Korea: The Danger We Can't Ignore," Column for Creators Syndicate, Inc., release date November 14, 1991.

Chapter 4

1. The United States was not a formal member of METO but clearly was the political godfather of the alliance.

2. J. K. McLay, "Perceptions from the Pacific Basin of the Atlantic Community and the Interrelationship of the Two Regions," *Atlantic Community Quarterly* 5 (Winter 1985–86): 336.

3. David Lange, "New Zealand's Security Policy," *Foreign Affairs* 63 (Summer 1985): 1013.

4. Paul Dibb, *Report to the Minister of Defense: Review of Australia's Defense Capabilities* (Canberra: Australian Government Publications Service, March 1986), p. 5.

5. For analyses of the dispute, see Ted Galen Carpenter, "Pursuing a Strategic Divorce: The U.S. and the ANZUS Alliance," Cato Institute Policy Analysis no. 67, February 27, 1986; Joseph Camilleri, *The Australia, New Zealand, U.S. Alliance: Regional Security in the Nuclear Age* (Boulder, Colo.: Westview, 1987); Stuart McMillan, *Neither Confirm Nor Deny: The Nuclear Ships Dispute between New Zealand and the United States* (New York: Praeger, 1987); Doug Bandow, "ANZUS: A Case of Strategic Obsolescence," in *Collective Defense or Strategic Independence? Alternative Strategies for the Future*, ed. Ted Galen Carpenter (Lexington, Mass.: Lexington Books, 1989),

pp. 121–32; and Michael C. Pugh, *The ANZUS Crisis: Nuclear Visiting and Deterrence* (Cambridge: Cambridge University Press, 1989).

6. Don Oberdorfer, "U.S. Withdraws New Zealand's ANZUS Shield," *Washington Post*, June 28, 1986, p. A1. The United States did not try to oust New Zealand formally from the alliance because the treaty has no provision for expelling a signatory.

7. Paul Wolfowitz, "The ANZUS Relationship: Alliance Management," *Department of State Bulletin*, September 1984, p. 62.

8. See William S. Tow, "The ANZUS Dispute: Testing U.S. Extended Deterrence in Alliance Politics," *Political Science Quarterly* 104 (Spring 1989): 117–49; and Carpenter, pp. 8–11.

9. Ron Scherer, "New Zealand Would Welcome U.S. Ship Visit," *Christian Science Monitor*, October 8, 1991, p. 4.

10. Bob Drogin, "No Nukes, No Ties: U.S. and Ally Mend Fences," *Los Angeles Times*, August 16, 1991, p. 5.

11. David Barber, "NZ May Scrap Nuclear Ship Ban," *Independent*, October 1, 1991, p. 12.

12. See, for example, Richard H. Solomon, "The Evolving Security Environment in the Asia-Pacific Region," Statement before the Subcommittee on East Asian and Pacific Affairs of the Senate Foreign Relations Committee, October 30, 1991, *U.S. Department of State Dispatch*, November 4, 1991, pp. 818–20. One of the most outspoken cases for reviving ANZUS is made in Richard D. Fisher, Jr., "How to Reinvigorate America's Alliance with Australia and New Zealand," Heritage Foundation Asian Studies Center Backgrounder no. 114, July 15, 1991.

13. Bill Gertz and Rowan Scarborough, "Soviet Navy Called Home in Disarray," *Washington Times*, January 10, 1992, p. A1.

14. Amitav Acharya and Daniel Mulhall, "Australia's Defense Strategy in Transition," *International Defense Review* 20, no. 7 (1987): 827.

15. International Institute for Strategic Studies, *The Military Balance, 1991–1992* (London: Brassey's, 1991), pp. 164–65.

16. Ibid., pp. 157–58.

17. Author's conversations with various defense and foreign policy officials, Canberra, September 3–4, 1991.

18. International Institute for Strategic Studies, p. 174.

19. Fisher, p. 8.

20. L. R. Vasey and Robert L. Pfaltzgraff, Jr., "U.S. Policy toward the South Pacific," *The South Pacific: Emerging Security Issues and U.S. Policy*, ed. John C. Dorrance et al. (Washington: Brassey's, 1990), pp. 103–4.

21. Peter Costigan, "Australia, N. Zealand Boost Ties," *Washington Post*, April 6, 1985, p. A10. For a discussion of Australia's cultivation of ties with both Washington and Wellington throughout the nuclear ships dispute, see Pugh, passim.

22. International Institute for Strategic Studies, pp. 158–59, 175.

23. Robert Hawke, "Australia's Security in Asia," Address at the Asia-Australia Institute, University of New South Wales, Sydney, Australia, May 23, 1991. Public Affairs Office, Embassy of Australia, transcript, p. 7.

24. William Branigin, "'Declining Asset' in Philippines," *Washington Post*, July 7, 1991, p. A22.

25. Aquino, Enrile, and Solanga are quoted in William Branigin, "Base Treaty Rejected by Philippines," *Washington Post*, September 17, 1991, p. A21.

26. Ibid.

217

27. Kenneth M. Quinn, "Update on the Philippines," Statement before the Subcommittee on Asian and Pacific Affairs of the House Foreign Affairs Committee, September 25, 1991, *U.S. Department of State Dispatch*, September 30, 1991, p. 730.

28. "Aquino Backs Down in Conflict over U.S. Bases," *New York Times*, September 20, 1991, p. A12.

29. Even after efforts to get an agreement for a three-year withdrawal period failed, some members of the U.S. foreign policy community still urged the Bush administration to wait until after the May 1992 elections before beginning the departure. See Richard D. Fisher, Jr., "Debasing the Philippines," *National Interest* 26 (Winter 1991–92): 90–94.

30. David E. Sanger, "Philippines Orders U.S. to Leave Strategic Navy Base at Subic Bay," *New York Times*, December 28, 1991, p. A1. Amazingly, neither Aquino nor U.S. officials entirely abandoned the hope of retaining a U.S. military presence in some form. The last ploy was to convert the Subic Bay installation into a commercial port with large dry docks that would service the U.S. Seventh Fleet. Indeed, under Aquino's scheme the fleet would be given preference in the use of those facilities. "Aquino Asks Bush to Let Bitterness Pass on Bases," *Washington Times*, February 18, 1992, p. A9.

31. Standard arguments along those lines can be found in Gregory P. Corning, "The Philippine Bases and U.S. Pacific Strategy," *Pacific Affairs* 63 (Spring 1990): 7–23; and A. James Gregor and Virgilio Aganon, *The Philippine Bases: U.S. Security at Risk* (Washington: Ethics and Public Policy Center, 1987). For criticisms of the thesis that the bases are important to U.S. security interests, see "U.S. Bases in the Philippines: Unneeded at Any Price," *Defense Monitor* 10, no. 5 (1990): 1–8; and Ted Galen Carpenter, "The U.S. Military Presence in the Philippines: Expensive and Unnecessary," Cato Institute Foreign Policy Briefing no. 12, July 29, 1991.

32. For a discussion of the marginal relevance of the Philippine bases for Far Eastern missions, see Paul Kattenburg, "New Strategies for U.S. Security Interests in Southeast Asia, the Indian Ocean, and the South Pacific Region," in *Collective Defense or Strategic Independence?* pp. 135–38.

33. Ibid., p. 136.

34. Ibid., pp. 136–39; Doug Bandow, "Does Uncle Sam Really Need the Bases?" *Defense and Diplomacy* 8 (November/December 1990): 38–41.

35. For criticisms of that assumption, see various chapters in *America Entangled: The Persian Gulf Crisis and Its Consequences*, ed. Ted Galen Carpenter (Washington: Cato Institute, 1991).

36. William E. Berry, Jr., "The Effects of the U.S. Military Bases on the Philippine Economy," *Contemporary Southeast Asia* 11 (March 1990): 306–33.

37. That long, unsavory association is described in Raymond Bonner, *Waltzing with a Dictator: The Marcoses and the Making of American Policy* (New York: Times Books, 1987).

38. See, for example, the comments of *National Review* Washington Bureau chief William McGurn. "Goodbye Subic Bay," *Wall Street Journal*, November 11, 1991, p. A20, and "Yankees Go home," *American Spectator*, January 1992, pp. 42–45. McGurn and others repeatedly refer to polls allegedly showing that an overwhelming majority of Filipinos favored the U.S. military presence. Some of those polls, however, apparently never existed. Following the senate vote, one American embassy official conceded, "I made the numbers up." Bob Drogin, "U.S. Overplayed Hand in Bid to Hold onto Bases," *Los Angeles Times*, September 28, 1991, p. A3.

39. Bob Drogin and Jim Mann, "U.S. Forces Recharting the Pacific," *Los Angeles Times*, October 15, 1991, p. A1; and Martin Walker, "U.S. Turns Expulsion into Expansion on Pacific Rim," *Guardian* (U.K.), October 23, 1991, p. 10.

40. John E. Yang, "Singapore Agrees to Host Navy Unit," *Washington Post*, January 4, 1992, p. A13. For a critique of that move, see Samuel Francis, "Needless Shift from Subic to Singapore?" *Washington Times*, January 9, 1992, p. G1.

41. George Bush, "U.S.-Australian Friendship Remains Firm and Deep," Excerpts from address to the Australian parliament, Canberra, January 2, 1992, *U.S. Department of State Dispatch*, January 13, 1992, p. 15. See also George Bush, "The U.S. and Singapore: Opportunities for a New Era," Address before the Singapore Lecture Group, Singapore, January 4, 1992, ibid., p. 19.

Chapter 5

1. Text of agreement, in U.S. Department of State, *U.S. Treaties and Other International Agreements*, vol. 5, part 1, 1954 (Washington: U.S. Government Printing Office, 1955), pp. 854–58. Provisions for CIA access can be inferred (despite the diplomatic jargon) in article V.

2. For a detailed account of the rationale for that "tilt" toward Pakistan, see Henry Kissinger, *White House Years* (Boston: Little, Brown, 1979), pp. 842–918.

3. The rationale for that policy reversal is described in Zbigniew Brzezinski, *Power and Principle: Memoirs of the National Security Adviser, 1977–1981* (New York: Farrar, Straus, Giroux, 1983), pp. 429, 432, 444, 448–49.

4. Murray Waas and Douglas Frantz, "Despite Ban, U.S. Arms Are Sold to Pakistan," *Los Angeles Times*, March 6, 1992, p. A1; and Steve Coll and David Hoffman, "Shipments to Pakistan Questioned," *Washington Post*, March 7, 1992, p. A1.

5. Leon T. Hadar, "The 'Green Peril': The Making of the Islamic Fundamentalist Threat," Cato Institute Policy Analysis no. 177, August 27, 1992, p. 5.

6. Accounts stressing the alleged threat of Islamic fundamentalism include "Fear of Fundies," *The Economist*, February 15, 1992, pp. 45–46; Amos Perlmutter, "Wishful Thinking about Islamic Fundamentalism," *Washington Post*, January 19, 1992; Barbara Crossette, "U.S. Aide Calls Muslim Militants Big Concern," *New York Times*, January 1, 1992; Robert S. Greenberger, "Islamic Fundamentalism's Rise in Sudan Sparks Concern over Movement's Spread," *Wall Street Journal*, March 16, 1992; and Craig Forman, "Islamic Resurgence Sweeps Soviet South," *Wall Street Journal*, October 9, 1991. More skeptical analyses include Douglas E. Streusand, "Abraham's Other Children: Is Islam an Enemy of the West?" *Policy Review* 54 (Fall 1989): 50–54; David Ignatius, "Islam in the West's Sights: The Wrong Crusade?" Outlook Section, *Washington Post*, March 8, 1992; and Hadar, "The Green Peril."

7. Pakistan's support for Hekmatyar has apparently been motivated more by calculations that such a strategy would prevent other *mujaheddin* leaders from creating a strong Afghan central government than by any enthusiasm for his brand of fundamentalism. Pakistani leaders across the political spectrum fear that a stable, united Afghanistan might act as a magnet for the Pushtun population in western Pakistan, thereby creating yet another threat to Pakistan's fragile sense of national unity. Conversely, Hekmatyar's willingness to act as an ally might enable Islamabad to influence the populations of eastern Afghanistan.

8. U.S. Department of State, *United States Treaties and Other International Agreements*, vol. 10, part 1, 1959 (Washington: U.S. Government Printing Office, 1960), p. 318.

9. Kissinger, p. 905.

10. *Congressional Record*, 85th Cong., 2d sess., March 6, 1958, 104, part 3, pp. 3537–38. For a discussion of the Eisenhower Doctrine and its implications, see Stephen E. Ambrose, *Eisenhower: The President* (New York: Simon & Schuster, 1984), pp. 381–83, 397, 463–75.

11. Kissinger, p. 895.

12. Kissinger, p. 1488 n. 7.

13. For a discussion of both nations' programs, see Leonard S. Spector with Jacqueline R. Smith, *Nuclear Ambitions: The Spread of Nuclear Weapons, 1989–1990* (Boulder, Colo.: Westview, 1990), pp. 63–117. The National Intelligence Council, a group of analysts in the office of the CIA director, reportedly has concluded that both India and Pakistan already have nuclear arsenals. Bill Gertz, "Israel, Pakistan, India Have Nuclear Bombs, Experts Say," *Washington Times,* June 20, 1991, p. A6. In early 1992 Pakistan's foreign secretary, Shahryar Khan, conceded publicly that his country had all the components necessary to build a nuclear explosive "device." R. Jeffrey Smith, "Pakistan Can Build One Nuclear Device, Foreign Official Says," *Washington Post,* February 7, 1992, p. A18.

14. Steve Coll, "South Asia Retains Its Nuclear Option," *Washington Post*, September 30, 1991, p. A1.

15. Steve Coll, "India Rejects Pakistani Bid for Talks on Nuclear Ban," *Washington Post,* June 8, 1991, p. A17.

16. Quoted in Edward A. Gargan, "U.S. Official in India to Discuss Limiting Spread of Nuclear Weapons," *New York Times,* November 11, 1991, p. A8.

17. International Institute for Strategic Studies, *Military Balance 1991–1992* (London: Brassey's 1991), pp. 161–63, 175–76. For a general discussion of the Indo-Pakistani political and military relationship, see Rodney W. Jones, "Old Quarrels and New Realities: Security in Southern Asia after the Cold War," *Washington Quarterly* 15 (Winter 1992): 105–28.

18. Quoted in Edward A. Gargan, "Diplomats Are Edgy As India Stubbornly Builds Its Nuclear Arsenal," *New York Times,* January 21, 1992, p. A13.

19. Steve Coll, "India Tests Controversial Agni Missile," *Washington Post,* May 30, 1992, p. A13.

20. Gargan, "Diplomats are Edgy."

21. Quoted in Steve Coll, "South Asia Retains Its Nuclear Option," p. A1.

22. Kissinger, pp. 895–96.

23. Jim Rogers, "Memo Asks Services to Draft Response to Possible India-Pakistan War," *Inside the Air Force,* May 8, 1992, p. 1.

24. Barbara Crossette, "Russia's Rocket Deal with India Leads U.S. to Impose Trade Bans," *New York Times,* May 12, 1992, p. A8.

25. The depth of Indian suspicions about U.S. intentions can be gauged from an incident in early 1991. In an effort to promote its proposal for a "next generation" cruise missile, General Dynamics Corporation prepared a briefing packet for think tank experts and other interested parties. To lend urgency to its call for a new missile, General Dynamics presented five illustrative war scenarios. One of those scenarios, set in the year 2000, posits a conflict with India when New Delhi prepares preemptive nuclear missile strikes against Pakistan because of an escalation of the crisis in Kashmir. In the ensuing clash, the United States ends up firing 190 "new generation" cruise missiles at a variety of Indian targets.

Even though the U.S. government was not involved in the preparation of the General Dynamics scenario, there was a firestorm of criticism throughout India. The

Telegraph, a Calcutta-based daily, gave the story front-page coverage with a banner headline, "Top Defense Firm Briefs Pentagon on How to Neutralize India." Other newspapers and magazines were only slightly less alarmist, and the public reaction was quite hostile to the United States. Selig S. Harrison, a senior associate at the Carnegie Endowment for International Peace, acknowledged that the incident had created "quite a sensation" throughout India. David C. Morrison, "Phony War Scenario Stirs India," *National Journal,* April 6, 1991, pp. 804–6.

26. For a discussion of the serious political tensions afflicting India, see Mohammed Ayoob, "Dateline India: The Deepening Crisis," *Foreign Policy* 85 (Winter 1991–92): 166–84.

Chapter 6

1. James F. Schnable, *The Joint Chiefs of Staff and National Policy, 1945–1947* (Wilmington: University of Delaware Press, 1979), chap. 8; and F. Parkinson, *Latin America, the Cold War, and the World Powers, 1945–1973* (Beverly Hills: Sage, 1974), pp. 11–12.

2. Text of the Rio Treaty, in *The Major International Treaties since 1945,* ed. J. A. S. Grenville and Bernard Wasserstein (London: Mathuen, 1987), pp. 88–92.

3. Ibid., p. 92.

4. The best account of that operation is Richard H. Immerman, *The CIA in Guatemala* (Austin: University of Texas Press, 1982).

5. Gerald K. Haines, "Under the Eagle's Wing: The Franklin Roosevelt Administration Forges an American Hemisphere," *Diplomatic History* 1 (Fall 1977): 373–88; David Green, *The Containment of Latin America: A History of the Myths and Realities of the Good Neighbor Policy* (Chicago: Quadrangle, 1971); and Donald M. Dozer, *Are We Good Neighbors? Three Decades of Inter-American Relations, 1930–1960* (Gainesville: University of Florida Press, 1959).

6. Walter LaFeber, *Inevitable Revolutions* (New York: W. W. Norton, 1984), pp. 92–95.

7. Alexander M. Haig, Jr., *Caveat: Realism, Reagan, and Foreign Policy* (New York: Macmillan, 1984), p. 90.

8. Carlos Andrés Pérez, "OAS Opportunities," *Foreign Policy* 80 (Fall 1990): 53.

9. For further discussions of that thesis, see Ted Galen Carpenter, "Back to a Monroe Doctrine," *Wall Street Journal,* May 8, 1988; and Alan Tonelson, "A New Central American and Caribbean Strategy," in *An American Vision: Policies for the '90s,* ed. Edward H. Crane and David Boaz (Washington: Cato Institute, 1989), pp. 183–202.

10. For a discussion of Latin American reactions to the U.S. invasion of Panama and other manifestations of aggressive unilateralism, see Abraham F. Lowenthal, "Rediscovering Latin America," *Foreign Affairs* 69 (Fall 1990): 31–32.

11. Text of resolution, in *U.S. Department of State Dispatch,* October 7, 1991, p. 750.

12. Robert A. Pastor, "Haiti Is Not Alone," *New York Times,* October 4, 1991, p. A31.

13. "Backing Up Principle with Justified Muscle," *Los Angeles Times,* October 3, 1991, p. B10.

14. Georgie Anne Geyer, "Without a Helping Hand," *Washington Times,* November 22, 1991, p. F1. An equally ambitious nation-building scheme was offered by

Peter Hakim, a senior fellow of the Inter-American Dialogue. Peter Hakim, "Saving Haiti from Itself," *Washington Post*, May 31, 1992, p. C1.

15. See David J. Scheffer, "Toward a Modern Doctrine of Humanitarian Intervention," *University of Toledo Law Review* 23 (Winter 1992): 275, 292; and Barbara Crossette, "U.S. Is Discussing an Outside Force to Stabilize Haiti," *New York Times*, June 6, 1992, p. A1.

16. Robert A. Pastor, "Establish a Collective Defense of Democracy," *Miami Herald*, February 9, 1992, p. C1.

17. "A Military Force for the Americas," editorial, *New York Times*, March 24, 1992, p. A20.

Chapter 7

1. Charles Krauthammer, "The Unipolar Moment," *Foreign Affairs* 70, no. 1 (1992): 23–32; Charles Krauthammer, "Bless Our Pax Americana," *Washington Post*, March 22, 1991, p. A25; Ben J. Wattenberg, "Neo-Manifest Destinitarianism," in *America's Purpose: New Visions of U.S. Foreign Policy*, ed. Owen Harries (San Francisco: ICS Press, 1991); pp. 107–14; and Joshua Muravchik, "At Last, Pax Americana," *New York Times*, January 24, 1991, p. A19.

2. Tom Bethell, "Pat's Answers," *American Spectator*, February 1992, p. 14.

3. Quoted in Scott Sullivan, "The Birth of a New NATO," *Newsweek*, November 18, 1991, p. 32.

4. Ann Devroy and Michael Dobbs, "Bush Warns Ukraine on Independence," *Washington Post*, August 2, 1991, p. A1.

5. Thomas L. Friedman, "Baker Urges End to Yugoslav Rift," *New York Times*, June 22, 1991, p. A1.

6. David Binder, "U.S. Deplores Moves," *New York Times*, June 26, 1991, p. A7.

7. See, for example, Charles Krauthammer, "Good Morning, Vietnam," *Washington Post*, April 19, 1991, p. A23; Charles Krauthammer, "Tiananmen II," *Washington Post*, April 5, 1991, p. A19; Samir al Khalil, "Do It Right; March to Baghdad," *New York Times*, March 27, 1991, p. A23; Laurie Mylroie, "Help the Iraqi Resistance," *Wall Street Journal*, March 26, 1991, p. A22; Flora Lewis, "America Deserts the Rebels Cynically," *New York Times*, April 3, 1991, p. A21; Richard Cohen, "A Moral Failure," *Washington Post*, April 5, 1991, p. A19; Joshua Muravchik, "The Right to Intervene," *Washington Post*, April 23, 1991, p. A19; and A. M. Rosenthal, "Mistakes of the War," *New York Times*, July 12, 1991, p. A29.

8. David Ignatius, "A Coup in Iraq: Why It Failed and How It May Yet Succeed," *Washington Post*, July 21, 1991, p. C1; William Safire, "The April Surprise," *New York Times*, January 13, 1992, p. A15; William Safire, "Declaring a War of Nerves," *New York Times*, January 20, 1992, p. A19; and Patrick E. Tyler, "Plan on Iraq Coup Told to Congress," *New York Times*, February 9, 1992, p. A1.

9. William Safire, "Saddam's Deadline," *New York Times*, July 22, 1991, p. A15.

10. Joseph Albright, "Schwarzkopf: Bush Right to End War," *Atlanta Constitution*, October 24, 1991, p. 2.

11. That was a strategy strongly embraced by many of the policy experts who subsequently advocated military action to prevent Iraq's preeminence in the region. See, for example, Laurie Mylroie, "The Baghdad Alternative," *Orbis* 32 (Summer 1988): 339–54; and Daniel Pipes and Laurie Mylroie, "Back Iraq," *New Republic*, April 27, 1987, pp. 14–15.

12. Youssef M. Ibrahim, "Assad and Mubarak Meet and Oppose Breakup of Iraq," *New York Times*, April 2, 1991, p. A8; Laurie Mylroie, "Led Astray by the Saudis in Iraq," *Wall Street Journal*, April 10, 1991, p. A22; and Andrew Rosenthal, "U.S., Fearing Iraqi Breakup, Is Said to Rule Out Action to Aid Anti-Hussein Rebels," *New York Times*, March 27, 1991, p. A1.

13. George Bush, "Toward a New World Order," Address before a joint session of Congress, September 11, 1990, *U.S. Department of State Dispatch*, September 17, 1990, p. 91; George Bush, "U.S. Increases Commitment in Operation Desert Shield," Opening remarks at a news conference at the White House, November 8, 1990, *U.S. Department of State Dispatch*, November 12, 1990, p. 258; and James A. Baker III, "Why America Is in the Gulf," Address before the Los Angeles World Affairs Council, October 29, 1990, *U.S. Department of State Dispatch*, November 5, 1990, p. 235.

14. Robert W. Tucker and David C. Hendrickson, *The Imperial Temptation: The New World Order and America's Purpose* (New York: Council on Foreign Relations Press, 1992), p. 99. The odious record of the Kuwaiti government since its restoration to power is also increasingly apparent. See *A Victory Turned Sour: Human Rights in Kuwait since Liberation* (New York: Middle East Watch, 1991).

15. John M. Goshko, "Wary U.S. Declines to Criticize Algerian Moves," *Washington Post*, January 14, 1992, p. A16. The State Department subsequently adopted a more critical position, but the initial response seems more indicative of the administration's inclinations.

16. Discussions of that theme include Earl C. Ravenal, "The Case for Adjustment," *Foreign Policy* 81 (Winter 1990–91): 3–19; David C. Morrison, "Old World Disorder," *National Journal*, March 30, 1991, p. 766; Thomas L. Friedman, "Today's Threat to Peace Is the Guy Down the Street," *New York Times*, June 2, 1991, p. E3; and Ted Galen Carpenter, "The New World Disorder," *Foreign Policy* 84 (Fall 1991): 24–39.

17. Krauthammer, "Unipolar Moment," p. 23.

18. Ibid., pp. 24, 33.

19. See, for example, Stanley Meisler, "Adjusting to a Unipolar World," *Los Angeles Times*, April 5, 1991, p. A5; Bob Drogin, "U.S.-Manila Rift over War Reopens," *Los Angeles Times*, February 2, 1991, p. A10; Urban C. Lehner, "More Japanese See a 'Fearsome' U.S. after Gulf Victory," *Wall Street Journal*, March 14, 1991, p. A15; "Mitterrand a Pawn of U.S., Foe Charges," *Washington Times*, March 19, 1991, p. A5; and Tom Wicker, "A Not-So-New World Order," *New York Times*, June 5, 1991, p. A29.

20. William Drozdiak, "Tensions between France and U.S. Said to Turn Allies into Rivals," *Washington Post*, January 22, 1992, p. A25. A few month earlier, French officials, including Foreign Minister Roland Dumas, had issued similar warnings at a meeting of the Socialist party. "France Warns U.S. on World Role," U.S. Department of Defense *Current News*, September 3, 1991, p. 16.

21. Important discussions of that tendency include Kenneth N. Waltz, *Theory of International Politics* (Reading, Mass.: Addison-Wesley, 1979); and Stephen M. Walt, *The Origins of Alliances* (Ithaca, N.Y.: Cornell University Press, 1987).

22. White House, Office of the Press Secretary, Text of State of the Union Address, January 28, 1992, p. 2.

23. Patrick E. Tyler, "U.S. Strategy Plan Calls for Insuring No Rivals Develop," *New York Times*, March 8, 1992, p. A1; and Patrick E. Tyler, "Excerpts from Pentagon's

Plan: Prevent the Emergence of a New Rival," *New York Times,* March 8, 1992, p. A14. After the adverse diplomatic fallout caused by the comments in the leaked draft, the offending passages were, of course, deleted from the final version. Instead, there was the usual pablum about enduring allied solidarity and cooperation. Barton Gellman, "Pentagon Abandons Goal of Thwarting U.S. Rivals," *Washington Post,* May 24, 1992, p. A1.

24. Text of President Bush's address to the nation, *Washington Post,* September 28, 1991, p. A22.

25. Examples of such calls include "Backing Up Principle with Justified Muscle," editorial, *Los Angeles Times,* October 3, 1991, p. B10; Robert A. Pastor, "Haiti Is Not Alone," *New York Times,* October 4, 1991, p. A31; Joel Dreyfus, "Don't Forget Haiti," *Washington Post,* November 12, 1991, p. A21; and Georgie Anne Geyer, "Without a Helping Hand," *Washington Times,* November 22, 1991, p. F1.

26. "Blessed are the Peacemakers: Troops—Not Sanctions—Needed to Halt Yugoslav Carnage, Milosevic's Aggression," Center for Security Policy Decision Brief no. 92-D57, Washington, May 29, 1992, p. 4. For a discussion of the efforts of opinion makers to persuade the Bush administration to intervene militarily in the Yugoslavian conflict, see Ted Galen Carpenter, "Foreign Policy Masochism: The Campaign for U.S. Intervention in Yugoslavia," Cato Institute Foreign Policy Briefing no. 19, July 1, 1992.

27. Monteagle Stearns, *Entangled Allies: U.S. Policy toward Greece, Turkey, and Cyprus* (New York: Council on Foreign Relations Press, 1992).

28. Dita Smith, "Cyprus Talks Gain Tentative Approval," *Washington Post,* August 3, 1991, p. A4.

29. Quoted in "The Bomb Club," *Indianapolis Star,* January 27, 1992, p. 8.

30. See, for example, William H. Lewis and Christopher C. Joyner, "Proliferation of Unconventional Weapons: The Case for Coercive Arms Control," *Comparative Strategy* 10 (Fall 1991): 299–309.

31. For discussions of the expanding role of the military in the war on drugs, see Ted Galen Carpenter and R. Channing Rouse, "Perilous Panacea: The Military in the Drug War," Cato Institute Policy Analysis no. 128, February 15, 1990; Charles Lane et al., "The Newest War," *Newsweek,* January 6, 1992, pp. 18–23; David C. Morrison, "Police Action," *National Journal,* February 1, 1992, pp. 267–70; and David Isenberg, "The Pentagon's War on Drugs: The Ultimate Bad Trip," *Defense Monitor* 21, no. 4 (1992): 1–8.

32. For examples of this thesis, see Joshua Muravchik, *Exporting Democracy: Fulfilling America's Destiny* (Washington: AEI Press, 1991); Larry Diamond, "An American Foreign Policy for Democracy," Progressive Policy Report no. 11, Progressive Policy Institute, Washington, July 1991; Michael Ledeen, "The Second Democratic Revolution," *American Spectator,* October 1990, pp. 19–22; and Samuel P. Huntington, *The Third Wave: Democratization in the Late Twentieth Century* (Norman: University of Oklahoma Press, 1991).

33. Jacquelyn Walsh, "Big Weapon in Anti-Drug War," *Bulletin of Atomic Scientists,* June 1990, p. 5.

34. Quoted in R. W. Apple, Jr., "Battle Cry in Congress," *New York Times,* October 1, 1991, p. A10.

35. Gregory Vistica, "U.S. Economic Recovery Slowed by Military Cuts, Cheney Says," *San Diego Union,* November 13, 1991, p. 1. There was a veritable flood of press accounts in late 1991 and early 1992 echoing the arguments of Cheney et al.

concerning the potential adverse effect on jobs of lower military spending. Most of those stories also stressed the impact on the local economy. For representative examples, see Ted Shelsby, "Sword Hangs over State," *Baltimore Sun*, February 2, 1992, p. D1; Ralph Vartabedian, "200,000 State Jobs Seen Periled by Defense Cuts," *Los Angeles Times*, January 30, 1992, p. A1; Art Pine, "Danger to Jobs May Limit Defense Cuts," *Los Angeles Times*, January 31, 1992, p. A1; George Judson, "For the People of Groton, Peace Pays No Dividend," *New York Times*, January 30, 1992, p. A16; Ron Hutcheson and Dave Montgomery, "Defense Cuts Drop a Bomb on North Texas," *Fort Worth Star-Telegram*, January 30, 1992, p. A4; Helen Dewar, "With Cold War Won, Jobs Are Being Lost," *Washington Post*, February 14, 1992, p. A1; Elizabeth Ross, "Two States Hit by Defense Cuts," *Christian Science Monitor*, February 11, 1992, p. A6; and "Arms Cuts: At War with Recovery," *Business Week*, February 17, 1992, p. 29. Some of the stories may have reflected an understandable desire to address an important issue, but the number of articles and their common "spin"— several "news" stories were little more than thinly disguised editorials—had all the earmarks of a propaganda campaign by the venerable Cold War foreign policy issue network.

36. *Newsweek*, April 22, 1991, p. 19.

37. Elizabeth Shogren, "Powell, Soviet Brass Bemoan Budget Slashes," *Los Angeles Times*, July 24, 1991, p. A4.

38. Rowan Scarborough, "Hill Gets Way on Defense," *Washington Times*, November 23, 1991, p. A1. On the pervasive role of congressional vested interests, see Robert Higgs, "Beware the Pork Hawk," *Reason*, June 1989, pp. 28–34.

39. "House Defense Funding Bill Keeps Cuts in SDI and B-2," *Congressional Quarterly*, June 8, 1991, pp. 1518–19.

40. Jerome R. Watson, "Guard Facing Its Toughest Battle," *Chicago Sun-Times*, September 16, 1991, p. 5.

41. Don M. Snider, "Why Is Congress Scared of the Reserves?" *New York Times*, August 5, 1991, p. A13.

42. Higgs, "Beware the Pork Hawk."

43. Barton Gellman and Tom Kenworthy, "Pentagon Outlines Plan to Shut Bases in Europe," *Washington Post*, July 31, 1991, p. A9. For a discussion of the long-standing pattern of congressional obstruction of domestic base closures, see Charlotte Twight, "Department of Defense Attempts to Close Military Bases: The Political Economy of Congressional Resistance," in *Arms, Politics and the Economy*, ed. Robert Higgs (New York: Holmes and Meier, 1990), pp. 236–72.

44. James M. Buchanan and Gordon Tullock, *The Calculus of Consent* (Ann Arbor: University of Michigan Press, 1965), p. 286.

45. For a discussion of issue networks and their roles, see Hugh Heclo, "Issue Networks and the Executive Establishment," in *Public Administration: Concepts and Cases*, 4th ed., ed. Richard J. Stillman II (Boston: Houghton Mifflin, 1988), pp. 408–17.

46. Robert Higgs, "U.S. Military Spending in the Cold War Era: Opportunity Costs, Foreign Crises, and Domestic Constraints," Cato Institute Policy Analysis no 114, November 30, 1988.

47. Quoted in Tom Wicker, "Questions at the CIA," *New York Times*, November 14, 1991, p. A29.

48. Ibid.

49. That sentiment had even begun to be reflected in portions of the journalistic and think tank communities. One of the earliest manifestations was a collection of

articles by Col. Harry G. Summers, Jr., Jack Beatty, Richard A. Stubbing, Richard A. Mendel, and David C. Morrison in the July 1989 issue of the *Atlantic*. During the spring and early summer of 1990, there was a spate of articles and studies suggesting reductions in the military budget of up to 50 percent over a 5- to 10-year period. See, for example, William W. Kaufmann, *Glasnost, Perestroika, and U.S. Defense Spending* (Washington: Brookings Institution, 1990); Stephen Alexis Cain and Natalie J. Goldring, "Restructuring the U.S. Military: Defense Needs in the 21st Century," Report by the Defense Budget Task Force of the Committee for National Security and the Defense Budget Project, Washington, March 1990; "$150 Billion a Year: Where to Find It," editorial, *New York Times*, March 8 and 9, 1990; and Lee Smith, "What We Really Need for Defense," *Fortune*, June 4, 1990, pp. 163–68.

50. Quoted in Eric Schmitt, "Pentagon Making a List of Choices for Spending Cuts," *New York Times*, November 24, 1991, p. A1.

51. Eric Schmitt, "Pentagon Says More Budget Cuts Would Hurt Combat Effectiveness," *New York Times*, February 1, 1992, p. A9.

52. Otis Pike, "Citizens Should Rule U.S. War Policy," *Chicago Sun-Times*, February 18, 1992, p. 25.

53. Quoted in David Steigman, "Pentagon Eyes Downsizing Carrier Force to 10," *Navy Times*, November 25, 1991, p. 26. Emphasis added.

54. "Sentiment Slowly Builds for Deep U.S. Defense Reductions," *Wall Street Journal*, September 27, 1991, p. A1.

55. Examples include Zbigniew Brzezinski, "Selective Global Commitment," *Foreign Affairs* 70 (Fall 1991): 1–20; Joseph S. Nye, Jr., "What New World Order?" *Foreign Affairs* 71 (Spring 1992): 83–96; David C. Hendrickson, "The Renovation of American Foreign Policy," ibid., pp. 48–63; Andrew C. Goldberg, "Selective Engagement: U.S. National Security Policy in the 1990s," *Washington Quarterly* 15 (Summer 1992): 15–24; James Chace, *The Consequences of the Peace: The New Internationalism and American Foreign Policy* (New York: Oxford University Press, 1992); James Schlesinger, "New Instabilities, New Priorities," *Foreign Policy* 85 (Winter 1991–92): 3–24; and John Lewis Gaddis, *The United States and the End of the Cold War* (New York: Oxford University Press, 1992). Despite the rhetoric about selectivity, the commitments that those writers recommend retaining are not very selective. None of the advocates of selective engagement, for example, proposes jettisoning NATO or the major East Asian alliances—or even eliminating the U.S. troop presence in the two regions. Unfortunately, most of the expense of Washington's overseas military obligations is due to such alliances, not peripheral commitments elsewhere. Eliminating minor commitments (formal or informal) in the Third World will, therefore, not produce much of a peace dividend.

Chapter 8

1. Patrick E. Tyler, "Pentagon Imagines New Enemies to Fight in Post–Cold War Era," *New York Times*, February 17, 1992, p. A1; Patrick E. Tyler, "7 Hypothetical Conflicts Foreseen by Pentagon," *New York Times*, February 17, 1992, p. A8; Barton Gellman, "Pentagon War Scenario Spotlights Russia," *Washington Post*, February 20, 1992, p. A1.

2. Earl C. Ravenal, *Designing Defense for a New World Order: The Military Budget in 1992 and Beyond* (Washington: Cato Institute, 1991).

3. "Pentagon Spurns Aspin's Budget Cuts as 'Political,'" *Washington Post*, February 28, 1992, p. A14. For a critique of the anemic and sometimes contradictory alternatives to the administration's strategy offered by Aspin and other congressional leaders, see Jeffrey R. Gerlach, "Pentagon Myths and Global Realities," Cato Institute Policy Analysis no. 171, May 24, 1992, pp. 12–14.

4. Barton Gellman, "Debate on Military's Future Crystallizes around 'Enemies List,'" *Washington Post*, February 26, 1992, p. A20.

5. Lyndon B. Johnson, "Peace without Conquest," Address at Johns Hopkins University, April 7, 1965, in *Public Papers of the Presidents: Lyndon B. Johnson, 1965* (Washington: Government Printing Office, 1966), p. 394.

6. Melvyn P. Leffler, "From the Truman Doctrine to the Carter Doctrine: Lessons and Dilemmas of the Cold War," *Diplomatic History* 7 (Fall 1983): 252–53.

7. Stephen E. Ambrose, *Eisenhower: The President* (New York: Simon & Schuster, 1984), p. 180; see also Robert A. Divine, *Eisenhower and the Cold War* (New York: Oxford University Press, 1981), p. 41.

8. Examples include Anthony Lewis, "Weakness and Shame," *New York Times*, June 14, 1992, p. E19; Leslie H. Gelb, "A Balkan Plan," *New York Times*, June 1, 1992, p. A17; and Center for Security Policy, "Blessed Are the Peacemakers: Troops—Not Sanctions—Needed to Halt Yugoslav Carnage," Decision Brief no. 92-D57, May 29, 1992. Critiques of such arguments include Christopher Layne, "Tragedy in the Balkans. So What?" *New York Times*, May 29, 1992, p. A29; Benjamin Schwarz, "Leave the Little Wars Alone," *Los Angeles Times*, June 8, 1992; Owen Harries, "Yugoslavia and the Politics of Memory," *Washington Times*, June 28, 1992, p. B3; and Ted Galen Carpenter, "Foreign Policy Masochism: The Campaign for U.S. Intervention in Yugoslavia," Cato Institute Foreign Policy Briefing no. 19, July 1, 1992, pp. 1–2, 8–10.

9. For a more detailed discussion of a coercive nonproliferation strategy and its problems, see Ted Galen Carpenter, "A New Proliferation Policy," *National Interest* 28 (Summer 1992): 66–68.

10. Robert W. Tucker and David C. Hendrickson, *The Imperial Temptation: The New World Order and America's Purpose* (New York: Council on Foreign Relations Press, 1992), p. 113.

11. W. B. Allen, ed. *George Washington: A Collection* (Indianapolis: Liberty Classics, 1988), p. 525.

12. See Richard N. Gardner, "The Comeback of Liberal Internationalism," *Washington Quarterly* 13 (Summer 1990): 23–39; Bruce Russett and James S. Sutterlin, "The UN in a New World Order," *Foreign Affairs* 70 (Spring 1991): 69–83; Brian Urquhart, "Who Can Stop Civil Wars?" *New York Times*, December 29, 1991, p. E9; Joseph S. Nye, Jr., "Create a UN Fire Brigade," *New York Times*, February 1, 1992, p. A21; and David J. Scheffer, "Toward a Modern Doctrine of Humanitarian Intervention," *University of Toledo Law Review* 23 (Winter 1992): 253–93. More critical analyses include Alan L. Keyes, "The UN, A Wobbly House of Cards," *Wall Street Journal*, August 30, 1990, p. A9; and Giulio M. Gallarotti, "The Limits of International Organization: Systematic Failure in the Management of International Relations," *International Organization* 45 (Spring 1991): 183–220.

13. For a discussion of that ploy, see Ted Galen Carpenter, "Direct Military Intervention," in *Intervention in the 1980s: U.S. Policy in the Third World*, ed. Peter J. Schraeder (Boulder, Colo.: Lynne Rienner, 1988), pp. 131–44.

14. For an early warning of log-rolling dangers in the United Nations—including citing the Yugoslavian crisis as a specific example—see Ted Galen Carpenter, "Collective Security Pitfalls," in *The Security Roles of the United Nations,* Proceedings of the Conference Sponsored by National Defense University's Institute for National Security Studies and the Joint Chiefs of Staff's Strategic Plans and Policy Directorate, October 9–10, 1991, Washington, D.C., pp. 17–19.

15. Robert A. Taft, *A Foreign Policy for Americans* (Garden City, N.J.: Doubleday, 1951), passim.

16. See, for example, Joshua Muravchik, *Exporting Democracy: Fulfilling America's Destiny* (Washington: AEI Press, 1991); Larry Diamond, "An American Foreign Policy for Democracy," Progressive Policy Institute Report no. 11, Washington, July 1991; and Bruce Russett, "Politics and Alternative Security: Toward a More Democratic, Therefore More Peaceful, World," in *Alternative Security: Living without Nuclear Deterrence,* ed. Burns H. Weston (Boulder, Colo.: Westview, 1991), pp. 107–35. Those authors rely extensively on earlier works, including R. J. Rummel, "The Relationship between National Attributes and Foreign Policy Behavior," in *Quantitative International Politics: Insights and Evidence,* ed. J. D. Singer (New York: Free Press, 1968), pp. 187–214; R. J. Rummel, "The Freedom Factor," *Reason,* July 1983, pp. 32–38; and Michael W. Doyle, "Liberalism and World Politics," *American Political Science Review* 80 no. 4 (December 1986): 1151–69.

17. Vladimir Bukovsky, "Drowning Democracy," *National Review,* September 13, 1991, p. 33.

18. Kenneth N. Waltz, *Theory of International Politics* (Reading, Mass.: Addison-Wesley, 1979); and Stephen M. Walt, *The Origins of Alliances* (Ithaca, N.Y.: Cornell University Press, 1987).

19. John Quincy Adams, Address of July 4, 1821, in *John Quincy Adams and American Continental Empire: Letters, Speeches, and Papers,* ed. Walter LaFeber (Chicago: Quadrangle, 1965), p. 45.

20. Text of Bush's speech, *New York Times,* December 8, 1991, p. A24.

21. David Boren, "The New Isolationism: A Threat to National Security," Speech at the American University, Washington, D.C., January 26, 1992, unpublished text, pp. 2–3.

22. "U.S. is Committed to Presence in Europe, NATO's Top Commander Asserts," *Baltimore Sun,* November 25, 1991, p. 6. Galvin used the same simplistic rhetoric in testimony before the Senate Armed Services Committee. John Lancaster, "Top General Supports 150,000 U.S. Troops in Europe as a Hedge," *Washington Post,* March 4, 1992, p. A20.

23. See, for example, George Weigel, "On the Road to Isolationism?" *Commentary,* January 1992, pp. 36–42; and Richard J. Barnet, "Domestic Urges, Foreign Obsession," *American Prospect* 8 (Winter 1992): 127–29.

24. Alan Tonelson "Fearful Opposition," *Washington Times,* February 18, 1992, p. E1. Tonelson did not need to look further than the op-ed page on which his article appeared for confirmation of his argument. Paired with his piece was a diatribe by Sen. Phil Gramm (R-Tex.), "Threadbare Philosophy," that was virtually nothing but a parade of caricatures and name calling.

25. Christopher Layne, "Bush's 'Isolationist' Straw Man," *Washington Post,* December 22, 1991, p. C7.

26. For arguments focusing on economic interdependence, see George Melloan, "'Bring the Boys Home' at What Price?" *Wall Street Journal,* September 23, 1991,

p. A15; Henry R. Nau, *The Myth of America's Decline* (New York: Oxford University Press, 1990); and Robert L. Bartley, "A Win-Win Game," in *America's Purpose: New Visions of U.S. Foreign Policy*, ed. Owen Harries (San Francisco: ICS Press, 1991), pp. 75–79. For a more general presentation of the interdependence argument, see Joseph S. Nye, Jr., *Bound to Lead: The Changing Nature of American Power* (New York: Basic Books, 1990); and for a very broad definition of the concept, see Jeremy Rifkin, *Biosphere Politics: A New Consciousness for a New Century* (New York: Crown, 1991).

27. David Hoffman and Patrick E. Tyler, "Bush Denounces Saddam as Threat to Arabs, West," *Washington Post*, August 15, 1990, p. A31. Les Aspin was equally alarmist, contending that "if we allow Saddam to control half of the world's oil supply, he will control our economy—determining our rate of inflation, our interest rates, our rate of growth." Les Aspin, "Define Our Goals in the Gulf," *Washington Post*, August 10, 1990, p. A15.

28. Andrew Rosenthal, "Seeking Voter Reward, Bush Still Predicts Fall of Hussein," *New York Times*, January 17, 1992, p. A8.

29. Doug Bandow, "The Myth of Iraq's Oil Stranglehold," *New York Times*, September 16, 1990.

30. Jonathan Marshall, "Economists Say Iraq's Threat to U.S. Oil Supply is Exaggerated," *San Francisco Chronicle*, October 29, 1990.

31. David R. Henderson, "The Myth of Saddam's Oil Stranglehold," in *America Entangled: The Persian Gulf Crisis and Its Consequences*, ed. Ted Galen Carpenter (Washington: Cato Institute, 1991), p. 43. See also David R. Henderson, "Do We Need to Go to War for Oil?" Cato Institute Foreign Policy Briefing no. 4, October 24, 1990.

32. The other justifications offered by the Bush administration and its supporters do not hold up either. See Christopher Layne, "Why the Gulf War Was Not in the National Interest," *Atlantic*, July 1991, pp. 55, 65–81; and Tucker and Hendrickson, pp. 80–119.

33. See, for example, Michael Shafer, "Mineral Myths," *Foreign Policy* 47 (Summer 1982): 154–71.

34. Patrick J. Buchanan, "America First—and Second, and Third," *National Interest* 19 (Spring 1990): 77–82; and "Now That Red Is Dead, Come Home America," *Washington Post*, September 8, 1991, p. C1.

35. James D. Richardson, ed., *A Compilation of the Messages and Papers of the Presidents, 1789–1897* (Washington: Government Printing Office, 1898), vol. 1, p. 323.

36. For an articulate example of such reasoning, see Eugene V. Rostow, "A Breakfast for Bonaparte: There Is No Alternative Strategy," in *Collective Defense or Strategic Independence? Alternative Strategies for the Future*, ed. Ted Galen Carpenter (Lexington, Mass.: Lexington Books, 1989), pp. 3–20.

37. Carpenter, "A New Proliferation Policy," pp. 63–66.

38. Carl Kaysen, Robert S. McNamara, and George W. Rathjens, "Nuclear Weapons after the Cold War," *Foreign Affairs* 70 (Fall 1991): 95–110.

39. For examples of that reasoning, see David C. Morrison, "Where's the Threat?" *National Journal*, October 26, 1991, p. 2629; "A Meaningful SDI Mission," editorial, *Boston Globe*, November 2, 1991, p. 18; and Matt Hansen, "Sounding Taps for Star Wars and the Stealth Bomber," *Defense Monitor* 20, no. 5 (1991): 1–8.

40. Gerlach, pp. 3–6. A Congressional Budget Office Study concluded that to maintain the base force structure outlined by the Bush administration, expenditures

would have to rise by $20 billion to $65 billion by the middle of the next decade. "Fiscal Implications of the Administration's Proposed Base Force," CBO Staff Memorandum, December 1991, p. 11.

41. International Institute for Strategic Studies, *The Military Balance, 1991–1992* (London: Brassey's, 1991), pp. 55, 58, 165.

42. One especially unpleasant consequence of an interventionist foreign policy has been the inexorable expansion of the powers of the federal government and the corresponding erosion of individual liberties. The best discussion of the connection between Washington's involvement in wars and other international crises and the growth of federal power is Robert Higgs, *Crisis and Leviathan: Critical Episodes in the Growth of American Government* (New York: Oxford University Press, 1987).

Index

nuclear arms control initiative, 97;
policy of continued U.S. Pacific
presence, 111–12; policy toward
Japan, 60, 71; position on alliance
with Pakistan, 115–16; position on
ANZUS revival, 98; position on
military commitment to South
Korea, 74, 87–90; support for
NATO, 11–13; thwarts independent
European military initiatives, 3, 17

Cam Ranh Bay naval base, Vietnam,
98, 108
Caribbean Basin, 132
Carter administration: human rights
policy of, 130; proposal for troop
withdrawal from Korea, 87; relations
with Pakistan, 114–15
Castro, Fidel, 130, 131
Chace, James, 35
Cha Young Koo, 68, 89
Cheney, Richard B.: on effect of
defense spending cuts, 158; on
Japan's role in world, 60–61; on
proposed defense spending cuts,
159–60; on threats, 164; on U.S.
commitment to Asia-Pacific region,
80–81; on U.S. military presence in
Europe, 43
Chile, 129
China: economic performance of, 50;
intervention in Korean War, 74, 77;
as military threat, 47, 49–50, 79–80,
99, 108; navy of, 108, 211 n. 12, 214
n. 9; relations with South Korea, 78;
U.S. relations with, 173
CIA (Central Intelligence Agency):
justification for, 162–63; military
assistance to *mujaheddin*, 117; power
base of, 140; proposed destabilizing
role in exporting democracy, 184–85;
sponsors coup in Guatemala (1954),
129
CIS. *See* Commonwealth of
Independent States (CIS)
Clark Air Base, Philippines, 103–4,
105, 107, 110–11
Cobden, Richard, 195
Cohen, Richard, 35
Commonwealth of Independent States
(CIS), 14; nuclear weapons in,
31–32; as potential threat, 45, 98;
uncertainty about, 31–33

Communism: in Cuba, 130–31; in
Latin America, 129
Conference on Security and
Cooperation in Europe (CSCE):
approval of post–Cold War NATO
role, 16–17; growing importance of,
40; relation of NATO to, 34
Connally, Tom, 77
Conventional Forces in Europe (CFE)
Treaty, 13
Corbin, Marcus, 81
Crazy-state phenomenon, 200–201
Crimea, 33
Crowe, William, 48
CSCE. *See* Conference on Security and
Cooperation in Europe (CSCE)
Cuba, 5, 130, 132
Cyprus, 154–55

Daisy chain reasoning, 171–72
Decisionmaking: flexible and
autonomous, 7; proposal for U.S.
autonomous, 179–83
Defense spending. *See* Military
spending; Military spending, U.S.
Defense system, U.S., 196–202
de Gaulle, Charles, 23–24, 39
Democracy: exportation of, 156–57; as
global system, 184–87. *See also*
National Endowment for Democracy
(NED)
Democratic People's Republic of Korea
(DPRK). *See* North Korea
Deng Xiao Peng, 50
Dependence: alleged U.S. resource,
191–92, 194; European military,
38–45; Japanese military, 50–67;
Korean military, 74, 82–86
Deterrence strategy, U.S., 196–202
Dibb report, 96
Dixon, Alan, 160
Dominican Republic, 129, 133
Domino theory, 171–72, 178
DPRK (Democratic People's Republic
of Korea). *See* North Korea
Draft Extension Act, 26
Drug war, 156, 157

Eagleburger, Lawrence S., 142
East Asian nations: fear of Japan,
67–68; U.S. desire for stability
among, 69–71, 80–81; as U.S.
security interest, 80, 177
Eastern Europe: interest of Western
Europe in, 34; military and political

232

conflict in, 3–4, 6, 33–34. *See also* Yugoslavia

Economic assistance: from Japan, 56, 59, 63; from United States to Latin America, 129; from United States to Pakistan, 115

Economic interdependence theme, 191–92

The Economist, 36

Eisenhower, Dwight D.: domino theory of, 171–72; on U.S. troop presence in Europe, 12, 22–23

Eisenhower administration: isolation policy for Cuba, 131; Korean War strategy of, 78; relations with Pakistan, 113

Eisenhower Doctrine (1958), 118

Enrile, Juan Ponce, 104

Eto, Jun, 64

Europe: devolution of responsibility to, 46; U.S. strategy to maintain dependence of, 38–45. *See also* Eastern Europe; Western Europe

European Community (EC): economic strength of, 45; growing independence of, 2–3; Maastricht meeting (1991), 40; role in East European conflict, 41–42

Evans, Rowland, 44

Exon, J. James, 170

Falkland Islands, 132

Fallows, James, 55

Fisher, Richard, 100

Foglietta, Thomas M., 161

Foreign policy: Cold War iron triangle in United States, 162–64; of global democracy, 184–85; global stability as basis for U.S., 141–47; justification for interventionist, 163; less interventionist, 167; proposal for post–Cold War, 183–89. *See also* Interventionist policy, U.S.; Military alliances; Military spending, U.S.

Forward defense doctrine, 75–77

France: expanded military force of, 2–3, 46; independent security policy of, 23–24, 39, 151

Friedman, Milton, 193

Fujimori, Alberto, 135–36

Funabashi, Yoichi, 58

Gaddis, John Lewis, 32

Gaffney, Frank, 154

Galvin, John, 43, 190

Gelb, Leslie H., 35

Gemayel, Amin, 185

General Agreement on Tariffs and Trade (GATT), 43, 44

George, Aurelia, 65–66, 71

Georgia, republic of, 33

Germany: assertiveness of, 36–37, 39; expanded military force of, 2–3, 46; goal of subordinating, 34–38; independent security policy of, 151; as military threat, 34–38; Ostpolitik policy of, 39; suspicions of United States, 9

Geyer, Georgie Anne, 134

Glenn, John, 156

Goose, Stephen D., 85

Gorbachev, Mikhail, 78–79, 141

Government expansion, U.S., 230 n. 42

Government spending, U.S., 203. *See also* Military spending, U.S.

Graham, Daniel, 14–15

Great Britain, 56

Greece, 155

Gregor, A. James, 48

Grenada, 129, 133

Guatemala, 129

Haig, Alexander M., Jr., 130

Haiti: coup in, 133; OAS embargo of, 134; proposals for U.S. intervention in, 154

Harriman, W. Averell, 18

Hawke, Robert, 102

Hekmatyar, Gulbuddin, 117

Henderson, David R., 193–94

Hendrickson, David C., 145, 173

Heritage Foundation, 48

Hickenlooper, Bourke, 20

Hidaka, Yoshiki, 65

Hishhiro, Seiki, 56

Holbrooke, Richard, 61–62

Hollings, Ernest, 65

Hormats, Robert D., 14

House, Karen Elliott, 14

Human rights: abuses in China, 142; abuses in Latin America, 130; abuses in Pakistan, 114, 115

Hungary, 33

Hunt, Kenneth, 59

India: as military threat, 119–20; relations with Pakistan, 119–22;

233

relations with United States, 122–25, 220–21 n. 25
Indonesia, 99–100
Indo-Pakistani wars (1965, 1971), 114, 118, 121
Inoguchi, Takashi, 66
Interamerican Treaty of Reciprocal Assistance (1947). *See* Rio Treaty (1947)
Intercontinental ballistic missiles (ICBMs), 200
Interest group activity, 161–62
Intermediate Nuclear Forces Treaty (1988), 27
International Atomic Energy Agency (IAEA), 92
International Missile Technology Control Regime, 124
International stability: goal of, 139–41; unattainable, 147–49; U.S. actions to maintain, 141–47
International system: anarchic nature of, 188; bipolar, 167; changes in, 1–7; changing role for United States in, 167–68; multipolar post–Cold War, 40–41, 167; trend toward multipolar, 25; U.S. interventionist policy for, 184; unipolar perception, 149–53
Interventionist policy, U.S.: arguments for using, 154, 172–73; a consequence of, 230 n. 42; criticism of, 190; efficacy of, 180–81; enthusiasm for, 139–41; justification of, 163, 167; in Korea, 181; in Latin America, 129, 133; in Panama, 17, 129, 133; in Persian Gulf War, 181; in Vietnam, 178–79
Iraq: arguments for war against, 192–94; Kurds and Shi'ites in, 143–45; nuclear weapons program, 92; role of NATO members against, 29–30
Ireland, Andy, 27
Ishihara, Shintaro, 64, 70
Islamic fundamentalism, 116–17, 145–46
Ismay, Lord, 36
Isolationism: accusation of, 25, 190–91; avoidance of, 8, 189–90, 195
Issue networks, 161–64
Ito, Kan, 65

Japan: assertiveness of, 3; economic performance of, 4; foreign aid

contributions of, 56; intelligence plan of, 56; as military threat, 67–69, 99; nuclear power program of, 57; resentment of United States, 9, 63–66; response to dependence strategy, 52–59; U.S. defense commitment to, 47; U.S. policy for military dependence of, 50–52, 60–67; U.S. relations with, 70–71
Jefferson, Thomas, 195
Jeremiah, David E., 168
Johnson, Louis, 19
Johnson, Lyndon B.: embargoed arms aid to Pakistan, 114; on United States in Vietnam conflict, 170–71
Johnson administration: attitude toward de Gaulle, 24; policy against European self-sufficiency, 23; position on U.S. troops in Europe, 25; promise of assistance to Pakistan, 119; response to Mansfield Amendment, 25

Kaifu, Toshiki, 56, 57, 60, 68
Kakizawa, Koji, 56
Kenbei attitude, 64–65
Kennan, George F., 12, 18
Kennedy administration: attitude toward de Gaulle, 24; isolation policy for Cuba, 131; policy against European self-sufficiency, 23; promise of assistance to Pakistan, 119
Kim Il Sung, 73
Kim Kook Chin, 89
Kiribati, 98
Kirkpatrick, Jeane, 45
Kissinger, Henry: response to Mansfield Amendment, 26; on U.S actions in Indo-Pakistani crisis, 118–19, 123
Kohl, Helmut, 37, 40, 44
Korean Peninsula: division of, 73–74, 77; potential for nuclear war on, 122; as proposed nuclear-free zone, 91, 93; U.S. risk in commitment to, 82; as vital U.S. security interest, 93–94. *See also* North Korea; South Korea
Krauss, Melvyn, 62
Krauthammer, Charles, 149–50
Kurds, 144
Kuwait, 29–30, 145–46

Lange, David, 96
Layne, Christopher, 190–91

234

relations with ANZUS members, 96–98; relations with neighboring countries, 101–2. *See also* ANZUS alliance

Nicaragua: Soviet role in, 131; U.S. security concern with, 132

Nixon, Richard M.: on future role of NATO, 28; on U.S. role in Pacific, 67

Nixon administration: assistance to Pakistan, 118, 119; on India's war with Pakistan (1971), 123; reaction to Mansfield Amendment, 26; relations with Pakistan, 114; troop reduction and withdrawal from Korea, 74, 86

Noriega, Manuel, 185

North Atlantic Cooperation Council, 16

North Atlantic Treaty Organization (NATO): as commitment to secondary U.S. security interest, 177–78; cost of, 1, 17; European dependence as agenda for, 38–45; Germany on agenda of, 34–38; justification for preserving, 5, 27–34; original provisions of charter, 18–21, 45–46; as potential out-of-area problem solver, 14–17, 28–30; to preserve European stability, 15–17, 30–34; proposed intervention in Yugoslavia, 154; proposed transformation of, 2, 14–15, 21; reasons for creation of, 12; supporters and opponents of, 11–18, 27; U.S. dominance in, 23–28

North Korea: creation of, 73; economic performance of, 4, 83, 92; as military threat, 80; nuclear weapons program of, 82, 87–92

Novak, Robert, 44

Nuclear nonproliferation policy: coercive, 156, 172–73; effect of, 197–98

Nuclear Nonproliferation Treaty (NPT), 50, 91, 196–97

Nuclear power program, Japan, 57

Nuclear war potential, 122

Nuclear weapons: accidental or unauthorized launch of, 200, 201; of China, 49–50; circumstances for Japan to consider, 91; of former Soviet Union, 31–32, 180; French arsenal, 24; in hands of adversaries, 197–98; in Iraq, 92; Japan's potential

for, 57, 68–69; in NATO deterrent strategy, 23; New Zealand's ban on, 96–98; North Korean program for, 82, 87–92; rivalry of India and Pakistan, 120–22; ROK-DPRK agreement to renounce (1991), 92; South Korean program for, 91; with strategic independence, 196; withdrawal from Korea of some U.S., 87–88. *See also* Nuclear nonproliferation policy

Nunn, Sam, 26

Oakes, Robert, 35

Odom, William E., 35

Olsen, Edward A., 62

Organization of American States (OAS): creation and functions of, 127–28, 130; proposals to strengthen, 133–35; recommendation for U.S withdrawal from, 136–37

Pakistan: relations with India, 119–20, 120–22; secular government of, 116; U.S. defense treaty with, 5

Panama, 17, 129, 133

Pastor, Robert A., 133–35

Peace Constitution, Japan, 51, 52, 53–55, 62, 67

Peace dividend: benefit of, 9; circumstances for lack of, 153; sentiment for, 163; source of and use for, 202–3

Pèrez, Carlos Andrès, 130

Persian Gulf War: arguments for, 192–94; political fall-out from, 193–94; Japanese contribution to, 63; NATO members' forces in, 29–30; role of UN Security Council in, 181

Peru, 5, 133, 135, 136

Philippines: U.S. military relationship with, 95, 103; U.S. trade with, 105

Pike, Otis, 164

Poland, 33

Police Reserve Corps, Japan, 54

Policy networks, or iron triangles, 161–62. *See also* Foreign policy; Issue networks

Political symbolism, 96

Powell, Colin, 158

Pressler Amendment, 115, 116

Quayle, Dan, 43, 44

Quinn, Kenneth M., 106

236

Ravenal, Earl C., 77, 169
Reagan administration: confrontation with New Zealand, 96–97; isolation policy for Nicaragua, 131; position on NATO, 26–27; relations with Angola, 194
Republic of Korea (ROK). *See* South Korea
Rhee, Syngman, 73, 74
Rio Treaty (1947): preservation of, 1, 5; proposal for U.S. withdrawal from, 136–37; provisions of, 127–28; question of continued importance of, 131–37
Roh Tae Woo, 79, 91–92
ROK (Republic of Korea). *See* South Korea
Roosevelt, Franklin D., 128
Rostow, Walt W., 25–26
Russia: as military threat, 30–31, 79–80, 98; Pacific fleet of, 98–99

Saddam Hussein, 29, 142–44, 181, 192
Safire, William, 144
Santiago Declaration (1991), 133
Scarborough, Rowan, 159
Schroeder, Patricia: on Japanese military expansion, 62, 63; opposition to base closings, 160; troop withdrawal proposal of, 26–27
Schwarzkopf, Norman, 144
Scowcroft, Brent, 3, 13, 17
SDF. *See* Self-Defense Forces (SDF), Japan
Secular governments, Middle East, 116
Security interests: of Australia and New Zealand, 101; conditional or secondary, 176–78; conflicts irrelevant to U.S., 3–4, 6, 33; focus of United States on own, 187–88; nations with common, 188; peripheral U.S., 75, 81, 93, 178–79; of United States in Cuba and Nicaragua, 132; vague definition of U.S. post–Cold War, 169–70; vital U.S., 7, 75, 80, 170–76; of Western Europe, 39–41
Self-Defense Forces (SDF), Japan, 54–55
Shining Path guerrillas, 5, 133, 135, 136
Singapore, 111–12
Singh, Jasit, 121
Singh, Satinder, 120

Snider, Don M., 160
Snowe, Olympia, 160
Solanga, Jovito, 104
Solomon, Richard H., 49, 87, 88
South Asia, 122
Southeast Asian Treaty Organization, 95, 113
South Korea: creation of, 73; economic performance of, 4, 83; military significance to United States, 77–78; objection to U.S. commitment to, 90–91; as peripheral U.S. security interest, 75, 80, 81, 93–94; trade with Soviet Union, 79; U.S. military commitment to, 73; as U.S. trading partner, 75
Soviet Union: control in Eastern Europe, 34; goals in Latin America, 129; influence in Latin America, 129–31; as military threat, 32, 45, 47, 76; reduced threat of, 13–14; relations with South Korea, 78–79; role in Latin America, 130–31; role in North Korea, 73–74; as threat to Japan, 70; trade with South Korea, 79; troops in Afghanistan, 115; U.S. response to aggression of, 75–77
Stackpole, Henry C., 66, 70
Stearns, Monteagle, 154–55
Steel, Ronald, 39, 42
Strategic Defense Initiative, 201
Strategic independence: basis for policy of, 9, 203–4; benefits of policy of, 195, 202–3; elements of, 189; equated with isolationism, 195; force structure based on, 198; as new security doctrine, 165; principles and focus of, 7–8, 10, 170
Subic Bay Naval Base, Philippines, 103–11
Submarine-launched ballistic missiles (SLBMs), 157, 200
Sundarji, K., 122

Taft, Robert, 177, 183
Taylor, William J., Jr., 84
Threat procurement, 153–54
Tito, Josip Broz, 148, 176
Tobin, James, 193
Tonelson, Alan, 41, 190
Truman, Harry S, 18, 52
Truman administration: commitments to NATO, 18–22; Korean War strategy of, 74, 77–78

237

238

About the Author

Ted Galen Carpenter is director of foreign policy studies at the Cato Institute. He is the editor of *Collective Defense or Strategic Independence? Alternative Strategies for the Future, NATO at 40: Confronting a Changing World, America Entangled: The Persian Gulf Crisis and Its Consequences,* and *The U.S.–South Korean Alliance: Time for a Change* (with Doug Bandow).

He has contributed chapters to 14 books on foreign affairs, and his work has appeared in numerous policy journals including *Foreign Policy, International History Review, National Interest,* and *Politique Internationale.*

Carpenter received his B.A. and M.A. in U.S. history from the University of Wisconsin at Milwaukee and his Ph.D. in U.S. diplomatic history from the University of Texas.

Cato Institute

Founded in 1977, the Cato Institute is a public policy research foundation dedicated to broadening the parameters of policy debate to allow consideration of more options that are consistent with the traditional American principles of limited government, individual liberty, and peace. To that end, the Institute strives to achieve greater involvement of the intelligent, concerned lay public in questions of policy and the proper role of government.

The Institute is named for *Cato's Letters*, libertarian pamphlets that were widely read in the American Colonies in the early 18th century and played a major role in laying the philosophical foundation for the American Revolution.

Despite the achievement of the nation's Founders, today virtually no aspect of life is free from government encroachment. A pervasive intolerance for individual rights is shown by government's arbitrary intrusions into private economic transactions and its disregard for civil liberties.

To counter that trend, the Cato Institute undertakes an extensive publications program that addresses the complete spectrum of policy issues. Books, monographs, and shorter studies are commissioned to examine the federal budget, Social Security, regulation, military spending, international trade, and myriad other issues. Major policy conferences are held throughout the year, from which papers are published thrice yearly in the *Cato Journal*. The Institute also publishes the quarterly magazine *Regulation* and produces a monthly audiotape series, "Perspectives on Policy."

In order to main its independence, the Cato Institute accepts no government funding. Contributions are received from foundations, corporations, and individuals, and other revenue is generated from the sale of publications. The Institute is a nonprofit, tax-exempt, educational foundation under Section 501(c)3 of the Internal Revenue Code.

CATO INSTITUTE
224 Second St., S.E.
Washington, D.C. 20003